W9-BLF-249

WITHDRAWN

WITHDRAWN

Taking Women Seriously
Lessons and Legacies
for Educating the Majority

by
M. Elizabeth Tidball
Daryl G. Smith
Charles S. Tidball
Lisa E. Wolf-Wendel

Foreword by
Jill Ker Conway

AMERICAN COUNCIL ON EDUCATION ★
ORYX PRESS ★
Series on Higher Education
1999

© 1999 by The American Council on Education and The Oryx Press
Published by The Oryx Press
4041 North Central at Indian School Road
Phoenix, Arizona 85012-3397

Library of Congress Cataloging-in-Publication Data

Taking women seriously : lessons and legacies for educating the
majority / by M. Elizabeth Tidball ... [et al.].
    p. cm.—(American Council on Education/Oryx Press series on
higher education)
    Includes bibliographical references (p.) and index.
    ISBN 1-57356-092-8 (alk. paper)
    1. Women's colleges—United States—History—20th century.
2. Women—Education (Higher)—United States—History—20th century.
I. Tidball, M. Elizabeth. II. Series.
LC1756.T26 1998
378'.0082'0973—dc21   98-36328
                                               CIP

We dedicate this book to
the founders, supporters, and leaders of women's colleges,
by whose vision, diligence, and generosity has been
made manifest the meaning of *taking women seriously*,
so that the education of women might flourish
throughout all of higher education—

And we further dedicate this book to
all students, parents, faculty, administrators, and
concerned alumni and alumnae of coeducational institutions,
that their trustees, governors, and regents
may establish *taking women seriously*
as a guiding principle for the new millennium.

CONTENTS

LIST OF FIGURES

LIST OF TABLES

FOREWORD

by Jill Ker Conway

The four authors of *Taking Women Seriously: Lessons and Legacies for Educating the Majority* represent three generations of research on American higher education and a variety of different disciplinary backgrounds. Consequently, this volume, focused on the outcomes of women's education within women's colleges, brings together history, social theory, statistical analysis, and case studies to illuminate just what it is about women's colleges that continues to produce graduates whose career achievement is significantly higher than that of peers educated in coeducational settings.

The question, first researched by Lee Tidball when she encountered debate about the value of women's colleges during the vogue for coeducation of the early 1970s, has given rise to a large and growing body of research on the significance of gender in the educational process. Lee Tidball's initial work was questioned when first published in 1970 because her critics thought, mistakenly, that she had based her research on data collected from the Seven Sisters, whose students, critics argued, were among those most likely to succeed in their generation because of social background, level of college preparation, and familial support. In fact, Tidball's 1970 study was based on a much larger group of women's colleges. Later, to dispose of the critics' insistence that the 1970 data did not resolve the question, Tidball analyzed outcomes for elite women's and elite coeducational colleges—with the same results.

Almost three decades later, her original conclusions hold up, now applied over three decades of women's access to elite, formally all-male institutions, and across the outcomes of education for women in women's colleges from small, Historically Black institutions, to Roman Catholic colleges serving inner city populations, to the Seven Sisters. The results of the more than 200 research papers and surveys documenting this trend are incorporated in the four sections of this book, offering the reader a handy guide to the way research in educational outcomes has developed, and of the developing sophistication in studying educational institutions and their culture.

We owe Lee and Charles Tidball, Daryl Smith, and Lisa Wolf-Wendel much for the painstaking way they have summed up research on the subject, indicated earlier criticisms, and showed how new research has been developed to answer the questions of critics. The simple words "college outcomes" can look narrowly social-scientific, but the four authors make clear that what they are talking about is the manner in which a college experience can convey the capacity to act on one's own behalf, drawing on informed judgment, using the focused energies of a well-integrated personality.

A finely nuanced understanding of this question of outcomes is of critical importance for policy at every level in the education system, since educational institutions today fail most notably in achieving such outcomes for disadvantaged populations. Moreover, it is of critical importance for efforts to bring literacy and the capacity for abstract critical thinking to third world populations where women, especially rural women, are the most strikingly disadvantaged group.

This volume also breaks new ground by spelling out what we know about the ways in which the total context of an institution—from who is most frequently called on in class to who serves on the board of trustees—conveys subtle educational messages. The authors supply a list of factors to consider when striving to demonstrate that women students are taken seriously; guidelines that can be utilized in any school or college and that could be transposed to deal with other populations accorded minority status, whether or not their numbers warrant the designation. So this book is not just one more polemic about single-sex education versus coeducation. It's a guidebook for anyone anywhere who wants to take educating women seriously.

Best of all possible recommendations—this book is written without jargon, in language that the nonspecialist can understand. Complex issues in statistical analysis are described in plain English accompanied by simple, down-to-earth examples. Moreover, the student who wants to become versed in this subject can find her or his way through a complex literature from the detailed scholarly bibliography and bibliographic essays that conclude this well-written and painstakingly researched book.

ACKNOWLEDGMENTS

Many people have been extraordinarily helpful to us from the outset of our earliest tentative discussions. Together, the four of us join to thank, first, the folks at the American Council on Education, where we ventured to take our prospectus: Jim Murray, Donna Shavlik, Judy Touchton, Madeleine Green, and Barbara Hill each played an important part in the generation or completion of this book. At Oryx Press, we are grateful for the enormous encouragement and steadying hands of Susan Slesinger and our tireless, talented editor, Liz Welsh. When the going became rough, they were steadfast in their support, and when the sailing was smooth, they never failed to tell us how great was our progress. Jadwega Sebrechts, executive director of the Women's College Coalition, has been a loyal friend and thoughtful adviser, as well as a dependable spokesperson among coalition members.

Our collegiate connections have been important to our progress: at Hood College, Martha Church, Joy Derr, David Hein, Yeny Orellana, Shirley Peterson, and Tom Samet; at the Center for Educational Studies at The Claremont Graduate University, the staff and faculty, along with Teresa Wilborn; at Scripps College, many faculty, staff, colleagues, and alumnae; at The George Washington University, Jim Kendrick; at the Population Reference Bureau, Carl Haub; and at the University of Kansas, Christine Keller-Wolff and Susan Twombly.

Beyond our institutional supporters have been friends near and far. We would like especially to thank Anne Worley Hummer, Sharon Ringe, Larry Stookey, and Ellie Wilson; Barbara Bergmann, David Smith, Hillary Bergmann, and Adrienne Rich; Lillian Brauman, Doug Wendel, Aron Wolf, and Pat Wolf. Charlie and Lee Tidball are thoroughly indebted to one another.

ABOUT THE
AUTHORS

T he corporate history of the four authors of this book prefigures the book itself, in that the totality of their lives and work is greater than the sum of their parts. There is a synergy in their relationship that accounts for a wider perspective than could have come from merely combining what each could write alone. Because they come from diverse academic disciplines, intellectual histories, and experiences, they have been able to contribute material not generally provided exposure beyond the immediacy of the venue for which it was prepared. Additionally, they have occupied all of the roles of which they write in a variety of academic institutions: student, faculty member, administrator, trustee, alumna, friend, guest, honoree. Appreciating that this book has resulted from the integration of efforts and individualities, the authors nonetheless have provided separate vitae below, while also noting some of the places of interconnectedness that have been significant to their mutual accomplishment.

Lead author **M. Elizabeth Tidball**, known as Lee, has earned degrees from Mount Holyoke College (B.A. 1951 in chemistry and physiology), the University of Wisconsin–Madison (M.S. and Ph.D. in physiology, 1955 and 1959), and the Wesley Theological Seminary (M.T.S. in education and liturgy, 1990). She also studied at the Universities of Rochester and Chicago and held a United States Public Health Service postdoctoral fellowship at the National Institutes of Health in Washington, D.C. At the department of physiology of The George Washington University Medical Center in Washington, D.C., she became the first woman to reach full professorial status (1970); in 1994, she was named professor emeritus of physiology.

From the 1950s into the early 1970s, she compiled a significant record of research and publication on the physiological function of neurotransmitters. In recognition of her work, she was elected to membership in the American Physiological Society in 1962. Noting the struggles of younger women in their efforts to gain postbaccalaureate education in science and medicine, she began her lifelong thrust to improve educational and professional opportunities for women. In 1972, she was a cofounder of the master's degree program in women's studies at The George Washington University (GW); in 1973, she was founder and chair of the Task Force on Women for the American Physiological Society; from 1975 to 1979, she was a faculty member for the Carnegie Foundation Intern Program for Women in Higher Education Administration; from 1975 to the present, she has served on the final selection panel for the Woodrow Wilson National Fellowship Foundation Doctoral Dissertation Awards in Women's Studies and Women's Health; she was GW's first institutional liaison officer for women to the Association of American Medical Colleges, from 1976 to 1987; in 1977, she was responsible for establishing the Committee on the Education and Employment of Women in Science and Engineering for the National Research Council/National Academy of Sciences, later serving as vice-chair; and, in 1987, she founded Summer Seminars for Women, a residential conference for adult women in Michigan, directing it until 1995. Also benefiting women and other marginally represented groups, she served more than 13 years on GW's Medical Admissions Committee, and as chair of the entirety of the Dedication of Ross Hall of Health Sciences and Himmelfarb Library of the Medical Center, ensuring the participation of the diverse constituencies of the wider Washington community.

Beyond George Washington, she served as a trustee of Mount Holyoke, Hood, Sweet Briar, Salem, and Skidmore Colleges, as well as chairing the boards of several cultural and educational organizations. In recognition of her contributions to science, to education, and to women, she has been honored with five distinguished visiting professorships, the Mary E. Woolley Fellowship and Alumnae Medal of Honor from Mount Holyoke, and the Chestnut Hill College Medal, and she has been cited for service to many other civic organizations. Additionally, she has received 17 honorary doctorate degrees from American colleges and universities in science, humane letters, humanities, letters, and laws.

In 1988, during her tenure on the editorial board of the *Journal of Higher Education*, she first became aware of Daryl G. Smith through an article Daryl submitted: "Women's Colleges and Coed Colleges: Is There a Difference for Women?" Although neither author nor reviewer knew the identity of the other, Lee was enormously impressed with the research and its presentation. In her review, she wrote to Bob Silverman, editor of the *Journal*, ". . . rush to the printer!" Upon reading the review, Daryl asked Bob if she might learn its author, and thereon hangs a tale of colleagueship and friendship that has resulted in many shared adventures over the years.

Daryl G. Smith received her B.A. in mathematics from Cornell University (1965); M.A.s from Stanford (1966) and The Claremont Graduate University (1975); and a Ph.D., also from Claremont, in psychology and higher education (1976). From 1966 to the early 1980s, she served as dean of students, or of women, or of freshmen, variously, at St. Lawrence University, Pomona College, and Scripps College. At Scripps, she subsequently became vice president for planning and research and associate professor of psychology, with a concurrent faculty appointment at The Claremont Graduate University. In 1986, she moved full time to Claremont where, in 1989, Lee provided an outside evaluation for Daryl's tenure nomination. In 1995, Daryl became professor of education and psychology, with Lee again serving as an outside evaluator for this career passage.

Daryl has continued her research, writing, and speaking on women's colleges; additionally, she has devoted substantial attention to issues of diversity in higher education, to other special-purpose institutions such as Historically Black colleges and universities, and to organizational topics such as planning, assessment, and evaluation. Most recently, she was selected to participate as part of the United States delegation to a Ford Foundation–sponsored trinational seminar on campus diversity in higher education held in South Africa.

She serves as a consultant to colleges, universities, and foundations; as a member of the National Science Foundation visiting panel for the Chemlinks Chemistry National Reform Project; and on a research task force for the National Association of Student Personnel Administrators (NASPA). She has been chair of the editorial board of the *Journal of Higher Education,* serves on the board of the Association for the Study of Higher Education (ASHE), and as a consulting editor for the ASHE-ERIC monograph series. She received the ASHE award in 1995 and the NASPA Region VI award in 1996, both for distinguished service.

Charles S. Tidball (Charlie) holds a B.A. in chemistry from Wesleyan University (1950) and received an M.S. in pharmacology from the University of Rochester (1952), a Ph.D. in physiology from the University of Wisconsin–Madison (1955), and an M.D. from the University of Chicago (1958). Following a rotating internship, he joined the department of physiology of The George Washington University School of Medicine and Health Sciences in 1959. He held a National Institutes of Health Research Career Development Award until he became chair of the department of physiology in 1963. By 1961, he had become an active member and leader in the American Physiological Society and, in 1967, he received the Washington Academy of

Science Award for Scientific Achievement. In 1973, he founded the Office of Computer Assisted Education in the GW Medical Center, pioneering online instruction for training medical library personnel in computerized information retrieval. For more than 10 years, he participated in the Association for the Development of Computer-Based Instructional Systems (ADCIS) and was both incorporator and officer of the Health Education Network, an outgrowth of the Lister Hill National Center for Biomedical Communication of the National Library of Medicine. While on sabbatical leave in 1977–78, he served as consultant to the deputy director of the clinical center at the National Institutes of Health, where he developed a multimedia training program to assist physicians in learning computerized patient management. On loan from the medical center to the department of education at GW, he developed the Educational Computing Technology Program, which he directed for two years. In 1984, he became a staff physician in the department of computer medicine at GW and a civil surgeon of the U.S. Department of Justice. He was named professor emeritus of computer medicine and of neurological surgery in 1992.

Charlie is the originator of the Small College Database, an online information source for demographic data from more than 1,100 four-year colleges, over three decades. In addition to his interest in small colleges, his concern for the education of women led to a nine-year tenure as a trustee of Wilson College, which subsequently awarded him the honorary doctor of humane letters degree in 1994. Currently, he is the volunteer manager of the Information Systems Program at Washington National Cathedral and distinguished research scholar and codirector, with Lee, of the Tidball Center for the Study of Educational Environments at Hood College.

Charlie and Lee married in 1952 and have made of their life a partnership both in physiology research and teaching, and in their education efforts, especially on behalf of girls and women. Unable to collaborate openly since their graduate student days on account of nepotism rules or others' fears, they are especially gratified to be working together at the Tidball Center and to be sharing with Daryl and Lisa in the development and production of this book.

Lisa E. Wolf-Wendel is an assistant professor at the University of Kansas. She received a B.A. in psychology and communications from Stanford University (1987), and both an M.A. and a Ph.D. in higher education from The Claremont Graduate University (1995). Lee had the privilege and pleasure of serving as outside examiner for Lisa's doctoral defense, which Daryl chaired. While a graduate student, Lisa was a residence life coordinator at Scripps College, where the women positively influenced her understanding of the power of a women-only educational environment. Even earlier, she had been strongly influenced by her grandmother, Lillian Brauman, a graduate of Douglass

College of Rutgers University, who frequently spoke of the positive effects of that women's college on her life.

Lisa has published several articles on women's colleges and has engaged in extensive research on the topic of environments conducive to the success of women. Her doctoral work explored the baccalaureate origins of African American, Latina, and European American women who earned doctorates and examined the characteristics associated with their institutions. Recent research endeavors include a study of the history and future of two-year women's colleges and an analysis of the relationship between the availability of financial resources and baccalaureate origins. She believes that her interest and passion for women's colleges and women's education have come from the mentoring, support, and scholarship of the book's coauthors. Further, she states that their contributions to the field and commitment to improving the education of women are inspiring examples she hopes to emulate throughout her life.

INTRODUCTION

Writing History Differently

. . . I realized that I'd write history differently in the future. The interaction of individual, institution, and environment was even more complex than I'd understood, and the tangible results often elusive.

—Jill Ker Conway, 1994

Writing about the education of women, even if limiting that princi-pally to women in higher education in the United States during the last half century, is a formidable task. It must be understood that such a history comprises stories, lists and numbers, disparate research method-ologies, informed opinions, personal experiences, philosophy, and a little bit of poetry—all intricately interwoven in a tapestry both tough and beautiful. Furthermore, the mix and proportion of each aspect of this history are not fixed for any given dimension of an institution's life nor for every moment of time. Nonetheless, out of the complexities of interactions are revealed pat-terns that serve as guides to what works for women.

This book constitutes a major effort to examine the situation for women in American higher education over the past several decades, a period during which powerful molding forces have forever altered women's educational opportunities. One might have hoped that women's increased access to higher education would have exerted a beneficial effect on their participation. How-ever, for many women, the quality of the education experience is overshad-owed by the pervasive mindset of a male-dominated academic environment that mirrors American life. Not only is the value of women's collegiate experience substantially compromised thereby, but contributions women might otherwise have made by their subsequent accomplishments are being lost to the wider society.

WHY WOMEN'S COLLEGES?

We are writing this book because we have found, in our own considerable work as well as that of many others, a consistent pattern showing that a high proportion of accomplished women have undertaken their collegiate education in women's colleges or in colleges formerly for women. In these institutions, the situation for women clearly is not only favorable but empowering: the education of women is the primary purpose of the institution, there is a critical mass of women faculty, women are nurtured and challenged in all realms, and woman-related issues dominate campus discussions—in short, at these colleges, the total development of women is taken seriously by the entirety of the community.

We do not, however, claim that women's colleges are "better" or that they are the best setting for all women. By no means! Rather, we write this book to document the qualities and programs of women's colleges that appear related to producing accomplished, achieving graduates. We do so to provide impetus and practical assistance to educators at *all* institutions that offer higher education to women, so that they may find ways to enhance their efforts and provide the most equitable opportunities for all of their students, faculty, administrators, trustees, and graduates. Indeed, it is in the national interest that there be such a resource as we strive to encourage and establish opportunities for women, not only during their collegiate sojourns but also continuing into the new century. We also do this to highlight for the record the steadfast and continuing contributions of this small group of institutions unique within American higher education from whom we have learned that it is the *entirety* of the education environment that impacts participants, not only during their student years but throughout their lifetimes. Surely this finding is not only of interest to women.

The lessons and legacies from women's colleges presented here are offered for the benefit of all women in academe, wherever they may be and in whatever capacity. They demonstrate that, for women students to flourish, all women associated with a college or university must be supported, encouraged, and empowered, so that individuals, institution, and environment are thoroughly interwoven in a fabric of recognized strength and value.

WHAT WE CLAIM

Colleges for women may be more effective for women than coeducational colleges, but women's colleges constitute such a small proportion of collegiate institutions that, until their benefits are more broadly appreciated, we cannot expect to see the improvement in women's education that our findings warrant and the nation deserves. We are concerned that there is a *loss* of women's talent in coeducational institutions: even though women meet the same admission requirements and pay the same tuition as men, many record but a marginal experience.

However, no one would assert that *all* women would be best served by attending a women's college, nor that all women's colleges have achieved the highest possible quality of educational environment for all who live and work there. Such claims would be frivolous. What we can say, from both research and experience (others' as well as our own), is that for many decades, women's colleges have been the foremost contributors of achieving women to the society. We further claim that the lessons and legacies from women's colleges regularly bespeak taking women seriously, as attested to by the consistent success of the graduates of these institutions. Thus, we now can look to the institutional priorities, patterns, and principles that have been developed and applied at women's colleges and know a great deal about what works for women. These are the findings and insights that we would share through this book with all of higher education.

The effort we present here capitalizes on what has been learned from a wide variety of studies of environments in which women either proceed to—or are lost from—the ranks of accomplished women. It is an issue of significance to all, men as well as women, who look to a future in which the necessity of providing first-class education opportunities for all participants is acknowledged.

OUR AUDIENCE

Taking Women Seriously has been written for, and is dedicated to, all who have a stake in the higher education of women; that is to say, *everyone*—especially to those involved in some way with coeducational colleges and universities. It has been designed to be useful to those outside the realm of academic research, although scholars will find methodologies and other supporting materials in a rich set of supplements. The book will enlighten academic administrators, trustees, parents, and students. It is a natural for classroom use in psychology, sociology, education, and women's studies. Indeed, it is a comprehensive presentation of what works for women in higher education and is a challenge to all to take women seriously.

HOW WE HAVE ORGANIZED THE BOOK

Taking Women Seriously is presented in four parts. Each part opens with a brief summary presenting the general thrust of the section. While we believe that there is value to reading the parts in order, each can be read or used

independently. At the end of the volume, a generous set of additional resources supplement Chapters 1–5.

Lastly, we have brought together a full assortment of more than 200
references that both support and extend the text, while the index is intended
to provide the greatest possible access to the contents. Indeed, the entirety of
the book is intentionally constructed to reflect the integration and wholeness
necessary for *taking women seriously*.

We believe that this organization itself serves as a metaphor for what it
means to educate the majority. On the one hand, we move from history as
story and perspective in Part One, to empirical research in Part Two, to
applications of experience in Part Three, to summation and philosophy in Part
Four. The education of women can be viewed from any or all of several angles
of vision. On the other hand, educating the majority is actually the composite
of all of these views, integrated and interdisciplinary, much as they have been
collated in this single volume—a composite that mirrors the complexity of
effort and energy that are required when women are taken seriously.

Part One

In Part One we provide two *contexts* in which to place women's colleges. One
is related to the history and development of the colleges themselves and their
relationship to women's education in the United States. The other involves
the demographics of small colleges in the United States as they have changed
during the last 40 years.

We begin by writing about six women's colleges and their founders; individual cases that serve as proxies and metaphors for the whole. They were
chosen to reveal, among other features: a range of sizes (from very small to
among the largest); different geographical locations (from east to south to
midwest to far west); venues from urban to relatively rural; varied governance
(from independent to church-related control); both predominantly white and
historically black; and curricula that emphasize the traditional liberal arts, as
well as those that have incorporated many new career-related programs.
Clearly, women's colleges are not a monolithic entity! Nonetheless, the six
exemplars demonstrate significant commonalities: all were founded by women;
all continue to this day as colleges for women; all have added educational
opportunities for women beyond the traditional collegiate age; and all have
regularly, often, and publicly stated missions that clearly designate women as
their first priority. In addition, we have associated with each of the six colleges
an attribute that has special meaning for the particular institution but, indeed,
is characteristic of all. The colleges selected demonstrate the diversity among
women's colleges yet also show that in many ways they have common roots
and shared values.

The stories of women's colleges do not end, however, with the retelling of their foundings and their early histories. Rather, we continue to the present by placing women's colleges within the larger scene of American higher education and the influences of national events that have affected all institutional life.

In response to cultural and demographic pressures on all colleges—especially small, private, residential institutions—many women's colleges rearticulated their commitment to the education of women. Additionally, they developed cooperative interactions that included regional and national conferences, symposia, centers for research, and publications. Such activities provided a means to report and call attention to what was becoming known and understood with respect to the education of women. Four such conferences were selected to represent the many kinds of communal initiatives that have blossomed and continue to appear. Again, we chose examples that show some of the diversity among the sponsors—a small college, a Roman Catholic college, one of the "Seven Sisters," and the Women's College Coalition—while also demonstrating their common agenda of discovering and articulating what works for women. We refer to this outreach by women's colleges as a level of maturity surpassing individual survival—as advocacy and action on behalf of women wherever they may be and whatever role they may occupy in the higher education world.

We also show that the development of women's colleges and women's education have taken place against a rapidly changing national scene in which all small colleges, of which most women's colleges are a part, have lost a substantial measure of their market share of students. It is important to appreciate these additional constraints and influences that come from outside the institutions themselves in understanding the enormous effort required to bring to light concerns for the education of women, an effort that is regularly and vigorously undertaken by women's colleges.

The two chapters of Part One thus serve to establish the contexts within which the education of women, small colleges, and women's colleges have operated, especially during the past 40 years. While the complexity of the education environment has by no means been reduced to simplicity, this analysis provides stimulation for further thinking and understanding to all who care about the education of women—the group that now constitutes the majority of participants in our institutions of higher learning.

Part Two

Formal studies by researchers from different disciplines using different methods are discussed in Part Two. These studies have built a powerful case that women's colleges are highly effective in producing achieving women. To date, however, there has been no recapitulation of this evidence; no systematic review of the research findings to edify boards of trustees, college administrators, faculty who direct relevant academic programs, parents, or the new generation of aspiring college women. This book speaks to these audiences.

It has been nearly 30 years since the publication of M. Elizabeth Tidball's earliest study of women achievers with its numerical evidence of the exceptional "productivity" associated with women's colleges—the disproportionate number of their graduates who later could be credited with significant accomplishments. These findings startled researchers and the general public alike, for they were contrary to the contemporary view that held coeducation as the ideal for everyone. The study also unsettled many educators, who would have preferred the simplicity of sameness; that is, they would have liked all institutions to be open to both men and women as the nation entered the era of Title IX. We show, however, that accepting both women and men students does not guarantee sameness among so-called coeducational institutions, nor can one infer an environment of equality just because both sexes have been admitted.

M. E. Tidball's data first appeared in print in 1970 and were reported at the national meetings of the American Association for the Advancement of Science (M. E. Tidball 1972). One result of these public presentations was their recording by the Carnegie Commission's *Opportunities for Women in Higher Education*. After summarizing Tidball's work, the editors stated, "These accomplishments of the graduates of women's colleges are worthy of emphasis . . . significantly in terms of potential influence as they suggest how changes in policies and faculty attitudes in coeducational institutions could affect the accomplishment of their women students" (Carnegie Commission on Higher Education 1973). That statement remains true to this day. Indeed, it is one impetus for the writing of this book, for we believe that there is still much work to be recognized and accomplished within coeducational institutions, and that the nature and extent of that work is made manifest by what has been learned about the education of women in women's colleges.

Two critical contributions of M. E. Tidball's early work have been of central importance to subsequent studies concerned with the higher education of women. Both have to do with the innovation of disaggregating data related to women and women's colleges. One is the separation of the sexes (sex disaggregation) in all categories of the education environment, which permits a look specifically at the situation for women, whose experience had been previously submerged in the generalities of "students" and "faculty," the majority of whom were men. The other is the separation of institutions by type (type disaggregation) so that the contributions of women's colleges can be assessed in their own right, rather than being submerged within another broader category such as "liberal arts colleges."

Combining these two methodological applications, many researchers began to evaluate the situation for women in various institutional settings of higher education by a variety of methodologies, principally those of the social sciences. Unfortunately, a few have used their energies attempting to disprove the contributions of women's colleges. Nor has the contention ceased as various persons pronounce which is "better" for women—women's colleges or coeducation. Such discussion further stimulates our present effort, for we assert that trying to prove which of two (only two?) education formats is better is decidedly wrong-headed (Tannen 1998, 275–76). We do not believe that this is the right approach (M. E. Tidball 1996). We have, instead, set about to direct attention back to learning what works for women—to taking women seriously—by whatever is shown to be of benefit to women in the several constituencies of the education enterprise.

The research presented in Part Two has been gathered from three broad methodological streams. We call these findings the *lessons* from women's colleges. In Chapter 3, studies of baccalaureate origins and institutional productivity consistently demonstrate the disproportionately high rate of accomplishment of women's college graduates by more than one measure of accomplishment. In Chapter 4, quantitative and qualitative social science research, which forms the largest base of studies in higher education, shows that women's colleges provide an unprecedented number of characteristics important to positive student outcomes on campus. In Chapter 5, case studies performed on site at two women's colleges offer an additional angle of vision on the nature of the positive environment of women's colleges. Data from these several types of research are discussed, and conclusions and inferences are drawn, with respect to what they tell us about taking women seriously. Further, we observe that although methodologies, researchers, and disciplines have varied across many years, there are common findings that demonstrate women's colleges to be foremost environments for the development of achieving women.

Part Three

In Part Three, we discuss some of the ways in which the lessons—the research findings—have been applied in the ongoing education environment. That is, we describe the *legacies* from women's colleges in terms of what works for women when they are an institution's first priority. Legacies from within the campus environment relate to faculty, students, administrators, and the personal and programmatic interactions among them. Beyond the campus, legacies emerge through the actions of boards of trustees and alumnae associations in ways that ensure women will always be taken seriously. These legacies are presented as models for other segments of the higher education community. Again, particular women's colleges have been chosen as examples to show ways in which many such environments have responded to their commitment to take women seriously. The examples are certainly not all-inclusive, but they provide a framework within which to appreciate some of the ways in which women's colleges have applied their understanding of what works for women. We see these applications as legacies, because they can be adapted by and transferred to coeducational institutions for the benefit of women in that broader sector of the education community.

Part Four

Part Four is an overarching *summary* of our thinking and work, in which we make note of the settings and circumstances that encourage or submerge the talents of women whose endowments warrant accomplishment. We offer a list of institutional characteristics that our work suggests are essential to taking women seriously, and we offer the entirety of our book as a challenge to all of higher education to make taking women seriously the highest of priorities.

Additional Resources

For each chapter of Part One and Part Two, we have provided supplementary resources. The Supplement to Chapter 1 has been gathered from a publication of the American Council on Education Office of Women in Higher Education, *Educating the Majority*, and several international sources that have included global issues for women's education. For the Supplement to Chapter 2, the multiplicity of national databases are detailed that have had to be addressed and coordinated in order to develop this unique presentation on small colleges. The Supplements to Chapters 3, 4, and 5 support the research presented in Part Two, including methodologies of the studies whose results are presented in the parent chapters.

We have intentionally separated the principal text of the book from these additional resources to avoid encumbering the reader with distracting technical details. However, we wanted the material available so that researchers and students will have at hand the necessary information on which to base their own assessments of the presented results. Primary sources are also included in the extensive compilation of references. By providing this wealth of resources we hope to encourage further research and interest in investigations that have captured our imaginations for many years.

● ●

Writing this book has forever changed the way we think about the education of women. It is our hope that it will likewise contribute new dimensions to the thinking and actions of all who have a stake in the education of women, so that both women and men may become importantly involved in the development of an equitable and humane society.

PART ONE

· · · · · · · · · · ·

Women's Colleges
within the Context of
American Higher Education

Two contexts are used to explore the evolution of women's colleges as they have participated in American higher education. In the first chapter, the founders and foundings of six women's colleges are described in order to highlight the diversity among women's colleges and to indicate some of the qualities they hold in common. Beyond their beginnings, women's colleges are followed into the present era, during which enormous cultural and social changes have markedly altered all of higher education. Additionally, women's colleges are celebrated as leaders in learning and sharing what works for women and for their active participation in demonstrating substantive ways of taking women seriously. In the second chapter, national statistics are used to study the demographic characteristics of groups of educational institutions. Changes during the past 40 years, particularly with respect to enrollment trends, curricular expansions, and selected campus qualities, are identified and verified as important molding forces for all of higher education. Within this context, the evolution of women's colleges is examined in terms of how these institutions have responded. The perspective offered by these two contexts sets the stage for an examination of the lessons and legacies available from women's colleges.

CHAPTER 1

From Vision to Reality

The work will not stop with this institution. This enterprise may have to struggle through embarrassments for years, but its influence will be felt.
—Mary Lyon, 1836

E lisabeth Oesterlein, Mary Lyon, Mother Theodore Guerin, Susan Tolman Mills, Sophia Packard, Harriet Giles, Indiana Fletcher Williams. Of these seven women, only one is listed in standard biographical dictionaries; three are included in *Notable American Women*. The others are known only to limited audiences with special interests. Some were foreign born; others, at most, second-generation American. Some were older, some younger; some poor in things, others wealthy by the standards of their day. The unique and important contributions they made were not limited to any one region of the country nor to any single religious or national group. Yet all hold a very special and singular achievement in common, an achievement of enormous importance to women and to the education of women. For all were founders of women's colleges—colleges that are still active and vibrant and continuing to serve women to this day. With such considerable accomplishments, it is not only appropriate but necessary to remember and record their gifts to women, to the nation, and, in any last analysis, to the education of women throughout the world.

MEETING THE NEED

Setting Priorities: The Moravians and Salem

Elisabeth Oesterlein received her schooling at the Moravian Seminary in Bethlehem, Pennsylvania, most likely under the tutelage of 16-year-old Benigna

Ludwig (Reichel and Bigler 1901, 21). There, girls were taught languages and literature, religion, history, music, and a panoply of natural sciences ranging from astronomy to biology to physics. (Indeed, by 1800, the school subscribed to the *Journal of the Academy of Natural Sciences* and the *Journal of the Franklin Institute*.) Such schooling was extraordinary for girls and young women of its time (Haller 1953, 244). Then, in 1766, Elisabeth, along with 15 other young women, walked (most likely barefoot) from Bethlehem to North Carolina. By 1772, she was teaching little girls in what grew to become a boarding school and eventually Salem Academy and Salem College in Salem, North Carolina (Griffin 1979, 21). The Moravian Seminary in Bethlehem, Linden Hall in Lititz, Pennsylvania (founded 1746), and Salem Academy were all established by Moravian settlers as schools for girls in prerevolutionary America, a re-markable and unusual distinction (Beck 1921, 3).

More commonly in colonial America, girls were excluded even from town elementary schools, and the occasional use of private tutors to teach girls reading and writing was available only to the wealthy (Goodsell 1931, 5–6). Salem, as one of the Moravian boarding schools, however, brought a whole new educational philosophy to the young colony: they were designed to provide a *total environment* supportive of mental, physical, spiritual, and social development. Each school was presided over by a principal and his wife in an atmosphere decidedly and deliberately that of a warm and loving— though disciplined— family. Housing arrangements for the girls were based on age, while classroom assignments were determined by academic ability. Unlike the children of other new settlers in America, Moravian girls were taught to speak, read, and write in both their ancestral language (German) and in English; one scheme was to use German for three days, English for three days, and then both languages on Sunday. In addition to classroom study, there were also practical lessons using maps, globes, and other equipment. Both girls and boys were taught to work with their hands and at physical labor, such as gardening and household chores, not simply because it was considered good discipline, but because Moravians were opposed to holding slaves. Time for play and exercise, and for music and reading, were integral parts of a balanced approach to living in the settings of great physical attractiveness, both natural and architectural, that characterized Salem (Haller 1953, 247–67).

By the end of the Revolutionary War, the Moravian schools were ap-plauded as the finest education available for girls. In response to popular demand, they opened their doors in 1785 to girls of all faiths, nationalities, and races in a spirit of genuine inclusiveness (Haller 1953, 354). Perhaps what is most impressive about these educational environments is that they have not only endured times of national political, social, military, and monetary strife, but they have also managed to flourish in the face of enormous antagonism toward substantive education for women. Historians of American education note that the colonial view of woman was "simply that she was intellectually inferior—incapable, merely by reason of being a woman, of great thoughts . . . Her place was in the home . . ." (Rudolph 1962, 307–8). Yet from Salem emerged a model of both the form and content of what was to follow, not just the Academy for girls but the College for young women as well. For out of these simple but deliberate beginnings grew an example of the crucial nature of interrelationships among all aspects of the collegiate environment that result in positive outcomes for women (M. E. Tidball 1973a; M. E. Tidball and Kistiakowski 1976; M. E. Tidball 1980a; Pascarella 1984; M. E. Tidball 1993).

Clearly, the roots of Salem College demonstrated that, among the Moravians, women were being taken seriously—even though the education of girls and women was of low priority in the community at large. Outward indicators today of the importance of women in women's college environments include such things as the telling of Sister Oesterlein's story each Founder's Day at Salem, her name gracing the highest honor bestowed upon a graduating senior; at Smith College, the presence of the Sophia Smith Collection; at Wilson College, the Sarah Wilson Scholarships; and in many institutions, women's names on campus buildings and women's portraits in college libraries. While it is not unusual for colleges to have such traditions and artifacts, what distinguishes women's colleges is that *women* are regularly and prominently recognized and celebrated for their important involvement in the life of the school. All contribute to the persuasiveness of this influential though subtle curriculum that bespeaks taking women seriously.

The Next Steps: Mary Lyon and Mount Holyoke

Further opportunities for collegiate-level education for women would have to wait more than half a century—until another teacher, Mary Lyon, began her amazing thrust to found Mount Holyoke in the outback of New England. Characterized as an individual who relied on prayer and gave unremitting attention to detail, she managed to collect funds, inspire helpers, and encourage parents to send their daughters to her school (Green 1979, 101–55). Indeed, it is reported of the founder that indifference and opposition to her project were so great that it was necessary for her "to trudge the hills of western Massachusetts pleading, arguing, and sometimes, in her great zeal, refusing to take her foot off the wheel of a wagon or rake until the farmer she was soliciting had vouchsafed to give at least a share of his crop to the seminary" (Curti 1936, 11). As for the male clergy upon whom she had expected to rely for financial assistance, even as they readily supported the education of men, Mary Lyon attempted many fund-raising efforts before she was forced to acknowledge the reality that they were not interested in educating women (Green 1979, 116–17).

Nonetheless, she persevered. And on November 8, 1837, some 80 young women converged upon South Hadley, Massachusetts, moving into a new five-story building and contributing their labor to the daily life and work of the school while they studied collegiate-level courses in the three-year curriculum (Green 1979, 173).

It must be recalled that women were thought incapable of higher learning on at least two counts: first, they were mentally inferior to men; and second, they were physically too frail for the rigors imposed by high levels of mental activity (Newcomer 1959, 26–28). If the former led to the inclusion of courses in the natural sciences and laboratories, the latter provided impetus for the development of programs in physiology, hygiene, and physical education. Even the work program at Mount Holyoke was viewed as contributing to the physical stamina of the students, thereby augmenting the overall fitness program (Green 1979, 114). By the 1870s, when Wellesley and Smith were founded, physical education was regularly included as a required part of the curriculum of women's colleges, while at Yale and Harvard, it was voluntary (Newcomer 1959, 28). One important lesson learned was that women *could* understand how their bodies worked; thus, the *participation of women in more academically oriented science studies* can be seen, in part, as growing out of efforts to maintain or improve physical health. These requirements served as the starting point for the subsequent and continuing preeminence of women's colleges in graduating disproportionately large numbers of women who become natural scientists. Not surprisingly, the most recent data available today show that women's colleges outrank all other institutions of higher education in their production of women who go on to earn doctorates in the natural sciences and women who enter schools of medicine, fields customarily associated with masculine undertakings (M. E. Tidball and Kistiakowski 1976; M. E. Tidball 1985; M. E. Tidball 1986b).

A First for Roman Catholic Women: St. Mary-of-the-Woods

Courage in the face of enormous struggle is a thread running through the stories of many early founders of women's colleges. In mid-nineteenth century America, Roman Catholic schools and convents were burned, nuns and sisters were blasphemed and assaulted, and Roman Catholics (especially women) were commonly demeaned and threatened (Stewart 1994, 80–93).

Into such an inhospitable climate came Mother Theodore Guerin. Leaving her home and friends in France in July 1840, journeying many months with five other women across the North Atlantic, Mother Guerin and her little band of colleagues at last climbed down the ladder from their ship on the East River into a rowboat, by means of which they finally made landfall in New York City. Then, in October, after three long and arduous months of travel, they reached Indiana where they found—nothing. Only dense woods. No school, no students, no teachers (Doherty 1993, 2; Stewart 1994, 137–38). As they gathered themselves together and surveyed the enormous task before them, they proceeded to found and build a college for women in the wilderness of southern Indiana. The year of founding was 1840. The college is St. Mary-of-the-Woods. Today, Sister Barbara Doherty retells this story so that all who hear it can be witnesses, adding that "stories which come from this holy place . . . touch something deep within our humanity that resonates with, and draws courage from, the power of myth and story" (Doherty 1993, 2).

Indeed, all the stories of the beginnings of women's colleges, and of courage in the face of struggle, make women proud and unerringly grateful to those who walked the road before, making possible the institutions that clearly have taken women seriously and clearly will always continue to do so, for that is an inextricable and nonnegotiable part of their mission as long as they continue to call themselves colleges for women. That *inspiring role models* continue to be of vital importance to women is regularly seen in studies that show a positive and statistically significant relationship between the presence of women faculty and the lifelong achievement of women students (M. E. Tidball 1973b; M. E. Tidball 1974b; M. E. Tidball 1986b; M. E. Tidball 1989).

The Second Generation: Mills as Daughter of Mount Holyoke

Yet the history of women's colleges is not only about women of humble backgrounds trudging their way to new beginnings. Women of greater privilege also committed their energies, their ideas, and their material resources to the cause of women's education. Susan Tolman and her five sisters were all graduates of Mount Holyoke Seminary. After completing her studies in 1845, Susan taught at the seminary for three years before leaving to marry the Reverend Cyrus Mills. Following 15 years as missionaries in Ceylon (now Sri Lanka), the Millses returned to the United States and settled in California (Green 1979, 235).

Mills College dates its founding to 1852, when its predecessor institution, an academy for girls at Benicia, was begun by a group of men whose daughters had accompanied them west in the rush for gold and who sought a quality education as well as protection from the roughness of mining camp life. To this scene, in 1865, came Susan and Cyrus Mills, who together purchased the Ladies' Seminary at Benicia, later moving the school to the foothills of Oakland. The principal building of the new site, with its running water and gas lights, was heralded as one of the finest educational buildings on the Pacific Coast. The teaching staff was improved, too—not least through the importation of other faculty from Mount Holyoke (Keep 1946, 11–97). The *network idea* had begun, and continues to this day, as women's college students, faculty, and alumnae support one another's development as individuals and as corporate members of the larger women's college community.

Networking can be seen today in incidents such as those of 1990 after the trustees at Mills College voted to admit men. Mills students went on strike, blockading buildings, shaving their heads, and taping shut their mouths to symbolize that they were not being heard. Joining them were thousands at women's colleges across the country, with the largest rally of all at Mount Holyoke. A 1993 *New York Times* article quotes a Mills graduate: "There was a feeling that we did something remarkable" (Quinn 1993). Indeed they did, for they not only re-energized Mills, but also the bond among students and alumnae from all women's colleges who learned what it means to be an educated and involved woman on behalf of other women in the closing decade of the twentieth century.

Two Women Reach out to the Margin: The Founding of Spelman College

They were both New Englanders from New Salem, Massachusetts, yet they did not actually meet until 1854, when Sophia Packard was 30 and Harriet Giles 21. They were then at the New Salem Academy, where Sophia was preceptress and Harriet a senior student. It was also there that they began their friendship and a lifelong working partnership, for they found they shared a common dream and vision to become teachers and eventually to establish a school of their own.

Little did they imagine, however, that their dream would materialize in the company of 11 African American girls in the basement of Friendship Baptist Church, in Atlanta, Georgia, on April 11, 1881. Yet there they were, under the sponsorship of the Women's American Baptist Home Mission Society and with the concurrence and joy of the 12 black pastors of Atlanta (Read 1961, 4–48). The women's long struggle had at last taken on recognizable form and content.

Throughout the history of Spelman College, there are many themes and many common threads with other colleges for women. One that stands out is the longstanding and strong bond of friendship between the founders, Sophia Packard and Harriet Giles, truly a model for friendship among the women of Spelman. Evidence of this today can be seen in the Sisters Chapel, dedicated in 1927 to the memory of the daughters of Lucy Henry Spelman, and the tribute from Laurence Spelman Rockefeller to his mother, Abby Aldrich Rockefeller, on Founders Day 1953: "She was a specialist in friendship" (Read 1961, 208, 342). Indeed, Spelman students continue to speak of *a tradition of friendship* "handed down through generations" as "a bond spanning time that turns classmates into sisters" (Spelman 1996a). Experienced more broadly are the enduring friendships among women who have shared the experience of living, working, and playing with others of their kind in a variety of supportive environments—from girls' schools and camps to women's colleges and substantive professional and volunteer enterprises by and for women, that is, venues whose first priority (and hence, mission) is to take women seriously (M. E. Tidball 1980b).

For the Love of a Daughter: The Establishment of Sweet Briar College

There is yet another attribute of the women's college culture that deserves attention, namely, *the generosity of women in behalf of others*, especially other women. It is a kind of service ethic that may be exemplified by the last will and testament of Indiana Fletcher Williams, which provided for the founding and early endowment of Sweet Briar College in southern Virginia in 1901. By the time Indiana Fletcher—Miss Indie to all who knew her—was 37 years old, in 1865, she had inherited a considerable amount of land known as Sweet Briar Plantation, where she lived alone, her parents having died and her siblings living at a remove. It was at that time in her life that Henry Williams, a graduate of Trinity College in Hartford, Connecticut, and the General Theological Seminary in New York, arrived at Sweet Briar and sought her hand in marriage. She accepted with delight, and the two subsequently divided their time between the culture and excitement of New York City and the restorative peacefulness of Sweet Briar.

Two years after their marriage, their only child was born— Maria to the family Bible, but Daisy to all who knew her. In January 1884 at the age of 17, Daisy died of pneumonia, a crushing loss from which her mother never recovered. Henry died in 1889. Then, in 1898, Miss Indie's brother-in-law died, leaving her the majority of his estate. Miss Indie had become very wealthy, but was very much alone, living for but another two years, until 1900 (Stohlman 1956, 27–37).

But what of the vast estate and the 6,000 acres of Sweet Briar Plantation? No one seemed to know— no one, that is, until the day of the funeral when a few friends and relatives were gathering at Sweet Briar House. Only then, serendipitously, was the will discovered in a little wicker basket that rolled out of the linen press as guest rooms were being prepared for the visitors. The paper was handed to a clergyman who read from it aloud. In this manner it was learned that virtually the entirety of the estate was to be used to "Procure the incorporation . . . of Sweet Briar institute . . . for the object . . . of establishing . . . a school or seminary . . . for the education . . . of young women." There were few additional directives, save that the school should be self-supporting and that the board might establish scholarships for deserving students (Stohlman 1956, 38–39).

In many ways, this was not only Miss Indie's legacy, but also Henry's and Daisy's—Henry's because he had often spoken of establishing a school for girls and young women, especially after Daisy's death, and Daisy's because she was the inspiration to both her parents. Nonetheless, it was through Miss Indie's ultimate generosity that both land and funds were provided for the building of a college for women. And like Miss Indie, thousands upon thousands of women's college alumnae continue in the spirit of her legacy as they participate in the marshaling of financial support for their colleges, whether by many small gifts such as Mary Lyon secured, or the largesse of a Miss Indie. If they have much, they give much; if little, then little. But what is important is that they are donors to the full extent of their capability. And the legacy continues to the present time: women who are graduates of women's colleges, both Roman Catholic and independent, are the most loyal contributors to their colleges of their material wealth and possessions of all donors, women and men, no matter how large or how small their gifts in monetary terms (Matthews 1991).

These six attributes of the women's college ethos, exemplified by the founders of six that have persisted to the present time, stand out as legacies of early women's colleges at which women were taken seriously. Through traditions built upon what works for women, these colleges have demonstrated the necessity and benefits of

- Involving the *total collegiate environment* in the education of women
- Ensuring women the opportunity to *study in all fields*, including those traditionally unwelcoming to them
- Providing a critical mass of *women role models*
- Demonstrating the principle of *networking*
- Creating a place and time for developing deep and lasting *friendships among women*
- Encouraging the *generosity* of women in behalf of others

These, then, are among the great legacies from the past, from women's colleges wherein women have been taken seriously.

HIGHER EDUCATION FOR WOMEN AS A GROWTH ENTERPRISE

There were many other collegiate institutions that also admitted women before the turn of the twentieth century, in particular, the land-grant colleges and many state universities, especially as an accompaniment to the westward expansion of the country. Women were valued as partners in the work of pioneering, and most men saw no reason why women might not also participate in higher learning. By 1869–70, 41 percent of all collegiate institutions in the United States were open to women, although the number of women actually receiving baccalaureate and first professional degrees was less than 1,400 that year, while some 8,000 men were graduated (Newcomer 1959, 37;

Snyder and Hoffman 1995, 250). More important, as access for women to higher education increased in coeducational settings, subjects of the curriculum regularly fell into two principal categories: those that were "useful, full-blooded and manly" and those that were "ornamental, dilettantish and feminine" (Rudolph 1962, 324). Segregation of women and men according to sex-traditional fields became a well-established practice in coeducational schools, while freedom to pursue studies of any sort was evident for both women and men in women's colleges and men's colleges. Reflecting this are data on fields of student concentration in 1956 in which women in coeducational institutions majoring in the sciences was 10 percent compared with 19 percent in women's colleges; and men in coeducational institutions majoring in the arts and humanities was 7 percent compared with 19 percent in men's colleges (Newcomer 1959, 95).

But the idea of higher education for women did catch on in some places, and by the closing decades of the nineteenth century, enrollments of women soared. Between 1875 and 1900, enrollments for women increased sixfold, twice that for the overall student population (Dexter 1906, 449), and although at the University of Michigan in 1870 there was but one woman student (and 429 men), by 1898, 53 percent of all degrees were awarded to women. Northwestern University found it judicious to add an engineering course to narrow the differences in enrollment between women and men, and Stanford instituted a quota for women "to preserve the college from an unwanted change in character" (Rudolph 1962, 323–24). That concern was reiterated nearly a century later when, in 1972, all-male Amherst College recommended the admission of women, but assured its male constituents that the college would still "preserve a sufficient number of male students for traditional activities of the college" (Ward 1972, 6).

Some coeducational colleges stand out as attempting to operate in a more equitable manner, most notably, Oberlin College, the first school to grant college degrees to both women and men, beginning in 1837. Founded upon a strong evangelical Protestant base that expected educated men to become ministers and educated women their wives, the college nonetheless permitted women access to all studies, even though the large majority of women chose to complete the Ladies' Course. Not only did curricular distinctions reinforce traditional views of women's intellectual inferiority, one professor was quoted asserting, "We find that the presence of the *girls* has a good effect upon the *men*" (emphasis added). Women students at Oberlin argued for a debating society and for a literary magazine, but both requests were denied (Solomon 1987, 82–87). Instead, many faculty continued to think of the presence of women chiefly as a "civilizing influence" upon men (Ginzberg 1987, 69). Thus, although Oberlin made a bold and worthy effort to advance coeducation–and was frequently used as a model for other colleges in this important initiative—

the meaning of coeducation was severely limited. As summarized by Florence Howe:

> . . . if we are looking for a coeducational institution that is a model of equality between the sexes, if we are looking for a coeducational curriculum, a coeducational faculty, coeducational assumptions about the rights of both sexes to work at the same jobs and for equal pay, even coeducational assumptions about the rights of men and women to share in the drudgeries and joys of family life: we will not find any of this in Oberlin's history. (Howe 1984, 209)

Cornell University, chartered in 1865, is recognized as the first important eastern institution and land-grant college to admit "anyone, to study anything," thereby serving as a prod—if not a model—to other colleges racked with continuing uncertainty about women's educability or the desirability of mixing the sexes in so crucial an enterprise for the nation (Rudolph 1962, 266). In any last analysis, however, it must be appreciated that the meaning of "coeducation" was often obscured in enrollment statistics, where but a single woman might be the justification for the co-.

Observers of these efforts over the years to include women among men, particularly in institutions that were founded for men only, have noted that women have been welcomed especially during those times when enrollments of men have been modest. These occasions have regularly included times of national military service when women, but not men, were available to become students (Newcomer 1959, 37–38). More recently, as financial pressures (particularly in private colleges and universities) have necessitated a larger pool of applicants who are not only academically qualified but also capable of paying tuition, the recruitment of women has been the salvation of formerly all-male institutions. The concerns for the present and future, however, relate to defining what constitutes equitable education for women and men and working toward goals by which it can be attained (M. E. Tidball 1983).

Women's Colleges Participate in the Growth

Most of the women's colleges that are present today were also founded during that halcyon time that led up to the turn of the century—Stephens, Wesleyan, The College of Notre Dame of Maryland, Hood, Wells, Wilson, Bennett, Bryn Mawr, Spelman, Randolph-Macon Woman's College, Smith, Chestnut Hill, and Barnard among them and in addition to those mentioned in this book. By 1900, there were some 150 women's colleges in the United States, and 71 percent of all collegiate institutions admitted women, albeit many quite reluctantly (Rudolph 1962, 322). Further development of women's colleges continued into the early new century, when Sweet Briar, Scripps, The College of St. Catherine, Emmanuel, Chestnut Hill, and Mount St. Mary, among others, were founded. Indeed, by 1930, 85 percent of all collegiate institutions were open to women, a proportion similar to that for men (Newcomer 1959, 37), although frequently equity did not accompany equality of access or equality of tuition charges (M. E. Tidball 1973b; M. E. Tidball 1976b). Except for ill-fated Kirkland and a few small Roman Catholic colleges, the establishment of women's colleges was complete by the 1940s. By 1960, 214 four-year women's colleges were recorded in the United States, among the largest number of any time (M. E. Tidball 1977b).

Global Events, National Responses

Then, the world changed dramatically. It would be impossible to enumerate the multiplicity of events, discoveries, and exigencies that overlapped and coalesced to change the academic world so radically in the late 1950s. A vignette from the lives of two academics suggests the unfolding drama:

> The alarm went off at three a.m. and, silent but very much alert, we moved into the routine laid out the evening before: start the water boiling for the hot chocolate; pull on the old wool ski pants and warm jackets; pick up the binoculars and the Thermos; set out in the bleak, clear night for the empty lot at 57th and Drexel; and wait and watch. Soon, across the still-dark sky, eerily and precisely on schedule, moving inexorably—too rapidly for an airplane, too slowly for a shooting star or comet—across that Chicago sky and easily visible without the binoculars, Sputnik I entered our lives. We did not know then the extent to which it would influence our future as teachers and thinkers, or the roles of institutions, or the whole fabric of society. The star of science and technology had been revealed, and we responded collectively as did the Wise Men of old: "We have seen the star in the East and have come to worship . . ." (M. E. Tidball 1976a, 193–94)

There followed a period of intense male domination throughout all facets of American life, coincident with the growth of massive federal expenditures for scientific and technological development. That the national pursuit of science and scientific expertise should bias the goals and rewards of society in favor of men is suggested by data from the National Research Council, which revealed that 44 percent of all doctorates received by 1973 had been awarded to men in the sciences. The corresponding figure for women was 3 percent (National Academy of Sciences 1974). Thus, while postsecondary education for women had become more accessible, the work of society demanded participation in fields most rigorously associated with its concept of masculinity (M. E. Tidball 1976b). And although women's colleges contributed women graduates to the scientific endeavor in disproportionately large numbers and percentages (M. E. Tidball and Kistiakowski 1976; M. E. Tidball 1985; M. E. Tidball 1986b), this was rarely viewed as an attribute to be emulated or desired, either by applicants for admission or by other institutions. No one else, it seemed, was interested in taking women *that* seriously.

Higher Education Caught in the Crossfire

Where once there had been a will that motivated a way for the founders of women's colleges, the slogan now became, "Where there's a will, there's a death." The beginning of a societal sea change was underway, continuing with the onset of student unrest at the University of California, Berkeley, in 1964 and spreading rapidly throughout institutions of higher education (M. E. Tidball 1977, 4395). Student demands for change in virtually everything, along with disruptive and costly campus demonstrations and an emphasis on personal and sexual freedom, not only brought about a new era of redefinition but led also to the dissolution of many small, private, liberal arts colleges with limited resources—women's, men's, and coeducational, especially those closely church related. After 1960, the number of women's colleges declined. An even greater loss befell coeducational colleges of similar size and control (F. T. Smith 1974; see also expanded discussion in Chapter 2). Clearly, for the young, the place to be was large, coeducational, open, and pulsating with excitement—a kind of four-year Woodstock. Thus, at women's colleges, struggles for survival abounded, even as struggles for establishment had occupied the founders some hundred years before.

Virtually all women's and men's institutions convened committees to study what they called the coeducation question. What they really meant was simply the admission of students of the other sex. Princeton University, for example, was preoccupied with ensuring that the cost of additional dormitory and office space would be offset by the anticipated increase in tuition dollars; records of their discussions make no mention of the intellectual, philosophical, or social responsibilities or concerns arising from their decision to admit—and presumably, to educate—women. They were pleased to note a "surprisingly low" negative differential between annual expenses and income that would result from the admission of 1,000 women (in addition to 3,200 men), thereby encouraging the move to coeducation.

Financial matters regularly and clearly outpaced educational philosophy or gender and developmental issues (Patterson 1968, 5–56). Later, Princeton officials reported to a committee at Amherst College that they estimated it would take 15 years (i.e., until 1984) before they would have at least 33 percent women in their tenured ranks (Amherst Visiting Committee on Coeducation 1974). In fact, Princeton recorded only 5.6 percent of their faculty as tenured women by 1984 and, by 1996, this proportion had reached only 14.1 percent (American Association of University Professors 1984; 1996). "Our girls," announced a Dartmouth faculty member, "are just like our men." How reminiscent of Oberlin a century and a half before! So certain was the prevailing wisdom that coeducation was the only viable model that many were blinded from contemplating alternatives and regularly predicted—and even applauded—the total disappearance of women's colleges. For surely they would wisely imitate their brothers, as they had always done in the past, and they would see the light. But this time they didn't.

A NEW IDENTITY AND PURPOSE

Pauline Tompkins and the Cedar Crest Conference

In 1969, for perhaps the first time in their history, women's colleges began seriously to organize themselves to pool their collective wisdom and experience. The place was Cedar Crest College in Allentown, Pennsylvania. The occasion was an invitational conference on women's colleges. The instigator was Cedar Crest's new president, Pauline Tompkins, a Mount Holyoke graduate of the class of 1941.

The conference was truly a landmark event, not because some well-honed document on the benefits of women's colleges emerged, for it did not. Rather, it pointed to the desirability, if not necessity, for those convinced of the value of women's colleges as an option for the education of women to find ways to articulate that value in an increasingly combative marketplace and to join in a variety of cooperative ventures to share strategies, programs, and moral support with one another. Indeed, since 1969, many collaborations have developed, as well as a variety of regional and national organizations, alliances, and conferences for the study and support of higher education for women.

In her closing remarks at the Cedar Crest Conference, President Tompkins said, "what is really needed is that we embark on a process of transforming ourselves" (Cedar Crest 1969, 75). What prophetic words! For that is exactly what the survivors have done—every one of them. And the women's colleges that serve as the most inspiring institutional models today are those that did not passively endorse the status quo and remain "women's colleges" but those that made the deliberate and positive decision to become "colleges for women." Two indicators of that resolve are evident in small but important figures that surely owe the directions they signify to the self-consciousness of women and their colleges generated by the Cedar Crest Conference some three decades ago: of the 18 women's colleges represented there in 1969, 13 were headed by men; today, 16 of the 18 *continue* as colleges for women, and *all* have women presidents. What a transformation! What a legacy!

They Heard the Trumpet Call

The Women's College Coalition, established in 1972 under the aegis of the Association of American Colleges, responded to President Tompkins's challenge to undertake transformation. Guided by a committee of presidents and comprising colleges as institutional members, the coalition sought to increase the visibility and hence acceptability (if not the popularity) of women's colleges. At the committee's first meeting in 1973, a principal agenda item was the newly released report of the Carnegie Commission on Higher Education, *Opportunities for Women in Higher Education.* Included was a chapter on women's colleges, in which the editors offered the following assessment:

> These accomplishments of the graduates of women's colleges [as reported in M. E. Tidball 1973b] are worthy of emphasis, not only as they bear on decisions of women's colleges to continue or abandon their single-sex status, but also—and far more significantly in terms of potential influence—as they suggest how changes in policies and faculty attitudes in coeducational institutions could affect the accomplishments of their women students. (Carnegie Commission on Higher Education 1973, 74)

The presidents could be heartened by this national recognition of their institutions and their implied value for the education of women in a much wider context.

Wellesley Joins in the Renewal

Other substantive responses to the challenge were also in evidence. By 1974 Wellesley, with impetus from its president, Barbara Newell, a Vassar graduate of 1951, was off and running with plans for the Wellesley Center for Research on Women. In 1979, the Center, along with Wellesley College and the Federation of Organizations for Professional Women, sponsored a national research conference called "Educational Environments and the Undergraduate Woman." The list of 56 participants from academe, foundations, and government included such stalwarts as Jacqueline Fleming, Jill Conway, Carolyn Elliott, Carol Gilligan, Patricia Bell Scott, Florence Howe, Elizabeth Tidball, Adele Simmons, Susan Bailey, and Mariam Chamberlain. All were either presenting papers, chairing panels, or serving as discussants in such diverse areas as "Issues of Access and Selection," "Aspirations, Attainments and Outcomes," "Institutional Cultures," "Classroom Climates," and "Issues of Curricula in Liberal Education" (Wellesley College 1979).

Conferees' interest was in learning about environments for the education of women wherever they may be—the nature of interactions between and among women students, teaching faculty, and other elements of the total environment—in order to suggest ways most appropriate for the facilitation of learning for women. The scope was the entirety of higher education, though it was clear that colleges for women provided a wealth of critical contributions to the discussions. And it was clear to all that colleges for women were taking women seriously, providing considerable empirical research that has a bearing on the education of women.

The Immaculata Conference: Reports from the Community

A decade later, another major conference took place, this time for all with an interest in the education of collegiate women. Entitled "Women's Colleges— The 90s and Beyond," this national conclave was held under the leadership of Sister President Marian William Hoben at Immaculata College, in celebration of Immaculata's 80th anniversary in November of 1990. The Roman Catholic sisters had truly come a long way from the skepticism, if not suspicion, of the preceding decades. It was a bold move, and one that resulted in much shared information, opportunities for networking, and considerable good will. Included were discussions of an experiential nature—"Alumnae Achievers," "Preparing Women for Leadership Roles," and "Academic Programs: Courses That Challenge." There were panels on student life, athletics, careers, alumnae relations, and public relations programs for nontraditional students; roundtables for student leaders, admissions staff, and male teachers and administrators in colleges for women; and, at the close, a panel of presidents (Immaculata 1990). The exchanges within the sessions and around the coffeepots and dinner tables were serious, enthusiastic, spirited, and engaging.

One especially important feature of this conference was a detailed and open-ended questionnaire sent beforehand to all women's colleges of record, which garnered a 75 percent response. A summary of the questionnaire results, in a keynote address at the conference, noted the inclusion of many transforming initiatives, ranging from curricular programs—such as communications, computer science, deaf education, global awareness, Jewish studies, and gerontology—to considerations for special groups of women including the economically disadvantaged, Latinas, and single mothers with children, thereby attesting to concern and outreach to those not customarily served by the higher education system.

Getting It All Together

By this time, the Women's College Coalition had gained a measure of focus and direction. In addition to its regular meetings of presidents of women's colleges, surveys of contributions of women's college graduates, and frequent reports to the media, the coalition also received research moneys from the Jessie Ball DuPont Fund, enabling the establishment of a small grants project. The first nine awards were made in 1992–93 from among 55 proposals received; the eight 1993–94 awards were selected from 122 requests. Clearly, research focusing on the education of women had attained widespread scholarly acceptance, as well as intense interest in academic circles.

One facet of the DuPont grant provided for a conference so that research results from the funded projects, as well as other relevant communications, could be widely shared. "Studies in Success: Applying Effective Models to Educating Women and Girls," hosted by Mount Holyoke College in November 1994, was presented publicly to an enthusiastic and engaged audience that had grown from the 18 institutions present at the Cedar Crest Conference to some 300 women and men (Women's College Coalition 1994). Thus women's colleges had reached a new level of collective maturity through their participation in the coalition and in their outreach in the cause of women's education.

LEGACIES BECOME LESSONS BECOME NEW LEGACIES

The recounting of past deeds and present responses—of legacies and lessons—could go on and on, far too long to enumerate here. Yet even this brief sampling shows colleges for women to be imaginative, impressive, generous, and tough. Salem, Mount Holyoke, St. Mary-of-the-Woods, Mills, Spelman, and Sweet Briar serve as examples of institutions whose qualities characterize women's colleges more widely: engagement of the total environment in the education of women; commitment to assuring women opportunities to study in all fields; the presence of a critical mass of women role models; demonstrations of the principles of networking; a place and time for developing deep and lasting friendships among women; and the generosity of women in behalf of other women. They also celebrate the lives of some whose work has cast long shadows of inspiration and expertise upon their colleges. These are, indeed, rich legacies.

Cedar Crest, Wellesley, Immaculata, and the Women's College Coalition—all sponsors of substantive conferences on what works for women—are contemporary models of women's institutions exploring issues of educational philosophy, research, experience, and recognition. They and their sisters thereby bring lessons for the advancement of the education of women, regardless of the educational setting.

All of these diverse institutions serve as examples of a thoroughgoing dedication to the common cause of women as a first priority. All are continually transforming themselves, even as they exert leadership on behalf of women. All are receiving legacies, teaching lessons, and creating new legacies.

CHAPTER 2

A Half Century of Change

For different purposes human beings need different structures, both small ones and large ones, some exclusive and some comprehensive. Yet people find it difficult to keep two seemingly opposite necessities of truth in their minds at the same time. They clamor for a final solution . . .

—E. F. Schumacher, 1973

In order to understand the environment for women in American higher education, it is first necessary to appreciate the impact of recent demographic changes with respect to the different types of education institutions. At mid-century the largest number of students was enrolled in universities followed closely by smaller institutions that were primarily residential and featured a liberal arts curriculum. Most women's colleges were members of this latter group.[1]

The period between 1920 and 1950 has been described as one in which the number of women's colleges increased and the kinds of institutions intended only for women students became more diverse. It should be acknowledged that there were problems in collecting accurate educational statistics prior to 1970 (Harwarth, Maline, and DeBra 1997, 28 n. a). Table 1 lists approximations for the number of higher education institutions, by sex of student, for the period from 1870 to 1990. The number of women's colleges and universities peaked at approximately 300 institutions between 1950 and 1970; whereas men's colleges and universities peaked at about 400 institutions some 70 years earlier (Newcomer 1959, 37). In contrast to the declining number of institutions for men only and for women only, the increase from 1870 to 1990 in the number of coeducational institutions—from 169 to 3,318—exceeded the increase in the total number of institutions of higher education by 133 institutions. In 1870, coeducational colleges and universities represented only 29 percent of the total number of institutions; by 1990, that proportion had increased to 92 percent. Somehow, a mixture of social pressures (coeducation

19

seemed to some more "equitable" than men's colleges and women's colleges) and economic pressures (comparatively low tuition at public institutions and even lower at community colleges[2]) has justified coeducation, regardless of the broader educational consequences. This is exactly the kind of singular resolution that Schumacher warned about in *Small Is Beautiful* (1973, 66). Documenting some of the variables that have changed, their interlocking nature, and their impact on women's colleges is the subject of this chapter.

TABLE 1

NUMBER AND TYPES OF HIGHER EDUCATION INSTITUTIONS

Year	Total Number of Institutions	Men Only	Women Only	Coeducational
1870	582	343	70	169
1890	1,082	400	217	465
1910	1,083	292	163	628
1930	1,322	198	212	912
1950	1,808	228	267	1,313
1970	2,409	228	238	2,024
1990	3,598	174	106	3,318

Notes: Adapted from Newcomer 1959; her data were used for 1870–1930. Data for 1950 were from U.S. Department of Health, Education, and Welfare 1951 and include first professional degrees. Data for 1970 and 1990 were from U.S. Department of Health, Education, and Welfare 1970 and U.S. Department of Education 1996 and do not include first professional degrees.

Sources: Newcomer 1959; U.S. Department of Health, Education, and Welfare 1951; U.S. Department of Health, Education, and Welfare 1970; U.S. Department of Education 1996.

Characterizing the diversity among colleges for women only in the midtwentieth century becomes a matter of how to choose the distinctions. On the basis of contemporaneous categories, there were two-year institutions, four-year colleges, teachers' colleges, professional schools, master's-degree-granting institutions, and coordinate colleges, as well as full-scale universities. (The concept of "comprehensive institutions"[3] had not yet even been proposed.) Notwithstanding this variety, it must be acknowledged that the predominant institution type in higher education for women at the middle of the twentieth century consisted of a small, residential college featuring a liberal arts curriculum. Publicly supported teachers' colleges of this era were also small, residential colleges, although their curricula were more specialized. It is noteworthy that more than half of the women's colleges in the 1950s had a founding affiliation with the Roman Catholic Church. To understand the pressures on women's colleges as a group, it is first necessary to review the gross demographic changes that have taken place in American higher education since the 1950s. For introductory information on the frame of reference and the sources of information used to support the conclusions below, see the Supplement to Chapter 2.

THE MOLDING FORCES

American higher education changed considerably between 1953 and 1993. A number of molding forces in that 40-year interval can be identified. The increase in total enrollment during that period is the major molding force that brought about change. Disaggregations in larger categories are published annually, and they identify components of the total enrollment increase that are, themselves, molding forces: increases in part-time students, increases in women students, and increases in the number of public institutions. However, to obtain a better understanding, it is necessary to refine the view. This requires going beyond the disaggregations in the public documents and identifying changes in enrollment among four prototypical institution types: two-year institutions, small colleges, comprehensive institutions, and universities. To appreciate the impact of this and other molding forces on women's colleges, it is necessary to refine the view a second time and focus on the small colleges. Although this category has the smallest total enrollment of the four institution types, it does consist of approximately 1,000 accredited institutions and includes approximately 85 percent of the women's colleges that are of primary interest in this volume.

It is acknowledged that education parameters other than those presented here have also changed over this 40-year period. However, the forces selected for discussion in this chapter are those that can be documented; they also represent forces that have had a direct bearing on how women's colleges have fared.

Changes in Total Enrollment from 1953 to 1993

The total enrollment[4] in higher education in 1953 was 2.2 million students; by 1993, this number had increased to 14.3 million students (Badger and Rice 1956; Snyder and Hoffman 1995, 176). In Table 2, the total enrollment numbers are disaggregated by attendance status, by sex of students, and by control (governance) of institution.

Attendance Status   At the outset of this period, the approximately 430,000 students enrolled part time represented 20 percent of the total enrollment (Badger and Rice 1956, 42–43). By 1993, there were 6.4 million part-time students, who represented 45 percent of the total enrollment.

Sex of Students   In 1953, there were approximately 800,000 women enrolled in higher education, which constituted 36 percent of all the students. By

TABLE 2

TOTAL ENROLLMENT BY ATTENDANCE STATUS, SEX, AND INSTITUTIONAL CONTROL

Year	Total Enrollment	Attendance Status		Sex of Students		Control of Institution	
		Full-Time	Part-Time	Men	Women	Public	Private
1953	2.231	1.801	0.430	1.423	0.808	1.186	1.045
1963	4.780	3.184	1.596	2.962	1.818	3.081	1.698
1973	9.602	6.189	3.413	5.371	4.231	7.420	2.183
1983	12.465	7.261	5.204	6.024	6.441	9.683	2.782
1993	14.306	8.128	6.428	6.428	7.878	11.189	3.117

Notes: 1963 part-time data include resident students and all extension students; 1993 data are preliminary; enrollment figures are for millions of students.

Sources: Badger and Rice 1956, 42–43; Snyder and Hoffman 1995, 176.

1993, there were 7.9 million women students, who constituted 55 percent of that year's total enrollment.

Control of Institution   The enrollment in public institutions in 1953 was 1.2 million students, or 53 percent of the total enrollment. By 1993, there were 11.2 million students enrolled in public institutions, which represented 78 percent of all students.

A sevenfold increase in total enrollment over 40 years is a phenomenal change itself, but within that growth can be found three other substantial shifts: a doubling in the proportion of students enrolled part time, a 50 percent increase in the proportion of women enrolled (which resulted in the number of women enrolled exceeding the number of men by 1.45 million students), and a 50 percent increase in the proportion of students enrolled at institutions under public control.

Changes in Institution Types

The overall trends in total enrollment are of general interest, but it is necessary to disaggregate those data by institution type. To do so, it is necessary to depart from annual reports, define some terms, and use more than one source of information (see the Supplement to Chapter 2). Figure 1 shows total enrollment changes for both women and men combined as partitioned between two-year institutions, small colleges (see "Defining Small Colleges" in the Supplement to Chapter 2), comprehensive institutions (see note 3), and universities. The growth rates for the different institution types have varied substantially, not only in number of institutions but also in size (mean enrollment/institution).

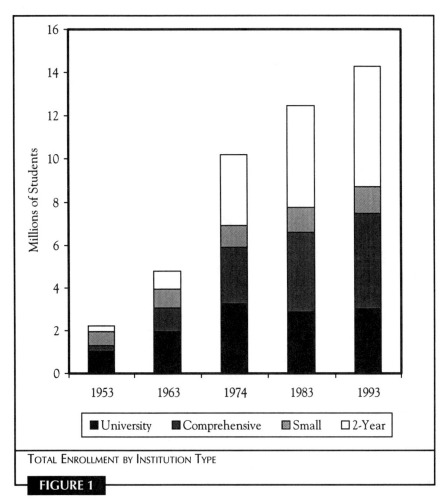

TOTAL ENROLLMENT BY INSTITUTION TYPE

FIGURE 1

Sources: Badger and Rice 1956, 42–43; Rice 1965, 93; Grant and Lind 1975, 98; Grant and Snyder 1986, 116; Snyder and Hoffman 1995, 216.

Two-Year Institutions   In 1953, there were 521 two-year institutions, with an average enrollment size of 510 students—representing only 12 percent of the total enrollment. Forty years later, their number had more than doubled, their size had quadrupled, and at 5.5 million students in 1993, they accounted for more of the total enrollment than any other institution type (Badger and Rice 1956; Snyder and Hoffman 1995, 176).

Small Colleges   Small colleges have experienced the greatest loss in share of enrollment (C. S. Tidball 1989). They did grow in number and size over the 1953–93 interval, but the increments were not very large. Their small growth in the face of rapid expansion of other institution types has left them with a decreased *share* of the total enrollment, from 29 percent in 1953 to 9 percent in 1993. Since women's colleges are primarily small colleges, the squeeze on small colleges has also affected colleges for women. The extent of this impact will be clarified in the section titled "Changes within Small Colleges" (below).

Comprehensive Institutions   Comprehensive institutions—though not yet well defined in 1953—have more than doubled in number, and there has been a sixfold increase in their average size. In 1993, their 4.5 million students represented 31 percent of the total enrollment. Thus, they ranked second among institution types in accounting for the number of students enrolled.

Universities   Universities were the leader in the number of students enrolled in 1953. They grew in enrollment share in 1963 and 1974, and then their enrollment plateaued for the next two decades. Their share of the total enrollment declined from 46 percent in 1953 to only 21 percent in 1993. Thus, today, universities rank below the two-year institutions and the comprehensive institutions in their share of the total enrollment.

Changes within Small Colleges

In order to focus on small colleges, it is necessary to refine the view again. Five subtypes of small colleges have been distinguished:

- Historically coeducational colleges
- Historically men's colleges
- Historically women's colleges
- Men's change colleges (colleges formerly for male students only that now also admit female students)
- Women's change colleges (colleges formerly for female students only that now also admit male students)

It is essential to make a distinction between the two categories of change colleges[5] identified above: neither type of change college approximates the institutional environment, as measured by quantities derived from demographic analyses, of the historically coeducational colleges and, more important, the women's and men's change colleges differ markedly from each other. In Table 3, the full-time enrollments for each of these five subtypes are shown for two of the four data points of the Small College Database.[6] The enrollment data are also shown as a percentage of the total small college enrollment.

Over the three-decade span from 1963 to 1993, the full-time enrollment at all small colleges increased by 8 percent.[7] The distribution of this change varied considerably among the five small-college subtypes. The enrollment data for 1963 are derived from 750 small colleges, whereas that for 1993 are based on 721 small colleges.

TABLE 3

CHANGES IN ENROLLMENT AND PERCENT ENROLLMENT FOR SMALL COLLEGES

College Subtype	1963		1993	
	Enrollment*	%†	Enrollment*	%†
Coeducational Colleges	462,241	69	515,575	71
Men's Colleges	73,154	11	7,385	1
Women's Colleges	115,391	17	46,200	6
Men's Change Colleges	14,355	2	83,460	12
Wom. Change Colleges	3,000	1	74,992	10
All Small Colleges	668,141	100	722,612	100

Notes
* Full-time enrollment.
† Percent of total full-time enrollment of all small colleges.

Source: C. S. Tidball 1996.

Although some small colleges were present at both time periods, it should be emphasized that each list contains a substantial number of colleges that are not on the other list; see the Supplement to Chapter 2 for a detailed analysis. The percentage figures, based on the full-time enrollment for all small colleges, clarify that the changes in the proportions of enrollment among the subtypes—except for coeducational colleges—have been marked: men's colleges decreased their share of enrollment from 11 percent to 1 percent, women's colleges decreased their share from 17 percent to 6 percent; men's change colleges increased theirs from 2 percent to 12 percent; and women's change colleges increased theirs from 1 percent to 10 percent.

Changes in Campus Characteristics   Two types of campus characteristics have been identified in the Small College Database.

1. Residential or commuter based. If more than 50 percent of the students reside on campus, the college is considered to be residential; otherwise, it is considered to be commuter-based.

2. Liberal arts curriculum or specialized curriculum. If more than 50 percent of the baccalaureate degrees are conferred in the traditional liberal arts subjects, the college is considered to have a liberal arts curriculum; otherwise, it is considered to have a specialized curriculum.

In Table 4, the full-time enrollments for the colleges that qualify as residential in the five subtypes of small colleges are presented.

TABLE 4

CHANGES IN RESIDENTIAL ENROLLMENT FOR SMALL COLLEGES

College Subtype	1963		1993	
	Residential*	%†	Residential*	%†
Coeducational Colleges	364,985	79	308,849	59
Men's Colleges	59,326	81	6,579	89
Women's Colleges	89,722	78	33,877	73
Men's Change Colleges	8,431	59	59,763	72
Wom. Change Colleges	2,521	84	30,782	41
All Residential Colleges	524,985	79	439,650	61
All Small Colleges	668,141	100	722,612	100

Notes
* Full-time enrollment at colleges that qualify as residential colleges, for each college subtype.
† The residential enrollment as a percent of the total enrollment for that college subtype as shown
  in Table 3.

Source: C. S. Tidball 1997.

The full-time enrollments at all residential small colleges decreased from 79 percent in 1963 to 61 percent in 1993. However, the variations among the five subtypes of small colleges were more pronounced. For example: enrollments at residential coeducational colleges decreased from 79 percent to 59 percent; enrollments at men's colleges increased from 81 percent to 89 percent; enrollments at women's colleges decreased from 78 percent to 73 percent; enrollments at men's change colleges increased from 59 percent to 72 percent; and those at women's change colleges decreased from 84 percent to 41 percent. The latter two comparisons demonstrate that the institutional environments for the two kinds of change colleges differ not only from those of historically coeducational colleges but also from each other.

In Table 5, full-time enrollments are tabulated for small colleges that qualify as having a "liberal arts curriculum" in the five subtypes of small colleges. Once again, the percentages shown in the table are based on the full-time enrollment for the college subtype previously shown in Table 3. The full-time enrollments for all colleges with a liberal arts curriculum decreased from 54 percent in 1963 to 27 percent in 1993. Here, too, the variations within the subtypes were greater than those for the entire liberal arts curriculum group. For example: the enrollments at coeducational colleges with a liberal arts curriculum decreased from 48 percent to 25 percent, those at men's colleges increased from 60 percent to 63 percent, those at women's colleges decreased from 68 percent to 41 percent, those at men's change colleges decreased from

60 percent to 40 percent, and those at women's change colleges decreased from 30 percent to 15 percent. The last two changes confirm that the two kinds of change colleges differ in their institutional environments from those of historically coeducational colleges, as well as from each other.

TABLE 5

Changes in Enrollment for Small Colleges with Liberal Arts Curriculum

College Subtype	1963		1993	
	Liberal Arts*	%†	Liberal Arts*	%†
Coed. Colleges	222,260	48	127,503	25
Men's Colleges	48,094	60	4,689	63
Women's Coll.	79,319	68	18,749	41
Men's Change Coll.	8,635	60	33,282	40
Wom. Change Coll.	912	30	11,416	15
All Liberal Arts Coll.	359,220	54	195,639	27
All Small Colleges	668,141	100	720,847#	100

Notes
* Full-time enrollment for colleges that qualify as having a liberal arts curriculum.
† Percent of college type full-time enrollment (see Table 3).
# This number differs from the total in Table 3 because 7 coeducational colleges did not have data in the primary source.

Source: C. S. Tidball 1997.

IMPACT ON WOMEN'S COLLEGES

Changes in seven molding forces have been identified:

1. Increase in total enrollment
2. Increase in part-time enrollment
3. Increase in the enrollment of women students
4. Increase in enrollment at public institutions
5. Redistribution of enrollment at institutional subtypes among small colleges
6. Decrease in enrollment at small residential colleges
7. Decrease in enrollment at small colleges with liberal arts curricula

In all instances, the impact of these forces has tended to work against enrollments at women's colleges that, for the most part, are small, residential communities where embracing a liberal arts curriculum permitted a focus on lifelong learning. In spite of the fact that the decrease in enrollment share for women's colleges between 1963 and 1993 was from 17 percent to 6 percent of the small college enrollment, women's colleges in the 1990s have achieved higher-than-average residential enrollments (73 percent as compared with 61 percent for all small colleges), as well as higher-than-average enrollments with liberal arts curricula (41 percent as compared with 27 percent for all small colleges).

The number of women who undertake part-time programs is greater than that for men; in 1993, part-time women students were 44 percent of the total enrollment, while the corresponding proportion for men was 38 percent (Snyder and Hoffman 1995, 189). Thus, the head count of women has increased, but as a group, women's utilization of the education environment has decreased due to their increased proportion of part-time enrollment. The impact on women's colleges has been particularly great, since their increase in part-time enrollment in the period from 1976 to 1993 was 60 percent greater than that for all institutions in higher education (Harwarth, Maline, and DeBra 1997, 50).

As shown in Figure 1, the increase in enrollment has varied substantially among the four large categories of educational institutions: two-year institutions, small colleges, comprehensive institutions, and universities. Although the total enrollment in small colleges doubled from 600,000 to 1.2 million from 1953 to 1993, their *share* of the national total enrollment decreased over this same period, from 29 percent to only 9 percent. In addition to these demographic changes in the number and distribution of students, there have also been changes that made college communities less nurturing and more impersonal: the loss of ideological support from a decrease in church affiliation (see the Supplement to Chapter 2 for details); the major increases in part-time students, which enhanced the shift away from residential communities to commuter-based ones; and the decreased emphasis on lifelong learning as a by-product of a liberal arts education to an emphasis on preparation for immediate postcollegiate employment, based on a more specialized curriculum. To be sure, the best-endowed and most selective colleges and universities have relatively few part-time students in their baccalaureate programs, are still residential, and adhere to a liberal arts curriculum; however, they represent but a small proportion of the total enrollment.

Another perspective on the impact on women's colleges from these major shifts can be provided by an analysis of the enrollment options for bright, motivated, young women from 1953 to 1993. At one time, the only competition women's colleges faced in attracting such students came from the historically coeducational colleges and the few large universities that did not restrict the entry of women. Today, with the changes in policy that have made the former men's universities, men's change colleges, and women's change colleges all aggressively seeking women students, as well as the large increase in economically favorable public education options, coupled with the decreased availability of enrollment opportunities at women's colleges, the situation has changed markedly. The result of this change is that fewer women in higher education are at colleges whose foremost purpose is to take women seriously.

Constancy amid Changing Dynamics

Now it is possible to appreciate how the reality has changed regarding the higher education of women in the United States in general, and at women's colleges in particular. At the midpoint of the twentieth century, undergraduate education for women was available at approximately 270 women's institutions of various kinds, plus 1,313 coeducational institutions. At that time, the total enrollment of women in higher education was 711,222 students, which represented 32 percent of the total degree-credit enrollment (Snyder and Hoffman 1995, 176). By 1990, the number of women's institutions had decreased to 85, and the number of coeducational institutions had increased to 3,300. By then, the total enrollment of women was 7.5 million students, which represented almost 55 percent of the total enrollment.

These substantive increases suggest considerable improvement of opportunity for women. Without a doubt, there is now greater access to the education establishment for women. However, the critical issue is the *quality* of that access. With few exceptions, the colleges where women have thrived have been small colleges—the very group whose *share* of the total national enrollment has decreased over the last 40 years. In fact, today there are probably fewer than 100,000 women in American higher education who have the benefit of attending a women's institution for their baccalaureate education. This hardy band of women's colleges continues to operate a disproportionately large number of residential colleges and colleges that feature a liberal arts curriculum. In short, they are education environments that take women seriously. In so doing, they provide the nation with more women leaders than their enrollments would predict—a higher proportion of achieving women than their coeducational counterparts. How it is known that this is the case, and how women's colleges have accomplished this feat, are the lessons and legacies that are presented in the following chapters.

NOTES

1. A complete history of the development of women's colleges in the United States is beyond the scope of this volume. Two treatments of this subject are available (Newcomer 1959; Solomon 1985). A shorter version can be found in *The International Encyclopedia of Higher Education* (M. E. Tidball 1977, 4392–98). The most recent review of this topic can be found in a report from the U.S. Department of Education (Harwarth, Maline, and DeBra 1997, 1–20).

2. Average tuition, by institution type, for 1993–94: all institutions: $3,827; 2-year institutions: $1,399; public universities: $2,820; public other 4-year: $2,360; private

universities: $13,874; private other 4-year: $10,100 (Snyder and Hoffman 1995, table 306).

3. The term "comprehensive institution" was introduced by the Carnegie Commission on Higher Education in the late 1970s in early versions of the classification scheme developed to recreate functional categories eliminated by the National Center for Education Statistics of the U.S. Department of Education during the 1960s (then a part of the U.S. Department of Health, Education, and Welfare). There were three criteria for this categorization: (1) graduate education through the master's degree but not including doctoral programs, (2) awarding of a high proportion of baccalaureate degrees in occupational or professional disciplines, and (3) size of institution (from 1,500 to 2,500 students for the smaller division and over 2,500 students for the larger division). The new scheme was based on demographic information submitted in the Higher Education General Information Survey (HEGIS).

4. As used in presentations of statistical data maintained by the United States government, the term "total enrollment" is understood to mean full-time students *plus* a head count of part-time students.

5. The term "change college" was first used in the late 1970s to refer both to changes in affiliation, e.g., Catholic-change or Protestant-change, and to changes in the sex of the student body, i.e., male-change or female-change (Anderson 1977, 6–8). This is more than a fine point. In most instances, there are campus vestiges of decades of church affiliation or attitudes relating to educating only men or only women students. Since these do not disappear at the time of declaring "independent" or "coeducational" status, it is helpful to designate such colleges as change colleges. In this volume, *formerly church affiliated* is used to designate a change in religious emphasis (from church affiliated to non–church affiliated). However, *men's change* and *women's change* are used to indicate a college that formerly enrolled students of only one sex and has changed its policy to also admit students of the opposite sex.

6. The Small College Database was developed by Charles S. Tidball during the late 1980s at which time there were only three datapoints: 1963, 1973, and 1983. The 1993 datapoint was added in 1995 and additional variables including faculty data have been added since. The database contains demographic information on 1,109 accredited colleges that ever had a full-time enrollment of fewer than 2,000 students. It is not available in print but is stored in a computerized version at the Tidball Center for the Study of Educational Environments at Hood College. For further details, see the Supplement to Chapter 2.

7. This increase differs slightly from the change that could be calculated from the numbers in Figure 1 because the frame of reference is different. For additional details, see the Supplement to Chapter 2.

PART TWO

· · · · · · · · · · ·

Three Major Ways of Knowing
Provide Lessons
from Women's Colleges

The following chapters report research results from three broad methodological approaches to investigating education environments. One approach is both objective and quantitative and relies on interrogating national, demographic databases in order to determine institutional productivities of women and men who subsequently become successful. Another uses both qualitative and quantitative social science methods to analyze several forms of self-report in order to document attitudes and opinions of various campus constituencies. A third approach makes use of case studies obtained from on-campus visits, providing a narrow but in-depth view of the qualities that support women's success. The results from these three very different ways of knowing, and the interpretations generated by them, have been developed over many years by different researchers with different backgrounds, working at different institutions with different colleagues. Yet despite these differences, the extent of overlap, the consistency, and the corroboration in the research findings are so great as to warrant the conclusion that women's colleges are among the most accessible and promoting environments wherein women are taken seriously. The supporting methodologies for these researches are documented in detail in the Supplements to Chapters 3, 4, and 5.

CHAPTER 3

Measures of Success

Having read the unsatisfactory conjectures of several, it occurred to me that by fixing tubes in the arteries of live animals I might learn about the force of the blood.

—The Rev. Stephen Hales, ca. 1730

The experiment alluded to above represents a true classic of phenomenological, or observational, research. Hales placed a tube within the blood vessel of a horse and recorded the height of the blood that flowed into it, thereby making the first direct measurement of mammalian blood pressure. He wrote very clearly exactly what he did, how he did it, and what he could measure under the stated circumstances (Clark-Kennedy 1929, 24–30). Hales's work is often used to illustrate the basics of observational research, for it makes clear the need to define the conditions and then to observe the outcomes in as exacting a manner as possible. The *reasons* for the findings and the *meanings* of the resulting data are then drawn from logical inferences and thoughtful deductions, based upon the experimental results, current theories, and others' research, and may be used in the framing of hypotheses, the evolution of theories, or simply as a point of departure for subsequent experiments.

The baccalaureate origins of achieving students—as a marker for institutional productivity—has also been determined phenomenologically. That is, the researcher defines the conditions and observes the outcomes as carefully and accurately as possible. The number of women and men are counted who are graduates of a given institution or group of like institutions (by whatever definition of likeness) who have attained a predetermined and prestated achievement. Every institution that fits the definition is included. "I took a horse fourteen hands high," said Hales. Or a group of similar horses.

The primary investigative focus in the studies described here is on *institutions* rather than persons, even though information about people is used to characterize the educational climate of undergraduate institutions. Further, in many of these studies, *groups of institutions* that share a demographic characteristic are used to gain information about commonalities among climates that are conducive to achievement, rather than to highlight the particularities of any individual institutional example.

In order to obviate discrepancies introduced by virtue of different sizes of institutions, the number of postbaccalaureate achievers from any given institution or group of institutions is divided by the total number of baccalaureates earned at that institution or group of institutions for the same sex and appropriate time period. The resultant number is considered the *productivity* of the institution for the sex and circumstances stated. Where differences occur, they are real differences; therefore, there is no need to apply probability statistics to the numbers counted in order to approximate the situation in a larger universe. This *is* the universe.

To be sure, in this kind of science it is possible that the same data, even impeccably derived, can lead to more than a single interpretation. Thus, the most important aspects of such a research venture are thorough design and scrupulous execution in order to produce reliable numerical data. What is done with these results, or what they mean, are legitimate subjects for debate, reasoned speculation, or the design of further research. But the *existence* of the phenomena is not in question. The use of baccalaureate origins as a means of studying education environments associated with institutional productivity in this observational manner has evolved with time and experience, as described in the Supplement to Chapter 3.

BACCALAUREATE ORIGINS OF ACHIEVERS

Listings in *Who's Who* registries may be used to document women who have attained a measure of recognized career achievement and who are referred to here as achievers. In the first such study of women achievers (M. E. Tidball 1970), biographies of women college graduates, randomly obtained from *Who's Who of American Women*, were used to identify productive colleges, the assumption being that the percentage of achievers among the graduates of a given institution would bear a definite relationship to the degree of support within that environment. This study was the first to demonstrate that graduates of women's colleges are more likely—two to three times more likely—than women graduates of coeducational colleges to be cited in a nationally constructed register for their career achievement.

This signal finding, startling to some, was made possible through disaggregation, (i.e., sorting). Student populations were disaggregated by sex, and then by type of collegiate institutions, followed by other disaggregations according to several institutional demographic characteristics such as selectivity in admissions, size, and per-student academic expenditures. For both women's colleges and coeducational institutions, greater selectivity, higher academic expenditures, and relatively small institution size were associated with greater productivity of women achievers. However, these characteristics did not discriminate between the two college types in any way that could account for their striking differences in productivity. Thus, one cannot conclude that the reason for the greater productivity of the women's colleges as a group depended on these characteristics of selectivity, size, and academic expenditures, even though they are all relevant to enhanced student outcomes.

While qualities of the collegiate environment are not the only basis for a student's future accomplishment, they nonetheless must be seen as a major contributor, inasmuch as all studies have counted only women who have actually graduated from college. From this fact alone, it can be concluded that all subjects, in order to have found their way into these research studies in the first place, have shared a certain minimum level of intelligence, persistence, financial support, initiative, motivation, and other qualities deemed necessary for collegiate graduation. In addition, measurement of several demographic variables within the groups of subjects according to baccalaureate institution type revealed no differences in a number of personal qualities, e.g., proportion married, proportion divorced, time between degree and marriage, proportion engaged in postbaccalaureate studies, and proportion with earned doctorates. In other words, there are no differences between the two collegiate groups of achievers as persons: an achiever is an achiever is an achiever. But there is a considerable difference in the productivity of the two institution types. It is for these reasons that one can conclude that there has been a *loss of talent* in the coeducational institutions (M. E. Tidball 1973b; 1974a). Therefore, other institutional characteristics of sufficient import to women must be identified that are related to the differential productivity of women's and coeducational colleges for women graduates (M. E. Tidball 1974a).

In searching for a measure that would account for the difference in outcomes from the two institution types, the relationship between the number of women faculty and the number of women students who subsequently became achievers was investigated. This study was the first to demonstrate that the number of women faculty on campus is strongly and positively related to the production of women who become achievers *regardless of baccalaureate origin* (see Figure 2 and the Supplement to Chapter 3). That is, the more women faculty, the more women students become achievers, regardless of institution type.

For many investigators who had long searched for qualities of education environments that would help explain research findings, these data were greatly welcomed. Many referred to them as "statistical confirmation of role model theory," and the work was subsequently awarded status as a Citation Classic (M. E. Tidball 1986a).[1] Conversely, the number of men students on campus was found to be inversely related to women's subsequent achievement (M. E. Tidball 1970; 1973b; 1974a; 1975; 1980a).

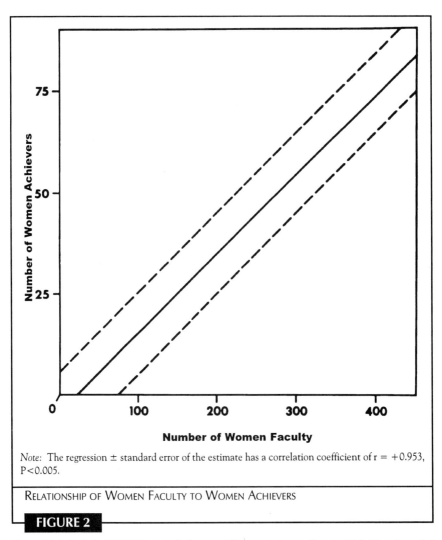

Note: The regression ± standard error of the estimate has a correlation coefficient of r = +0.953, P<0.005.

RELATIONSHIP OF WOMEN FACULTY TO WOMEN ACHIEVERS

FIGURE 2

Source: M. E. Tidball, 1980. "Women's Colleges and Women Achievers Revisited," In *Signs: Journal of Women in Culture and Society* 5: 504–17, Figure 1. Reprinted with permission from the University of Chicago. Copyright 1980 The University of Chicago. 0097-9740/80/0503-0010$01.23.

Variations on a Theme

Other research has corroborated the basic finding that graduates of women's colleges are more likely to be cited for career accomplishment than are women graduates of coeducational institutions (Oates and Williamson 1978; Rice and Hemmings 1988). Studies carried out by the Women's College Coalition, while not comparing women's and coeducational colleges, have provided information that women's colleges continue to be highly productive for women, in several contexts (Women's College Coalition 1995). In a recent doctoral dissertation, the most productive institutions for European American women, African American women, and Latinas have also been identified by listings of their graduates in *Who's Who in America, Who's Who among Black Americans,* and *Who's Who among Hispanic Americans,* respectively (Wolf-Wendel 1995). This disaggregation by race or ethnic background has provided yet another indication that women's colleges, along with some formerly women's colleges (designated as "women's change colleges," see the Supplement to Chapter 2), are disproportionately represented among institutions most productive of women who later were cited for their career accomplishments: among the top 10 institutions for European American women, all are women's colleges or women's change colleges; for African American women, 4 of 10 are women's colleges (8 are Historically Black institutions); and for Latinas, fully 60 percent are women's colleges or women's change colleges (Table 6). Once again, it is made clear that women's colleges, and colleges with a long history of serving women primarily, are taking women seriously. Additionally, for blacks and Latinas, it is clear that these women are especially well served by institutions with a specialized focus, many of which are relatively nonselective in admissions (Wolf-Wendel 1995). Important among all the studies reported here is the recognition that they were performed by different researchers, at different times, at different institutions, and by different approaches—and yet with mutually consistent conclusions.

BACCALAUREATE ORIGINS OF DOCTORATES

Subsequent studies of institutional productivity moved away from achievement associated with the self-reported material in a *Who's Who* registry to be focused, instead, on achievement defined by the attainment of a research or medical doctorate, based on information collected and recorded by the National Research Council of the National Academy of Sciences in their Doctorate Records File, or by the Association of American Medical Colleges, respectively. Such databases are subject to unique design and permit the achievement marker to be assessed closer to the time of graduation from college. More important, they provide an objective measure of accomplishment, inasmuch

TABLE 6		
BACCALAUREATE INSTITUTIONS IDENTIFIED AS *WHO'S WHO* PRODUCTIVITY LEADERS		
European American Women	African American Women	Latinas
Barnard College (Women's)	Bennett College (Women's)	Barnard College (Women's)
Bennington College (W. Change)	Fisk University (Coed)	Barry University (W. Change)
Bryn Mawr College (Women's)	Howard University (Coed)	Bryn Mawr College (Women's)
Connecticut College (W. Change)	Knoxville College (Coed)	Incarnate Word Coll. (W. Change)
Manhattanville (NY) (W. Change)	Lincoln University (PA) (Coed)	University of Miami (Coed)
Radcliffe College (W. Change)	Mills College (Women's)	New Mexico Highlands U. (Coed)
Sarah Lawrence College (W. Change)	Saint Mary College (KS) (Women's)	Our Lady of the Lake U. (W. Change)
Smith College (Women's)	Spelman College (Women's)	Pomona College (Coed)
Vassar College (W. Change)	Stillman College (Coed)	Texas A&I University (Coed)
Wellesley College (Women's)	Tougaloo University (Coed)	Texas Women's Univ. (Women's)

Notes: Productivity was measured by the proportion of graduates who were listed in the appropriate *Who's Who* volume for the particular group of women. The top 10 institutions are listed in alphabetical order.

Source: Wolf-Wendel 1995, 80, 106, 124.

as the attainment of a research or medical doctorate is undebatably an achievement. In early work, a 5 percent random sample of women doctorates was disaggregated such that women's college graduates and women coeducational college graduates who had received research doctorates were further characterized by the broad field in which the doctorate had been earned. In all fields combined, graduates of women's colleges were more than twice as likely to have received a doctorate than were women graduates of coeducational colleges. Especially of interest has been the much greater productivity of women's colleges of graduates continuing to the doctorate level in both the life and physical sciences, fields in which women have been traditionally underrepresented. Most striking are the very large difference in the arts and humanities (3.5 times more doctorates for women's college graduates) and the relatively small difference in the field of education (1.2 times more doctorates for women's college graduates), although the productivity of the women's colleges is greater than that of the coeducational institutions in *all* fields (M. E. Tidball 1974a; 1975; 1980a).

The Landmark Study of Baccalaureate Origins

Subsequently, a large study of research doctorate attainment was carried out that included data for women and men separately. By this means, it was possible to suggest attributes present in the education environment that affected women and men differently, and to assess differences in both rate and content of each sex's attainment of doctoral degrees. Specific measures were taken to adjust for baccalaureate degrees separate from first professional degrees in the years before 1961, and to attach doctorates earned to the actual baccalaureate recipients who earned them, thereby obviating the necessity to approximate the time between receiving the baccalaureate and doctoral degrees for each sex separately and for each field by sex separately (see the Supplement to Chapter 3).

While institutions were not specifically disaggregated by type for analysis, this is a landmark study by virtue of its assessment of institutional productivities for both women and men separately, along with their doctoral fields, over several time periods beginning in 1910 and running through the 1960s (M. E. Tidball and Kistiakowsky 1976). Although institutional productivities for men who earned doctorates had been investigated earlier (Knapp and Goodrich 1951), no one had ever attempted a study of institutional productivities designed to yield data on women and men separately. The significance of this work is that it provides a broader angle of vision with respect to the climate for women, which may be influenced by what is simultaneously occurring with and for men. The work involved in such a venture is truly enormous when baccalaureate graduates and the doctorates earned by them are disaggregated according to sex and field within several discrete time periods and recorded both by absolute numbers of doctorates and by doctorates earned as a percentage of graduates; i.e., by productivities of the institutions.

The conclusions and inferences from this work are focused upon outcomes revealed by listing the most productive institutions for women and those for men. First, there are distinct differences in the baccalaureate origins of women and men who have earned doctorates. Women are more likely to have graduated from a narrower range of institutions, the majority of which are small colleges, with women's colleges being predominant among these. Men, by contrast, are more likely to have graduated from universities, principally private but also several prestigious public universities. Second, many of the colleges especially productive of doctorate-earning women would not have surfaced at all if the productivity data had enumerated students of both sexes combined, inasmuch as the large majority of those earning doctorates were men; hence, institutions found to be productive would have been those

---

TABLE 7

NUMBER OF DOCTORAL FIELDS IN WHICH GRADUATES OF THE MOST PRODUCTIVE
INSTITUTIONS OBTAINED RESEARCH DOCTORATES

Patterns for Women	Patterns for Men
Five of the Five Fields	
University of Chicago	None
Four of the Five Fields	
Barnard College	University of Chicago
Bryn Mawr College	
Radcliffe College	
Vassar College	
Wellesley College	
Three of the Five Fields	
Cornell University	None
Mount Holyoke College	
Oberlin College	
Swarthmore College	
Two of the Five Fields	
University of Florida	Cornell University
Goucher College	Harvard University
University of North Carolina	University of North Carolina
Smith College	Oberlin College
Stanford University	University of Wisconsin
One of the Five Fields	
Brooklyn College	Amherst College
City College of New York	Brigham Young University
Columbia University	Brooklyn College
Hunter College	California Institute of Technology
Massachusetts Institute of Technology	Carnegie-Mellon University
New York University	Case-Western Reserve University
University of Pennsylvania	City College of New York
University of Pittsburgh	University of Florida
University of Wisconsin	State College of Iowa
	Iowa State University
	Mass. Institute of Technology
	University of Massachusetts
	University of Nebraska
	Princeton University
	Rensselaer Polytechnic Institute
	Temple University
	North Texas State University
	University of Utah
	Wayne State Univerity
	Yale University

Note: The five broad doctoral fields identified by the Doctorate Records File are: education, arts
and humanites, social sciences, life sciences, and physical sciences and engineering.

Source: Reprinted with permission from M. E. Tidball and V. Kistiakowsky, 1976, "Baccalaureate
Origins of American Scientists and Scholars," in Science 193: 646–52, Table 6. Copyright 1996
American Association for the Advancement of Science.

primarily noted for the accomplishments of their male graduates. Third, institutions that proved highly productive for women are more likely to have their women graduates go on to doctorates in a variety of fields, in contrast to the more circumscribed number that is the case for men, as shown in Table 7. This distinctive pattern suggests that institutions with a wide range of quality departments or fields of study are important for women students, who may be in the process of discovering their interests and hence are aided by a variety of quality offerings. Fourth, institutions highly productive for women are more likely to be those that enrolled a substantial number of women students; when they also had a high *proportion* of women students, as in the case of the women's colleges in the study, they were among the most highly productive institutions for women in the nation.

From such demographic data, it can be inferred that women who subsequently receive doctorates in each of the several broad fields recorded by the Doctorate Records File are more likely to graduate from institutions that enroll large numbers of women students, have a long and continuous history of women who have received doctorates, and offer strong academic preparation in several areas of study. It can further be inferred that a favorable climate for women students who are intellectually motivated and capable is one that conveys to them a sense of being in an environment where many other women are seriously engaged in a variety of academic pursuits. It is further apparent that a disproportionate number of women's colleges appear among institutions most productive of women who earn doctorates—and hence are to be numbered among those colleges that take women seriously.

Reinforcing the Basic Findings

Other research also contributes to the findings that a preponderance of women's colleges and women's change colleges are among the most productive of women who have earned research doctorates. In a report on the baccalaureate origins of Chicanas earning social science doctorates, the 3 most productive institutions in the country were women's colleges or women's change colleges (Solorzano 1995). Wolf-Wendel (1998) listed only 1 coeducational college along with 9 women's colleges and women's change colleges that were found to be the 10 most productive baccalaureate institutions for European American women earning research doctorates, while 2 of the 10 most productive institutions for African American women were women's colleges, and 6 of the 10 most productive institutions for Latinas were women's or women's change colleges (see Table 8). For both African American women and Latinas, both institutional gender and institutional race were important characteristics of institutions that graduated large proportions of women who subsequently earned doctorates. In fact, the coeducational institutions listed for these women were all special-focus colleges, either historically black or Hispanic-serving institutions. Further, if there had been no disaggregation by race or ethnic group, the productivity of these institutions would not have emerged.

The three additional results from Wolf-Wendel's research are important by virtue of confirming earlier findings: the admission selectivities of the most productive institutions vary across the range of selectivities, rather than being among the most selective colleges in the country; the most productive institutions comprise a quite small representation of the approximately 2,000 baccalaureate-granting colleges and universities; and the great majority of productive institutions are small colleges (M. E. Tidball 1974a; 1975; 1980a; 1985; M. E. Tidball and C. S. Tidball 1995).

TABLE 8

BACCALAUREATE INSTITUTIONS IDENTIFIED AS DOCTORATE PRODUCTIVITY LEADERS

European American Women	African American Women	Latinas
Barnard College (Women's)	Bennett College (Women's)	Barnard College (Women's)
Bryn Mawr College (Women's)	Fisk University (Coed)	Barry University (W. Change)
Goucher College (Women's)	Hampton University (Coed)	Bryn Mawr College (Women's)
Mount Holyoke College (Women's)	Howard University (Coed)	Incarnate Word Coll. (W. Change)
Radcliffe College (W. Change)	Lincoln University (PA) (Coed)	University of Miami (Coed)
Sarah Lawrence College (W. Change)	Morgan State Univ. (Coed)	Our Lady of the Lake U. (W. Change)
Smith College (Women's)	Spelman College (Women's)	Pan American, Univ. of Texas (Coed)
Swarthmore College (Coed)	Taladega College (Coed)	Pomona College (Coed)
Vassar College (W. Change)	Tougaloo University (Coed)	Texas A&I University (CoEd)
Wellesley College (Women's)	Tuskegee University (Coed)	Texas Women's Univ. (Women's)

Notes: Productivity was measured by the proportion of graduates for the particular group of women who obtained research doctorates. The top 10 institutions are listed in alphabetical order.

Source: Wolf-Wendel 1995, 79, 105, 123.

FROM BACCALAUREATE ORIGINS
TO INSTITUTIONAL PRODUCTIVITY

Women in Traditionally Male Fields

The next evolutionary turn in this method of research was applied to two parallel studies, one describing the baccalaureate origins of entrants into American medical schools (M. E. Tidball 1985) and the other, baccalaureate origins of recent recipients of natural science doctorates (M. E. Tidball 1986b). These studies reflect a transition from reporting only the rank-ordering of *individual institutions* to presenting data for *groups of similar institutions*. In order for a baccalaureate institution to be included in the study, the absolute number of its women or men graduates who subsequently entered medical school or earned a natural science doctorate was set after reference to earlier work by Manuel and Altenderfer (1961) for medical school entrants and Knapp and Goodrich (1951) for natural scientists. In both studies, several new categories of institution types were employed in order to provide more disaggregation opportunities and hence more clues to the nature of institutional climates associated with subsequent achievement. Because many men's and women's colleges had, by the time of this study, begun admitting students of the other sex, these institutions now rated their own separate categories; that is, men's change colleges and women's change colleges (see Chapter 2). Additional categories of institution type were devised in the study of medical degrees to include private and public universities with and without affiliated medical schools, and for the study of science doctorates, private and public universities with and without affiliated substantive graduate programs in the natural sciences (see the Supplement to Chapter 3).

Becoming a Physician   Medical school entry rates from the nine categories of institutions are depicted in Figure 3. For men, comparison with the data from 1950–59 (Manuel and Altenderfer 1961) showed that the number and proportion of colleges (as distinct from universities) important to the premedical education of men had been halved, and a concomitant rise in the importance of universities had occurred, especially universities with affiliated medical schools. This is consistent with the demographic changes discussed in the Supplement to Chapter 2. For women, the productivity of women's colleges was almost twice that of the nearest other institutional type, private universities with affiliated medical schools, and clearly greater than that of women's change, men's change, and historically coeducational colleges. From these and other findings, one can infer that, while the presence of notable science faculty and an abundance of state-of-the-art laboratory equipment (more likely to be found in prestigious universities than small colleges) may well be related to the production of those who continue to medical school, they are

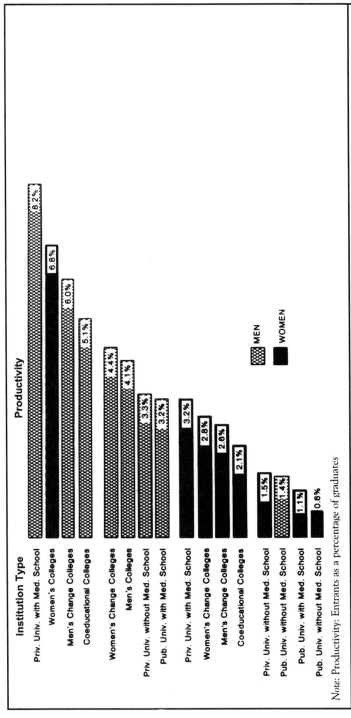

Note: Productivity: Entrants as a percentage of graduates

MOST PRODUCTIVE INSTITUTION TYPES FOR MEDICAL SCHOOLS ENTRANTS

FIGURE 3

Source: Reprinted, by permission, from M. E. Tidball, 1988, "Baccalaureate Origins of Entrants into American Medical Schools," in Journal of Higher Education 56, no. 4 (July/August): 385–402, Figure 1. Copyright 1985 by Ohio State University Press.

but a small factor in the extraordinary productivity of women's colleges (M. E. Tidball 1985).

For other aspects of the educational environment of these colleges that also play a significant role in the encouragement and development of women students, see also Chapters 4 and 5.

Becoming a Natural Scientist   In the study of recent natural science doctorates (M. E. Tidball 1986b), women's colleges topped the list in productivity for women, even more than private universities with substantive graduate programs in the natural sciences (Figure 4). In general, however, colleges as contrasted with universities were places from which women scientists were most likely to emerge. A recent report confirms this finding that small colleges, including several women's colleges, are highly productive for women who have received doctorates in the physical sciences (Sharpe and Fuller 1995). However, the Tidball data also show that the productivity (in terms of women earning doctorates) of both women's change colleges and men's change

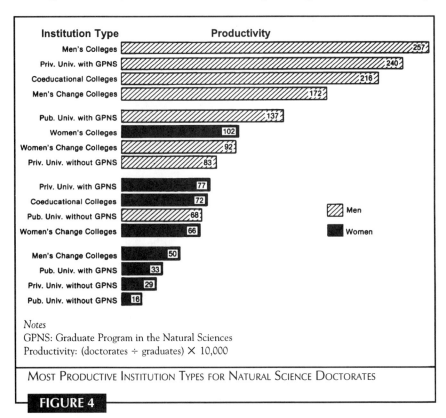

Notes
GPNS: Graduate Program in the Natural Sciences
Productivity: (doctorates ÷ graduates) × 10,000

MOST PRODUCTIVE INSTITUTION TYPES FOR NATURAL SCIENCE DOCTORATES

FIGURE 4

Source: From M. E. Tidball, 1988, "Undergraduate Institutions and the Natural Sciences," in Arco's *The Right College* 1989, The College Research Group of Concord, Massachusetts. Copyright 1988 by Arco Publishing. Reprinted with permission of Macmillan USA, a Division of Simon & Schuster, Inc.

colleges is less than that of the women's colleges, raising the question as to whether the presence of men students and faculty in the change colleges has altered these institutions' ability to encourage women to participate in traditionally masculine fields.

Additional Insights   For men, outcomes in medicine and the sciences are basically institution-specific, but this is not the case for women. By contrast, institutions especially productive of women in medicine and the natural sciences show considerable overlap in terms of their preparation and encouragement of women who subsequently enter health and science fields (Table 9). It is to be noted that there are no highly productive institutions whose male graduates enter all three areas of endeavor (life sciences, physical sciences, and medicine), while for women, relatively few institutions are preparation sites for only one or two of these areas of advanced scientific study. This pattern echoes that seen in Table 7, in which far more institutions prepared men for only one field of advanced study, while numerous institutions prepared women for three to five areas of advanced study. The point is thus made again that, for women to be taken seriously, there must be not only a wide selection of fields for significant study, but also sufficient and concerted preparation in each of these fields if women are to make their way into the postgraduate realms of medicine and science. It also reemphasizes the previously noted fact that the number of institutions important to women's postbaccalaureate achievement constitutes but a small portion of American colleges and universities.

In the studies of both medical doctorates and science doctorates, the relationship between women faculty and women students who proceeded to the advanced degree was calculated; in both studies, the findings were consistent with those from the original study of women listed in *Who's Who of American Women*; that is, the greater the number of women faculty, the more women who proceeded to the postcollege accomplishment under study, for all types of institutions. Clearly, women faculty—regardless of field or institution of employment—are important role models, if not mentors, for collegiate women and contribute to a climate in which women are taken seriously. Just as clearly, awareness of the importance of adult women to women students, along with the regular hiring, paying, and promoting of women faculty and, by extension, women administrators, are hallmarks of an institution that takes women seriously (M. E. Tidball 1974b, 56–59; 1976b).

TABLE 9

Most Productive Baccalaureate Origins for Doctoral Scientists 1910–69 and Medical School Entrants 1975–78

	Baccalaureate Origins	
Most Productive for:	**Women**	**Men**
Physical Science Ph.D.s *and* Life Science Ph.D.s *and* M.D. entrants	Barnard Cornell U. Harvard (Radcliffe) Mount Holyoke Wellesley	
both Physical Sc. Ph.D.s and Life Sc. Ph.D.s	Bryn Mawr U. Chicago Goucher Vassar	U. Chicago Cornell U.
either Physical Sc. Ph.D.s or Life Sc. Ph.D.s	Mass. Inst. Tech. Swarthmore	Calif. Inst. Tech. Carnegie-Mellon U. Case-Western Res. U. Iowa State U. Rensselaer Poly. Inst. U. Massachusetts U.N.C.-Chapel Hill U. Wisconsin
only M.D. entrants	Stanford U. Yale U.	Columbia U. Dartmouth Duke U. Harvard U. Johns Hopkins U. Northwestern U. Stanford U. Yale U.

Source: Reprinted, by permission, from M. E. Tidball, 1988, "Baccalaureate Origins of Entrants into American Medical Schools," in *Journal of Higher Education* 56, no. 4 (July/August): 385–402, Table 4.

POPULATION DEMOGRAPHICS AND INSTITUTIONAL PRODUCTIVITY

The most recent refinements of population demographic research include the calculation of individual institutional productivities for the majority of United States baccalaureate institutions, for women and for men separately, followed by the determination of the study population based upon matching its proportion of women and men achievers with those of the national population (M. E. Tidball 1994). A comparison of the numerical characteristics of the national and study populations is shown in Table 10, in which it can be seen that the

TABLE 10

Comparison of National and Study Populations

Category	National *	Study Population†
Women Baccalaureate Recipients	4,055,042	1,212,671
Men Baccalaureate Recipients	4,942,787	1,622,870
Number of Baccalaureate Institutions	2,036	316
Women Doctorate Recipients	70,038	39,621
Men Doctorate Recipients	142,650	82,526
Ratio of Men to Women Doctorates	2.04	2.08

Notes

* National data for baccalaureate recipients during the decade of the 1970s from the National Center for Education Statistics; that for doctorate recipients from the Doctorate Records File of the NRC-NAS through 1991.

† Study population data from the universe of institutions with 4% or more men graduates of the 1970s or with 2% or more women graduates of the 1970s who obtained research doctorates through 1991.

Source: M. E. Tidball and C. S. Tidball 1994.

ratio of men to women doctorates in the study population is essentially identical to that of the entire country (M. E. Tidball and C. S. Tidball 1994). This has been accomplished for baccalaureate graduates of the decade of the 1970s who received doctorates by 1991, resulting in a population of 316 institutions. For each institution, doctoral field data have been calculated and reaggregated for women and men separately, according to institution type, institution selectivity, and ratio of men to women doctoral productivities for each institution.

The resultant depictions for the study population by doctoral field participation for women and for men are shown in Figure 5. In the figure, male participation can be seen as increasing from education through the humanities, social sciences, and life sciences to its peak in the physical sciences. Female participation, by contrast, is described by an inverted V with its peak in the social sciences. In short, there are clearly different patterns of doctoral participation for the two sexes.

The grouping of institutions by type and selectivity reveals that the women's colleges of this study, while their overall selectivity is less than that of several other types of institution, have by far the greatest overall productivity of women who continue to complete doctorates (Table 11). This is a significant and consistent finding, having first been noted in the Who's Who study and reported in both verbal and graphic form (M. E. Tidball 1980a). It should be noted, however, that while admission selectivity is important with respect to future accomplishment, its relative importance is present only for the most selective institutions and, in addition, it appears to be more important for men

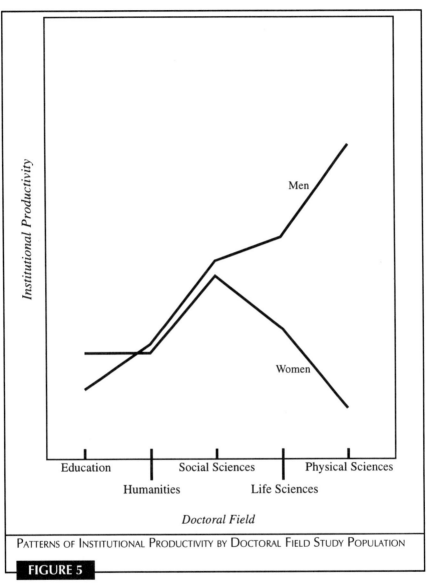

PATTERNS OF INSTITUTIONAL PRODUCTIVITY BY DOCTORAL FIELD STUDY POPULATION

FIGURE 5

Source: M. E. Tidball and C. S. Tidball 1994.

than for women. That is, for women, many varied qualities and characteristics of the education environment work together for women's encouragement and promotion, while for men, the support must be more focused, specific, and to the point (M. E. Tidball and C. S. Tidball 1994).

	TABLE 11						

DOCTORAL PRODUCTIVITY BY SELECTIVITY AND INSTITUTION TYPE—WOMEN

Selectivity*	Women's Colleges	Private Univ.	Men's Change	Women's Change	Coed Colleges	Public Univ.	Number of Institutions
Most Selective	2	13	2	0	4	0	21
High. Sel.+	3	4	2	0	5	0	14
High. Sel.	0	6	6	2	4	3	21
Very Sel.+	0	7	3	2	17	5	34
Very Sel.	6	6	2	1	20	10	45
Selective+	2	1	1	1	14	8	27
Selective	7	9	6	2	31	15	70
Not Sel.	5	1	4	2	36	11	59
Not Listed	1	0	0	0	9	0	10
Totals	26	47	26	10	140	52	301
Productivity†	505	426	387	344	317	273	[327]

Notes
* Cass and Birnbaum 1979.
† (doctorates ÷ graduates) × 10,000; doctorates earned through 1991.
[] Mean productivity as calculated for all 301 institutions.

Source: M. E. Tidball 1998.

A new parameter was studied using this refined database, namely, the ratio of productivity for men to productivity for women within the same institution for all the coeducational institutions. The ratios so calculated were then grouped within several ranges of ratios[2] and the patterns of doctoral productivities portrayed graphically by doctoral field, as before. The productivities by field for the five ratio ranges studied are shown for men in Figure 6. It is important to appreciate that alterations in institutional ratios do not alter institutional productivity for men. The five tracings all look very much alike, and like the aggregate male depiction for the study population of Figure 5. Ratio ranges for women, along with their productivities by field, are shown in Figure 7. By contrast with the situation for men, *as the ratio ranges increase, institutional productivities for women decrease* until they are exceedingly low.

Yet it must be remembered that the institutions being studied here are the most productive of students eventually earning doctorates among all coeducational institutions in the nation. These findings speak to institutional climate by suggesting that, even though an institution appears to have sufficient material supports and encouragement for men students' achievement, these advantages are not necessarily available to women to the same degree, by whatever definition of advantage and availability. Only in the 23 institutions where the ratio is less than one (that is, where the productivity for women is

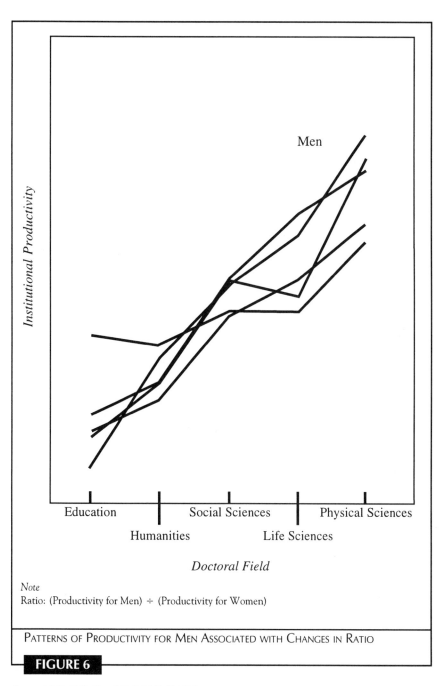

Men

Institutional Productivity

Education   Social Sciences   Physical Sciences

Humanities   Life Sciences

Doctoral Field

Note
Ratio: (Productivity for Men) ÷ (Productivity for Women)

PATTERNS OF PRODUCTIVITY FOR MEN ASSOCIATED WITH CHANGES IN RATIO

FIGURE 6

Source: M. E. Tidball and C. S. Tidball 1994.

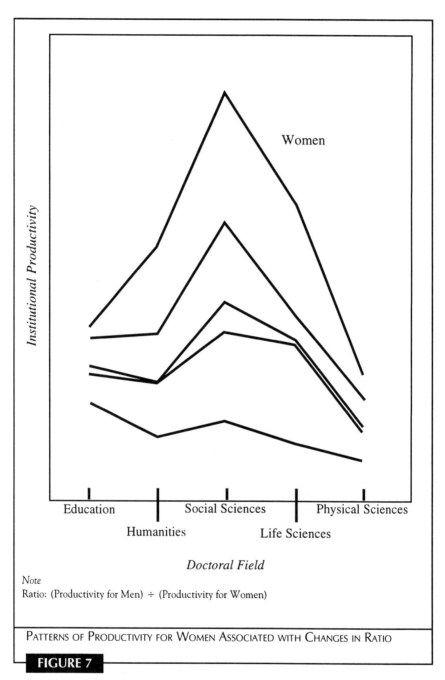

Women

Institutional Productivity

Education   Social Sciences   Physical Sciences

Humanities   Life Sciences

Doctoral Field

Note
Ratio: (Productivity for Men) ÷ (Productivity for Women)

PATTERNS OF PRODUCTIVITY FOR WOMEN ASSOCIATED WITH CHANGES IN RATIO

FIGURE 7

Source: M. E. Tidball and C. S. Tidball 1994.

greater than that for men) is the productivity for women substantial, comparing favorably with that of the women's colleges.

Again, studying what happens for women and men *in the same settings* provides important clues about the situation for women in American higher education. These results may be taken as a measure of institutional gender equity which, regrettably, has not yet arrived on the majority of campuses, or at least on the majority of campuses of the most productive institutions in the country. Moreover, these observations confirm the persistence of many institutions, otherwise accepted as leaders in higher education, wherein what works for women has not been incorporated into the campus environment and program.

LESSONS FROM THE CREATIVE INTEGRATION OF TABLES AND LISTS

The foregoing presentation has described several approaches to the observational study of institutional productivity by using student postbaccalaureate outcomes as indicators of institutional encouragement and support of women. The first principle in such studies is the separation of subjects by sex. Following this is the disaggregation of institutions by type, especially for assessing the productivity of women's colleges or other special-focus institutions. Subsequently, investigating the influence of particular variables on outcomes relies on the separation of the variables of interest (e.g., admission selectivity) by disaggregation, in order to establish and describe the population(s) under study. Repeatedly, using the methods of population demographics, it has been found that the patterns of women's participation in postcollege accomplishments differ from those of men. Additionally, women's colleges are seen to be disproportionately productive of women who have become career achievers in many kinds of endeavors, who have entered medical schools, and who have earned research doctorates in each of the broad doctoral fields, including both life and physical sciences, as compared with any of the several types of coeducational institutions.

Such studies have regularly demonstrated that institutional productivity for women follows from a set of characteristics that include some felicitous admixture of the following:

- A women's college or institution with a substantial history of successfully educating women
- A relatively small institutional size
- The presence of a large number of adult women, but relatively few men students in the environment
- A wide variety of scholarly fields of study

Not obligatory and not critical are

- High selectivity in admissions
- Generous academic expenditures
- Highly elite accompaniments, where elite is defined by standards set by institutions especially productive for men

Rather, from the data presented here, the overriding characteristic of institutions that are highly productive of achieving women is their focus on women.

Finally, it is clear that by developing and employing a demographic, observational approach characterized by determining institutional productivities of women and men of achievement, an angle of vision is gained that could not otherwise have been acquired. Findings from such work can then be joined with those from other research approaches, as discussed in Chapters 4 and 5, to form a larger and more integrated understanding of what works for women.

NOTES

1. A Citation Classic is a highly cited publication as identified by *Science Citation Index, Social Sciences Citation Index*, or *Arts and Humanities Citation Index*, published by *Current Contents*. For the work cited here, the *Science Citation Index* and the *Social Sciences Citation Index* indicate that this paper is the most-cited paper ever published in the *Educational Record*.

2. The ranges of ratios were as follows: <1.00, for which there were 23 institutions in which productivity for women was greater than that for men; 1.00–1.37, with 73 institutions; 1.38–1.74, with 74 institutions; 1.75–3.00, with 74 institutions; >3.00, with 27 institutions, some with ratios as great as 8.00.

CHAPTER 4

Making a Significant Difference

*The pretense that we can be external observers . . . without acknowledging
that we are parts of [what we observe] introduces serious distortions
into our scientific endeavors.*

—Ruth Hubbard, 1984

L ike the studies of institutional productivity, other types of research also
suggest that women's colleges have a significant positive impact on their
students. The studies described in the prior chapter focused primarily
on a number of important indicators of achievement, such as attaining a
doctorate, and looked back to the baccalaureate institutions that produce
these results. The studies described in this chapter build on this powerful
research, using a variety of quantitative and qualitative social science methodologies to investigate both the question about the impact of women's colleges
on students and the aspects of the women's college experience that leads to
such success.

Most college impact studies measure changes that occur during college.
Many also investigate the relationship among student characteristics, the
experiences students have in college, and changes that occur in college. The
most comprehensive of these use sophisticated statistical techniques on large
national databases to study complex relationships. Such studies allow researchers to look at the importance of a wide variety of factors, including
attendance at a women's college, while taking into account differences in
outcomes that might be explained because of the differences in those who
choose women's colleges. Other studies also rely on survey techniques to assess
satisfaction, educational attainment, occupational attainment, and levels of
engagement during and after college. Sometimes these involve graduates as
well as student participants. While much of the research is comparative,
asking about the *differences* between students at coeducational and women's

colleges, some are more interested in the actual experiences for women in one environment or the other.

Another group of studies, using more qualitative techniques, such as campus interviews and observations, attempts to understand more about the experiences students have and the ways in which institutional characteristics make a difference. While qualitative studies can be comparative, they need not be.

For the most part, both quantitative and qualitative studies have found that attendance at a women's college is associated with positive outcomes, and they have provided information about the elements of those institutions that facilitate success.

A Few Methodological Issues

As research is summarized in this chapter, it is important to be mindful of the kinds of methodologies employed. While this chapter cannot provide detailed information about methodological issues, the Supplement to Chapter 4 describes more about the nature of impact studies. The reader should keep in mind, however, that the studies reported in this chapter inevitably deal with "samples" of participants—often quite small—rather than entire populations. In addition, they commonly rely on surveys and student reports of their experiences in college. This helps to explain why the results are not always, under all circumstances, consistent. As such, these studies, taken one at a time, represent only pieces of the larger puzzle that help in the understanding of research on college impact. Research of this type, therefore, is most powerful when it is aggregated; that is, when conclusions are drawn from a wide variety of studies using different methods, sources of data, and time periods.

One major source of information has come from studies using the Cooperative Institutional Research Program (CIRP), a national longitudinal database that began collecting data on entering college freshman in 1966 with four-year follow-up studies of samples of college seniors. After more than 30 years, it constitutes the largest longitudinal database on college students. Other data sources are described in the Supplement to Chapter 4.

Research on college impact necessarily asks about the difference college makes in terms of some "outcome" or result. However, the distinction between the results of the college experience and the experiences during college becomes quite blurred in this area of research. For example, while satisfaction with college is often treated as an outcome of college because of its link to success, it is also clearly an indicator of the quality of the college experience. Similarly, while leadership opportunities during college are seen as important because of the preparation they provide for achievement and leadership after college, training students to lead and participate actively in their communities is also viewed as an important outcome from experiences in college, especially women's colleges.

Another issue centers on the role of the institution in contrast to the role of the student in accounting for achievement. For some researchers, the goal of a study is to separate what happens to a student as a result of the college experience itself from what the student brings to college. Indeed, some scholars have suggested that women's colleges have been so outstandingly successful merely because of the self-selection of the students. In other words, women at women's colleges are predetermined for success, and the college experience has almost no influence. Studies discussed in the prior chapter and in this one reveal that the findings about the impact of women's colleges emerge regardless of the selectivity of the institutions or the characteristics students bring with them (A. W. Astin 1993; Pascarella and Terenzini 1991).

However, it should also be noted that framing the research in this way reveals a troubling bias. In most other contexts, observers would agree that prestigious institutions are successful, in part, because of the elite students who attend. Indeed, one would expect outstanding results from these students. Few scholars ask Harvard, to name just one, to demonstrate its success independent of the entering characteristics of its students. Why is it, then, that women's colleges, or Historically Black institutions, are asked to demonstrate their contribution to their graduates' success by statistically "subtracting" the significance of the characteristics of the admitted students? Nevertheless, this is a common part of the research tradition on college impact. In spite of this defensive burden of proof, however, one sees consistent and important research support for the impact of women's colleges. Significantly, many of these institutions are successful in spite of a lack of resources. Indeed, in their massive review of the literature on the research looking at the impact of college on students over a 20-year period, Pascarella and Terenzini conclude:

> Even with student background characteristics and institutional selectivity held constant, a woman attending an all-women's college, compared with her coeducational counterpart, is more likely to emerge with higher educational aspirations, to attain a higher degree, to enter a sex-atypical career, and to achieve prominence in her field. (Pascarella and Terenzini 1991, 638–39)

COLLEGE AS A GENDERED EXPERIENCE

Before exploring the paths to success for women at women's colleges, it is important to acknowledge the context in which most women's education experiences take place—at coeducational colleges. Over the course of the last three decades, coeducation has spread to many colleges and universities that once educated either men only or women only. As this shift has occurred, the belief that coeducation is equivalent to equitable education for men and women has often been assumed. However, there is empirical evidence that suggests that the coeducational college experience is still a very "gendered" one—an experience that involves potential impediments to the success of women students (Smith, Morrison, and Wolf-Wendel 1994). That is, despite the fact that women and men can attend the same institution, men and women do not necessarily experience the institution in the same way and are not necessarily treated equitably either within the classroom, in athletics, or by their peers. The results suggest that even neutral approaches can have a negative impact on women. Indeed, numerous studies and reports have expressed alarm at what has been described as the "chilly climate" for women.

What is the chilly climate, and how do we know it exists? Looking at the in-class climate, Hall and Sandler were among the first to suggest that women are supported less in coeducational classrooms by peers and faculty than are men students. They came to these conclusions based on an examination of the literature, reports from numerous campus commissions, and anecdotal evidence from campus visits. Despite the fact that many people—men and women alike—believe that campus discrimination against women has ended, *The Classroom Climate* (Hall and Sandler 1982) identifies a host of subtle personal and social barriers that remain, including faculty calling on men more than women in class, and faculty and students making stereotyping comments about women's abilities. Hall and Sandler describe the existence of "micro-inequities" that discount women in male-dominated academic and student cultures. Similar inequities have been documented in the work environment, as well (Rowe 1990).

The existence of in-class micro-inequities is supported by the work of several authors who use slightly different methodologies. In a classic observational study, Catherine Krupnick (1985) observed the classroom participation of men and women at Harvard University. By viewing videotapes of classrooms, Krupnick found that male students talked much longer in classrooms than did their female peers, especially if the course was taught by a male faculty member. Further, the American Association of University Women's national report, "Shortchanging Girls, Shortchanging America," and Sadker and Sadker's (1994) research on the gendered classroom, also support the claim that faculty members do not give women (and girls) the same level of attention and support that men (and boys) typically receive. Similarly, in Ernest Boyer's national study of undergraduate education, he concluded: "We were especially struck by the subtle, yet significant, differences in the way men and women participated in class. . . . In many classrooms, women are overshadowed. Even the brightest women often remain silent. . . . Not only do men talk more, but what they say often carries more weight" (Boyer 1987, 150). It is important to note the consistency of these observation-based findings in contrast to the less-clear findings based on self-report.

Measuring the existence of the chilly climate outside the classroom has not been easy. Once colleges and universities eliminated many of the structural barriers to access, women continued to report gender discrimination, but the incidents were often more subtle, thus making them difficult to study using traditional methods. Pascarella et al. (1996), for example, conducted a longitudinal study of first-year students at 23 colleges and universities to determine whether the chilly climate existed, and if so, its effects on cognitive development. The researchers found that perceptions of a chilly climate for women were not pervasive and that the magnitude of negative effects stemming from it were not as severe as they had predicted. They did find, however, that women's perceptions of a chilly campus had a small, though significant, negative association with self-reported gains in academic preparation for a career. The researchers concluded that, though the effect may be small, it was present, and, thus, is an important factor and one to which institutions should pay heed.

Awareness of a climate in which issues such as gender or race are factors can influence individual performance. Using a classic experimental design, Steele (1997) has found dramatic differences on tests of academic performance, such as mathematics examinations, when white women and students of color perceive that their performance is being evaluated in the context of their race and gender. In his studies, students who take tests aware that their race or gender is known perform less well than those who cannot be stereotyped. Whether or not students perceive or experience specific behaviors, they are, he demonstrates, vulnerable to societal stereotypes, which can have dramatic effects on achievement.

Taking a more qualitative approach to the notion of chilly climate and its impact, Mills, London, Mills, and Shepala (1993) compared the climate for women at a women's college with that of women attending an adjacent coeducational institution. The researchers found that evidence of the chilly climate was most obvious to the students from the women's college who had begun to take classes and participate on the coeducational campus. The students at the women's college reported being taken seriously at the women's college while being devalued at the coeducational institution. The authors conclude that the presence of the chilly climate is hard to pinpoint—but those who have a heightened awareness of gender inequity can more easily see it and judge its impact.

Holland and Eisenhart also looked at out-of-class experiences to identify the effects that peer culture has on fostering a hostile environment for women at colleges and universities. They qualitatively examined the impact of peer relationships on both men and women and determined that for women, peers (both male and female) emphasize the importance of romantic attraction. Women are rewarded by their peers for spending time pursuing dates, focusing on their appearance, and being engaged in the social side of academia. At the same time, men students are rewarded by their peers for their academic and athletic abilities. Thus, women in college spend more time than men improving their social lives, while men in college spend more time achieving in the more traditional sense. The authors argue that the emphasis on social life impedes women's progress in coeducational environments, pulling women away from taking *themselves* seriously. They noted that "not being taken seriously as students has dire consequences for learning" (Holland and Eisenhart 1990, 203). As further evidence of this, Miller-Bernal (1989) found that women at coeducational colleges also reported that their peers were more likely to stress the importance of social life and were less likely to emphasize academic success.

In a recent analysis of a sample of college students in the 1990s, using the CIRP database, Smith, Morrison, and Wolf-Wendel (1994) found that for all the gains women have made in college attendance and in changes in the society, there are still profound differences by gender in the characteristics, attitudes, and values of women and men as they start college and as they change through college. One of the most striking findings in this study is the remaining differences in ratings of self-esteem and self-confidence for men and women. Women rate themselves lower at the beginning of college than men in these categories and continue to do so throughout college. Indeed, although both men's and women's self-confidence improve over time in college, men start out more confident than women and that difference increases over the four years in school. These findings have been documented by others (H. S. Astin and Leland 1991; Whitt 1994) and are significant because of how this shortage of self-esteem affects the way women think about their aspirations and also potentially interferes with their academic performance. Light (1990), as well, in the Harvard assessment studies, points to the very gendered perceptions of achievement and self-confidence.

Thus, despite the growth of women's participation in most sectors of education, the overall experience fails to develop women's full potential—a condition that is damaging not only to individuals, but to the entire nation. The environment for women, although it has changed dramatically in the last 30 years, remains problematic, but often in subtle and invisible ways. Whether environments are overtly hostile or simply "neutral" may not be as significant as the absence of positive intent concerning women's education.

PATHS TO SUCCESS

In what ways do women's colleges promote success? What are the paths to success that emerge from the research on women's colleges? What do they model for women, and for higher education as a whole? This section focuses on the evidence for the impact of women's colleges in terms of a broad array of indicators, using methods that ask students and alumnae directly. In addition, it focuses on the research that is attempting to understand the paths to that success.

Gendered Rewards

The research evidence generally focuses on a variety of success-related characteristics including satisfaction with the college experience, sense of competence, graduation, leadership, career aspirations, and choice of fields.

Satisfaction   Perhaps one of the most common indicators studied is satisfaction with the college experience. Not only do measures of satisfaction suggest "good feelings" about the collegiate experience, they also have been related to persistence and achievement (A. W. Astin 1985). Moreover, satisfaction can be related to higher levels of involvement and engagement with one's education, an important predictor of academic success (A. W. Astin 1984; Pascarella 1985).

A significant body of evidence suggests that women's college graduates are more satisfied with their college experience than women graduates of coeducational colleges. This conclusion has been reached consistently for over 20 years, based on a wide variety of studies. A.W. Astin's (1977) study using the CIRP databases from the entering classes of 1966 through 1969, followed 4–6 years later, concluded that women were more likely to be satisfied with college, to complete their undergraduate degrees, and (especially) to participate in leadership activities if they attended women's colleges rather than coeducational institutions.

In another study using CIRP longitudinal data from 1982 to 1986, and this time comparing women at women's colleges with women at comparably small, four-year, liberal arts institutions, D. G. Smith found that students at women's colleges were more satisfied with the following institutional characteristics:

> . . . overall quality of instruction, courses in the major, courses in the social sciences, opportunity to talk to professors, campus regulations, career counseling and advising, housing, contact with faculty and administration, relations with faculty and administration. (D. G. Smith 1990, 187)

Indeed, those attending women's colleges were more satisfied with every aspect of campus life except for social life. In addition, Smith found that students "evaluate [women's colleges] more positively on measures having to do with faculty and administrators, as well as perceived changes in values of tolerance and cultural awareness" (D. G. Smith 1990).

In another analysis of CIRP data for students entering college in 1985 and again as seniors in 1989–90, a sample of almost 25,000 students from over 400 institutions came to very similar conclusions. A. W. Astin found that women at women's colleges were more satisfied than women at coeducational colleges overall, and with faculty, overall quality of instruction, general education requirements, facilities, and support. He stated that women at women's colleges were more likely to trust the institution's administration, believed more strongly that the institution had a strong diversity orientation, and were more likely to believe the institution enhanced students' leadership and academic skills. He concludes by noting "most of the findings here are directly attributable to attending a women's college; that is, they cannot be entirely explained or accounted for on the basis of other characteristics (A. W. Astin 1993, 325).

A Sense of Competence and a Capacity for Leadership   One of the characteristics of women's colleges that has received a lot of attention is their ability to foster leadership skills and self-esteem among their students and alumnae (A. W. Astin 1977; 1993; Kuh, Schuh, and Whitt 1991; Pascarella and Terenzini 1991; Riordan 1992). The study of leadership and developing the capacity for leadership is important, in part, because of the explicit purpose of most institutions to develop leaders for roles in the larger society. Moreover, the research on the impact of college on students has suggested that involvement in leadership activities leads to student growth and development during the college years (Pascarella and Terenzini 1991; Kuh 1993). For women students, leadership activities have also been linked in important ways to a sense of competence, self-confidence, and self-esteem, and to the pursuit of nontraditional careers (H. S. Astin and Kent 1983; H. S. Astin and Leland 1991; Sagaria 1988; Pascarella and Terenzini 1991). The importance of experiencing leadership in all-woman settings has emerged not only from research at women's colleges. H. S. Astin and Leland (1991), in their study of important women leaders, found a consistent theme concerning the power of all-female settings, including Girl Scouts, sororities, and girls' high schools—along with women's colleges. Similar findings are mentioned by Sagaria (1988).

Once again, A. W. Astin's classic study (1977) may be cited. It reported that women at women's colleges were more likely to attain leadership positions and be involved in student government (among other outcomes). A study by Kim and Alvarez (1995)—a longitudinal study of women's colleges and women at coeducational schools, again using CIRP data—concluded that attending a women's college has a positive effect on students' self-perceived academic abilities and on social self-confidence. The authors suggest that women's colleges provide their students with profound opportunities to be actively involved in student organizations and to exercise leadership skills; this, they conclude, leads to the positive outcomes found in the study. The assumption made is that women's colleges provide more opportunities for women students to be involved in both curricular and extracurricular activities, thereby fostering a host of positive outcomes. Because women, in general, tend to underestimate their abilities, Kim and Alvarez's finding that growth in perception of academic ability is stronger for those at women's colleges is very significant. Being surrounded by a peer group that has strong intellectual self-esteem, along with institutional characteristics such as commitment to students, emerged as important factors in their study. They also found a positive relationship *between* institutional commitments to diversity, more typical at women's colleges, and student plans for graduate and professional preparation.

Indeed, the commitment to diversity, as a variable to be studied, and its potential impact on college outcomes, is relatively new. Its appearance as an important institutional commitment bodes well for all students and also for the diversification of women students at women's colleges (D. G. Smith, et al. 1997).

These outcomes are supported by an important qualitative study (Whitt 1994) of leadership opportunities at three women's colleges (Wellesley College, Randolph-Macon Woman's College, and Westhampton College). Whitt found great similarity among the institutions in institutional practices and student reports of their experiences. The results describe the important link between leadership opportunities and a variety of important outcomes related not only to social and political awareness, writing, thinking, and organizational skills, but also expanded notions of career opportunities. The study emphasized the intentional ways in which women's leadership was encouraged and taught through workshops, training for campus leaders, and the introduction of information about women's development and leadership issues. Some programs also integrate academic components, career development, and links to the community. Students at the three institutions also commented on the extensive opportunities to be significantly involved in college decision-making through membership on important committees, participation in curriculum development and admissions work, and involvement in student government. Whitt noted that students viewed these opportunities as being related in important ways to the college's emphasis on service and to assuming responsibility for the success of the college. One student noted, "This college encourages you to take charge. We're taken seriously—almost as seriously as the faculty" (Whitt 1994).

Indeed, there is a great deal of evidence of the power of all-woman settings in developing women's leadership skills and affirming women's self-esteem (A. W. Astin 1993 ; H. S. Astin and Leland 1991; Moos and Otto 1975; Sagaria

1988; Whitt 1994). Not surprisingly, students at women's colleges have been found to hold more leadership positions in campus activities than women at coeducational colleges (A. W. Astin 1977; 1991). However, the important finding may be not so much the evidence for experience in terms of numbers of activities, but rather the importance of providing an environment in which women participate fully in all kinds of leadership activities, women see women in leadership roles, and choices whether or not to participate are not mediated by gender. The participants in Whitt's study affirm the role of the faculty, administration, and student peers in creating an environment that encourages participation, leadership, and diverse styles of leadership. Moreover, experimental research looking at factors that contribute to women's leadership suggests that women who develop leadership in women's settings are more likely to take on leadership positions in coeducational settings than women who have not had such experience (Lockheed and Klein 1985). These results speak to the apparent contradiction in the capacity of women's colleges to educate women for the "real world."

The Pursuit of the Nontraditional   In addition to the powerful evidence reported in Chapter 3, there is other evidence suggesting that graduates of women's colleges have made great strides in the pursuit of nontraditional areas for study and work.

Bressler and Wendell (1980) studied the occupational choices of a national sample of women attending women's colleges and coeducational colleges between 1967 and 1971. According to this study, women at women's colleges were more likely to pursue nontraditional fields of study than women at coeducational colleges. Looking at women who changed their majors, the same study found that women at women's colleges were more likely than their coeducational counterparts to change from a traditionally female major to one that was more male dominated.

Solnick (1995) also explored the effect of college environment on women's choice of major. In a large-scale study of intended and final major fields at eight women's colleges and seven coeducational institutions for students graduating in 1992, she found that women at women's colleges were more likely than their coeducational counterparts to leave female-dominated majors for neutral or male-dominated majors. She also found that both women at women's colleges and women at coeducational institutions were equally likely to remain in and/or depart from a male-dominated major.

A recent report of the Women's College Coalition, using institutional and national data, found that women at women's colleges were three times more likely to earn bachelor's degrees in economics and one-and-a-half times more likely to earn bachelor's degrees in the life sciences, the physical sciences, or mathematics than women at coeducational institutions (Sebrechts 1993). A study by Scheye and Gilroy (1994) of 300 college students at four liberal arts colleges also found a positive impact from a woman-only environment on women's sense of competency in pursuing nontraditional careers.

There is no question that choice of major has a significant impact on wage differences between men and women. As such, it is not surprising that several studies have found that graduates of women's colleges are more likely to have higher salaries than comparable women at coeducational institutions. Riordan (1994), for example, found that attending a women's college had a positive effect on the prestige of one's occupation. This, in turn, has an impact on income. Riordan's study used data from another large database, the National Longitudinal Study of the High School Class of 1972 (NLS), sponsored by the National Center for Education Statistics. The database began with a large survey of over 18,000 high school seniors in 1972, with follow-up studies in the 1970s and finally in 1986. In that study, Riordan concluded, "Women's colleges attendees achieve higher occupational prestige positions and greater salaries despite the fact that they actually obtain no more education than their coeducational counterparts." In another nod to those concerned about "the real world" for women's college graduates, Riordan (1992) also found that graduates were more likely to have achieved marital happiness. A similar study by Conaty (1989), again using the NLS, followed high school seniors in 1972 and found that, by 1986, women who had attended a women's college earned, on average, between 20 and 25 percent more than similar women who attended coeducational institutions.

There is other evidence focusing on outstanding achievement. The Women's College Coalition reports that, in 1985, 30 percent of those on *Business Week's* list of 50 women "rising stars" in corporate America were graduates of women's colleges. Since less than 5 percent of women college graduates during the era studied graduated from women's colleges, women's college graduates are overrepresented 6 to 1. Additionally, one-third of the women board members of Fortune 1000 companies graduated from women's colleges, and 44 percent of the women in Congress attended women's colleges (Harwarth, Maline, and DeBra 1997). Similarly, Ledman and aassociates (1995) found disproportional representation of women's college graduates in management positions. In exploring the factors related to this outcome, they cite the important role of graduate education for women's college graduates. Finally, a recent report on women college and university presidents found that 63 percent of the women heading four-year independent colleges were graduates of women's colleges and that 22 percent of the women presidents of four-year public institutions were graduates of women's colleges (Touchton, Shavlik, and Davis 1993).

The Paths

Women's Places, Women's Spaces   In an attempt to look at the factors that lead to success, some research has focused on the atmosphere and behaviors that occur in classes and has compared classrooms for women with coeducational classrooms. The evidence suggests that some in-class environments are more conducive to student success than others (A. W. Astin 1977; 1991; Pascarella and Terenzini 1991). Some evidence suggests that women's colleges possess these favorable within-classroom traits. For example, Miller-Bernal (1993) found that students who had taken more courses whose subject matter dealt with women, who spoke up frequently in class, and who perceived their college to be concerned with students, were more likely to have positive self-esteem. Further, in a major observational study of 141 classes at 22 institutions (10 coeducational colleges, 10 women's colleges, and 2 men's colleges), designed to explore both student and faculty behaviors, Trice (1994) found that at women's colleges, students were given more opportunities for academic accomplishment than at coeducational institutions: their classes were more interactive and discussion-oriented, they showed more positive change in levels of participation, they were invited to participate more through faculty questions, and women were given more opportunities for academic interaction with peers and faculty members.

Ginorio and Wiegand (1994), while not directly studying women at women's colleges, compared participants in a woman-only science program with participants in a similar coeducational group. The students in the woman-only group reported that their experience in this group had a positive influence on their career choice and made them want to persist in science. These students were the only ones to report an increase in perceived ability in the physical sciences, which they attributed to the presence of a strong, academically based support network. The women students in the coeducational program also experienced some positive outcomes, but not to the same degree; moreover, their perceptions of their abilities declined.

Other researchers, comparing the experience of women in women's environments, such as all-woman residence halls, have also found that levels of career and academic aspirations are higher in such contexts (Ballou 1986; Moos and Otto 1975). These environments seem to create a climate of high expectations, supported by peer and faculty cultures.

Women and Supportive Men   In the context of the general condition of women in the nation and on most campuses, one cannot underestimate the power on the campuses of women's colleges of seeing women in all places. Most of the presidents are women, the faculty is balanced by gender in virtually all disciplines and ranks, and women assume positions of leadership everywhere. There is almost universal agreement about the importance of role models for women, and many studies support that contention (Bailey and Rask 1996; Bressler and Wendell 1980; Brown 1982; Noe 1988). The most dramatic impact of role models was cited in the prior chapter, with M. E. Tidball's data showing the striking relationship between women on the faculty and women's students' career achievement. Her study of male and female faculty attitudes was among the first to study gender differences among faculty using an extensive faculty survey developed by the American Council on Education (Bayer 1973). Looking at the data for men and women faculty from over 200 four-year institutions, Tidball documented differences in male and female attitudes toward women's issues, toward women students, and in the value placed on teaching and research. The study showed that woman-related issues and women students were relatively unsupported by male faculty across the country. Serious concerns were raised about the collegiate environment for women because of the realtively small number and proportion of women faculty (M. E. Tidball 1976b).

While the numbers and proportion of women faculty have grown since M. E. Tidball's (1976b) study, data from the Small College Database discussed in Chapter 2 and in the Supplement to Chapter 2 reveal significant disparities among institutional types even 20 years later. Table 12 shows the proportion of women on the faculty for five subtypes of small colleges. In 1983, women's colleges had 57 percent women on their faculties, the highest proportion of the institutional categories. Coeducational colleges were 28 percent and men's colleges—not surprisingly—were 8 percent. Between 1983 and 1993, the overall percentage of women faculty of small colleges grew from 32 percent to 36 percent. In 1993 women's colleges had 60 percent women faculty, coeducational colleges had 33 percent, women's change colleges had 54 percent, while men's change colleges were below the mean at 26 percent. The increase in the proportion of women faculty members in the nation's small colleges is a change in the right direction, although the increase is not very large. Moreover, closer inspection reveals even greater disparities in the numbers and proportions of women by disciplines. Here too, women's colleges show balance (Sebrechts 1993). This suggests that it will be some time before coeducational institutions support women faculty and provide the models for women students in the ways already being done at women's colleges. Considering that small colleges have higher percentages of women faculty than large comprehensive institutions and research institutions, where most of today's college women are studying, the data presented above, focusing on only small colleges, are troubling indeed.

At the same time, it is clear from other research that men can have an important influence on women's roles and aspirations. Indeed, Scheye and Gilroy's (1994) study of women and career choices found important roles for girls' high schools and women's colleges—and for men as role models in those environments. The evidence that men at women's colleges tend to have attitudes more supportive of women is, thus, very important. An earlier study by M. E. Tidball (1976b) documented the differences in attitudes of faculty by gender but also found significant differences at different institutions. She found that men teaching at women's colleges were more likely to hold supportive views about women and their potential and to value teaching than their male peers at other institutions. Moreover, findings of strongly shared values of male and female faculty at women's colleges have been reported in a

TABLE 12

PERCENT OF FEMALE FACULTY FOR SMALL COLLEGES

College Subtype	1983				1993			
	No.	MaF	FeF	%FeF	No.	MaF	FeF	%FeF
Coeducational Coll.	488	48	18	2.8	363	49	24	33
Men's Colleges	12	68	12	8	7	70	11	12
Women's Colleges	70	26	33	57	44	27	38	60
Men's Change Coll.	46	67	14	18	56	76	27	26
Wom. Change Coll.	58	25	27	52	67	31	37	54
All Small Colleges *	634	45	20	32	537	48	27	36

Notes

No.   The number of colleges for each subtype; the numbers are smaller than those tabulated in Table 17 because some colleges were not listed in *Academe*, the source for the faculty data.

MaF   Mean of the male faculty for the number of colleges in the type.

FeF   Mean of the female faculty for the number of colleges in the type.

%FeF Female faculty as a percent of total mean faculty for the number of colleges in the type.

Sources: Hansen 1983; Hamermesh 1993; C. S. Tidball 1997.

study of the learning environment at women's colleges. In that study of presidents and faculty, male faculty saw their role as contributing to the leadership of women, to raising aspirations, and to countering traditional role expectations (Women's College Coalition 1981).

Miller-Bernal (1993), in a comparative study of women students at four institutions (a women's college, a coordinate college, a coeducational college, and a men's change college), underscored the complex and important relationships between male and female faculty and students, the institutional ethos, and opportunities for involvement. She concludes that women at a women's college and women at a coordinate college have more female role models and supportive male faculty, are more involved in leadership activities, and sense a greater institutional commitment to students.

There is evidence for both propositions—the importance of women to women and the importance of men to women. The influence of classroom contexts, faculty, peer environments, and general institutional commitment to excellence, achievement, and women cannot be underestimated. Women's colleges are the only institution type with both substantial numbers of women faculty and supportive male faculty.

Institutional Ethos—Taking Women Seriously   Implicit and explicit, in many of the studies cited, are efforts to understand the factors associated with the success of women's colleges. Given the limits of research, many studies focus on single variables looked at in isolation. Taken as a whole, however, single characteristics, programs, or events reveal less than looking at the interrelationship among many factors embedded in an institutional ethos.

D. G. Smith, Wolf-Wendel, and Morrison (1995), using the CIRP databases for 1986 and 1990, found that women at women's colleges were not only more involved but also perceived that their institution was supportive of involvement and student learning. Specifically, students at women's colleges were more likely than their counterparts at coeducational colleges to perceive that their institutions cared about them and cared about their learning, to perceive that their institutions cared about civic involvement, and to believe that their institutions cared about multiculturalism. In turn, institutions that were perceived to hold these values were more likely to have students who were actively involved in the academic and extracurricular life of the college and who were more satisfied with their institution, held higher career and degree aspirations, and rated themselves higher in terms of sense of competence and leadership ability. In addition, even though attending a women's college negatively predicted social satisfaction, the negative component was mediated by women's colleges' perceived concern for student development. In other words, the negative impact was diminished when students perceived that their institution cared about their ability to learn and grow. Kim and Alvarez (1995) suggest further that the lower ratings of social satisfaction are not indicative of lower self-confidence. They found that attitudes about social life are unrelated to social self-confidence, which was developed more strongly at women's colleges.

In a study attempting to understand the success of women's colleges and the lessons for coeducational institutions, Whitt (1992) demonstrated the interrelationship of many institutional factors, all focused on taking women seriously. She highlighted institutional mission and culture, high expectations and an environment of support, a balance of role models who live women's experiences and support women's achievement, research and knowledge about women, and the development of strong women's communities. In her study, she saw dramatic evidence of women serving as peer models, as leadership models, and as faculty models. In addition, she pointed to the importance of male faculty role models in promoting student self-confidence and self-worth. Underlying each of the specific attributes is a fundamental commitment to women as women—on a campus that serves to develop the full potential of each student. Whitt emphasizes the important role of institutional mission that, at these institutions, permeates the culture, the programs, the curriculum, and the traditions. Echoing Wellesley's mission to "provide an excellent liberal arts education for women who will make a difference in the world," Whitt quotes an alumna who said, "People here are really conscious of the core mission of the place—education of women for leadership" (Whitt 1994).

CHAPTER

A Look Inside

A sheltered life can be a daring life as well. For all serious daring starts from within.

—Eudora Welty, 1983

To understand some of the ways that women's colleges take women seriously, it is helpful to visit a campus or two. This chapter presents information about the campuses of two women's colleges—Bryn Mawr College and Bennett College—through the lens of a researcher conducting qualitative case studies. Case studies allow a researcher to explore in-depth and holistic descriptions that represent people and institutions in their own terms (Lincoln and Guba 1985; Yin 1989). It has been suggested that case studies that demonstrate the inner workings and socialization processes of a campus can illuminate how and why some colleges achieve certain educational goals (Baldwin and Thelin 1991). Case studies also allow one to understand the nuances of complicated phenomena.

Bryn Mawr and Bennett were selected as case study sites because they both have a demonstrated record of facilitating the success of their women students. The characteristics of these institutions are not necessarily typical of women's colleges, if "typical" characteristics exist anywhere, but they do represent some of the variations that exist among women's colleges and they do exemplify institutions that take women seriously. By understanding how members of these campuses view their institution, it becomes easier to see how these places can be institutional models.

Bryn Mawr College is a prestigious, resource-rich women's college in an affluent suburb of Philadelphia, Pennsylvania. It has a national reputation for attracting bright women who go on to achieve great things. In particular, Bryn Mawr has graduated one of the highest proportions of white women who have earned doctorates and who have been listed in *Who's Who in America*. In contrast, Bennett College, located in Greensboro, North Carolina, is one of two Historically Black women's colleges in the United States. Although relatively resource-poor and "non-selective" in its admissions, Bennett also graduates women who achieve success. Bennett College was among the most productive institutions in graduating African American women who subsequently earned doctorates and who were listed in *Who's Who among Black Americans* (Wolf-Wendel 1998).

The case studies developed in this chapter are based on qualitative research; details on the methodology can be found in the Supplement to Chapter 5. Four-day site visits were conducted at each of these colleges during the spring of 1994. The visits consisted of hour-long interviews with approximately 30 individuals, including students, faculty members, alumnae, and administrators. In addition to the formal interviews, the site visit consisted of attending campus events, visiting residence halls, and informally interacting with a range of campus members. During the formal interviews, participants were asked to describe why they thought their institution was so successful with women students. The formal interviews, which were tape-recorded and transcribed, were coded to discover themes. Results of these interviews and observations are presented below.

BRYN MAWR COLLEGE

Bryn Mawr's campus has a very collegiate, studious look about it; so much so that a faculty member commented, "The somber, gothic architecture sets the mood for academic pursuits." Bryn Mawr, though it is a women's college, is not a cloistered convent—students from neighboring campuses, Haverford and Swarthmore, are present to take advantage of the reciprocal course-exchange policy. Further, men from Bryn Mawr's graduate programs are also around. Despite the presence of men, Bryn Mawr is clearly a campus for women. The campus today lives up to its original identity as a "college determined to prove that women could successfully complete a curriculum as rigorous as any offered to men in the best universities."

Bryn Mawr College is small, private, residential, and non-sectarian (see Supplement to Chapter 5 for details regarding the demographics of Bryn Mawr). Founded in 1885, Bryn Mawr was the first college to grant both undergraduate and graduate degrees in all departments to women. The undergraduate college still admits women exclusively; the graduate school, however, has admitted men since 1931. Institutional brochures describe Bryn Mawr as a school "dedicated to the classical humanist tradition."

Members of the Bryn Mawr community are very aware of their ability to graduate large numbers of successful women. An institutional publication from 1992 claims that Bryn Mawr "is the only women's college and one of five liberal arts colleges in the nation with the highest percentage of winners of the National Science Foundation Graduate Fellowships." Further, the publication notes that the percentage of graduates earning degrees in the physical sciences at Bryn Mawr is "five times the national average overall and nine times the average of degrees awarded to women. It is four times the rate for women at other highly selective liberal arts colleges and five times the rate for women at highly selective private research universities." In addition, the percentage of women completing the physics major at Bryn Mawr is 29 times the national average for women.

Students, alumnae, faculty members, and administrators credited eight institutional factors with influencing Bryn Mawr's high production of successful alumnae. These factors are presented in order of importance, as indicated by the frequency with which they were mentioned by constituents and by how much constituents emphasized them. The factors include the following:

- An institutional mission and history that takes women seriously
- A faculty penchant to treat students as colleagues and scholars and to hold students to the highest academic standards
- The presence of strong women role models at all levels of the institution; the ability of the school to attract and retain a critical mass of motivated, bright, and capable women students
- A recognition of the social realities facing women in the real world
- Extracurricular involvement opportunities
- Tempered personal support and advising
- The inclusion of women in the curriculum

Institutional Mission and History

The whole institution is one that takes women very seriously.

There was agreement among those interviewed that Bryn Mawr's mission was directly related to the success of its students. Bryn Mawr's mission has always been to provide women students with a "rigorous education that prepares them to accomplish any goal that they set for themselves." A fundamental component of this mission is that, at the undergraduate level, the institution is exclusively for women. According to an alumna, "Because it's a women's institution, they [the faculty and administration] really reinforce, support, and encourage whatever opportunities can be made from that fact." Indeed, those at the institution "expect women to have no artificial constraints on their intellectual aspirations."

Understanding Bryn Mawr's history seems to be a key to understanding its mission. Repeatedly, campus members talked about M. Carey Thomas, the founding dean and second president, who remains the central historical figure on campus. Members of the community believe that Thomas wanted to create a college that would be "a Harvard for women" where there would be "an educational experience equivalent to what was available to men at the time." Thomas's goal for the college was "to propel young women to careers primarily in the academy." Given this history, it was not a surprise to many of the respondents that Bryn Mawr continues to graduate a large proportion of women who receive doctorates. In fact, a faculty member stated, "Bryn Mawr was founded as an institution to train women for the Ph.D. . . . It's part of our history, part of our reason for being." As evidence of this, several respondents noted two campus rituals—Lantern Night and the May Day hoop race.

In the Lantern Night ritual, first-year students are each given a lantern; the woman whose lantern stays lit the longest is predicted to be the first who will acquire her doctoral degree. The student whose lantern goes out first is predicted to be the first to marry. Similarly, the May Day hoop race has the senior women racing with a hoop and a stick down a hill and across a finish line. Tradition suggests that the first across the line will be the first to earn her doctorate; the second to finish will be the first to get married. According to several respondents, marriage and doctorates are frequently "prizes" at Bryn Mawr events, dating back to Thomas's assertion that "our failures only marry." The impact of these rituals was summarized well by one faculty member who commented, "All of the traditions that have been accumulated . . . are geared to push you along the way to success as an intellectual."

High Academic Expectations

You have to believe that the students will do well.

High expectations at Bryn Mawr positively influence student achievement. Expectations for first-year and second-year students, and the type of encouragement they receive, differs slightly from that for upper-class women. During the first two years at Bryn Mawr, it appears that faculty and administrators concentrate on convincing women that they are capable students and encouraging them to pursue topics that interest them, particularly in nontraditional fields. The focus for upper-class women is on preparing them to handle graduate-level work and encouraging them to see themselves as scholars.

One of the things that Bryn Mawr does particularly early on is to reinforce the idea that students are capable. As one student said, "You are told all the time that you are a successful woman and that you are going places. After a while, you start to believe it." The school's honor code is one way that this gets conveyed. Through the honor code, students find themselves "treated like adults . . . capable of making [their] own decisions." The honor code gives students "full responsibility for the integrity of [their] academic work, from original research activities to self-scheduled exams." It establishes what one student called "a high degree of trust and responsibility." This message "sets the stage" for treating students like scholars and colleagues.

Professors at Bryn Mawr often demonstrate their high expectations of students by pushing students to succeed beyond students' own expectations. One student, for example, recalled a professor's reaction to a class assignment:

> I thought it was a tremendous paper. And I got it back, and she [the professor] had written "This is very good, but you haven't gone as far as I know you can." I kept getting those comments, and finally I wrote a paper that met her expectations. . . . It wasn't like she kept knocking me down, but she had high expectations for me.

Similarly, a faculty member talked about the effect of making students take responsibility for their education. He commented, "Once your expectations are set—that is, how a course should be—then I think that you carry those expectations from course to course to course, and what you expect of yourself is certainly shaped by that experience."

For students in their first two years at Bryn Mawr, the emphasis is on "leaving the door open for people to feel that they may succeed." This form of encouragement is particularly important for women students interested in nontraditional fields. Professors in mathematics and the sciences, for example, were adamant about the need to encourage women to consider majoring in these fields. Their methods of doing this varied, but all were based on the fundamental belief that women are capable of succeeding. For example, in the physics department, the faculty were careful to avoid unintentionally socializing women out of science. Bryn Mawr, it was explained, "started the sophomore lab with 15 people in the room, none of whom had spent their childhood fixing the old man's car." One physics professor added, "If you create an atmosphere where students are not penalized for the way they are brought up, then women will learn equally as well as men do. . . . Bryn Mawr's sophomore classes start at a lower level than Haverford but . . . by the end of the year, they are at exactly the same place."

Upper-class women at Bryn Mawr are directly encouraged to work at the level of graduate students and to consider themselves scholars. According to a professor, "In many ways they [the faculty] looked at their undergraduates, particularly as they got more advanced, as being very similar to their graduate students in ability, in seriousness, and motivation." This becomes possible because Bryn Mawr sees itself as "half-way between a normal liberal arts college and a research university." The result of this amalgamation, according to one faculty member, "breeds a kind of fierce independence, and as a consequence it attracts women who want to be hard-core researchers, but who recognize the importance of the liberal arts—women physicists who recognize the value of Shakespeare." In addition, the emphasis Bryn Mawr places on academic majors implicitly encourages women to achieve. One faculty member indicated that "graduating with a major in something [at Bryn Mawr] is almost equivalent to getting a master's degree in that subject."

In preparing students for the world "outside of Bryn Mawr," constituents stressed the importance of students developing strong research skills, which translates to providing opportunities for active learning. Through active learning, students are treated like colleagues. Scholarship and colleaguehood at Bryn Mawr means different things in different settings. "In archaeology, it means digging things out of the ground together. In the English department, colleaguehood means something like recommending readings to one another." Students "formulate [their] own ideas and present them to the class. . . . They [students] do not just sit in the lecture hall, listen passively to the revealed truth, take it down, and then reproduce it on the exam. That does not happen around here. We get them out in the field." Many classes, in fact, are taught like graduate seminars so that "once they are in graduate school, it's already a familiar setting, the method of teaching that inquires . . . rather than regurgitation."

Active learning also takes the form of working with faculty members and independently working on research projects. Most majors at Bryn Mawr require senior theses. In addition, students in all fields are given the opportunity to work on faculty research projects, many of which are published. One professor, for example, commented, "The work of my own most widely cited in the field was done in collaboration with a junior at Bryn Mawr." These kinds of research opportunities, according to one professor, help students "learn the dimensions of being independent, the dimensions of what research begins to mean." Another professor stated: "If you allow, at the undergraduate level, people to do something that is more advanced, then they can decide whether they can do it and whether they want to do it, and pursue it." A professor in the sciences summed up the preparation her students receive at Bryn Mawr:

> They will do research at the end of the freshman year, and then we try to get them into a good national program at the end of their sophomore year, and then another internship or something at the end of their junior year. They have probably done several research projects already, some of them over a long period of time. They tend to get internal awards, and then by the time they are ready for graduate school they look really different.

In addition to preparing students academically, respondents talked repeatedly about how the expectation of attending graduate school is conveyed to students. Most students interviewed mentioned being overtly encouraged to apply to graduate programs. Several students mentioned faculty members and administrators who took them aside and said something to the effect of, "You should think about going to graduate school," or, "Look, those are really good points that you made, would you like to go on with this?" It was said to be common for faculty to care about what happens to students after they graduate. Further, the prevailing attitude among all constituents is "that it just doesn't end after four years of college."

Role Models

Where the portraits on the walls are women.

For most of the respondents, it was important to student success that students could easily find powerful, successful, competent women at all levels of the institution to serve as role models. "To see women as leaders, as thinkers, as speakers, is not something the college has to make any special effort to do; it is just the way we are." Similarly, an administrator commented:

> I think it's just terribly exciting to young women to come to an institution where the portraits on the walls are women, where the people teaching them are women, where the president is a woman. . . . Young women at a very impressionable time in their development are in institutions where women have taken on the burdens and pleasures of leadership equally or with something of an advantage. And that is so different from the world most of them have known, and that has a lot more influence than they are conscious of in a lot of ways.

Role models at Bryn Mawr come in many forms. For example, administrators—who are predominantly female—were seen as positive role models for students. As one faculty member said, "I think the presence of highly competent, impressive women in the administration is definitely a plus in terms of role modeling, but also in terms of inspiration."

The presence and visibility of strong women alumnae and trustees also seemed to have a positive role-modeling effect on Bryn Mawr students. Specifically, one alumna stated, "The preponderance of high-achieving women means you have no questions that women can do anything that they want to do in society." The positive modeling from alumnae and trustees was said to have a potentially stronger impact for "students whose families have not provided access to a lot of women who have had high-powered careers."

The faculty, which is approximately 50 percent male and 50 percent female, were the most frequently mentioned group in terms of their role modeling potential. According to several people, the faculty at Bryn Mawr, regardless of their sex, model what it means to be an academic. "The faculty think of themselves as active scholars. . . . I would guess that is a significant factor behind the numbers of Bryn Mawr students that go on and get Ph.D.s. They are like kids who grow up on farms and they see their parents as farmers and it occurs to them that they might be farmers."

Women faculty, however, are the real role models on campus. The presence of women faculty, particularly in traditionally male-dominated fields, was said to be very important. For example, one student indicated that she had a female philosophy professor who was a "real positive role model. . . . Philosophy is one of the more male-dominated fields, and it is nice to see that a woman can make it through and to hear her personal experiences." A professor in the sciences commented:

> Mentors do not need to look like the students, but I think it is important to have women in departments. . . . I can't figure out what departments tell their women students . . . when there are no women faculty members. What actually are they training these women to do? It is such a glass ceiling message.

The students themselves were also said to serve as role models for one another. As one student commented, "You see everybody around you setting their sights very high academically and professionally, and you feel that you can do it too." A faculty member explained, "The smartest students at Bryn Mawr are also the highest-status students. That is not necessarily the case at a lot of places." Similarly, an alumna noted, "At Bryn Mawr, one of the up-sides of peer culture is its persistence of the sense that this is a place where you work hard and are taken seriously, and you are surrounded by other people who are high-powered and bright and ambitious, and that's a good thing." Looking up to other students as role models fosters competition among the students. This competition was credited with motivating students to succeed, but it was also credited with creating stress among the students. Several individuals talked about stress as "individually motivated, but socially acceptable." In fact, faculty members and administrators made comments to the effect that "stress is a badge of honor for many students." As one explained, "Certainly the notion that 'I am most put upon by my serious studies' is a favorite attitude to strike at Bryn Mawr. And the kids do a certain amount of one-upmanship on the amount of suffering that they have just undergone or have yet to do." One student added, half jokingly, that perhaps the stress has a positive side. "Bryn Mawr," she said, "can be a pressure cooker. . . . Women are forced to handle stress and pretty much bring it on themselves a lot of the time. And, if that is a good qualification for getting a Ph.D., then we are certainly on the right path."

Critical Mass of High Achieving, Motivated Women Students

This is a room of their own.

At the risk of stating the obvious, because Bryn Mawr is a women's college, it has a critical mass of women. This was one of the reported strengths of Bryn Mawr. As one administrator explained, "I think there is something very powerful for women about being at a place that is theirs; that the women students feel a kind of ownership to the history of the place, the traditions of the place. . . . They identify with the culture and see the culture as taking them seriously and really being invested in them." Another faculty member added, "I believe in Virginia Woolf's notion of 'a room of one's own.' This is a room of their own."

It is not just the presence of *any* women that makes Bryn Mawr successful—most respondents indicated that Bryn Mawr's success is tied to the kind of student who applies to and is admitted to Bryn Mawr. Students at Bryn Mawr were described as "predestined to achieve post-baccalaureate success." The combination of so many high-achieving, motivated women was said to create a "gendered intellectual density" that facilitated the success of women students. According to a student:

> Bryn Mawr is a place where intellectual women find camaraderie and colleagueship of other women who are trying to do the same thing. . . . You don't have to tough it out on your own. . . . You find other people who have the same feelings, and I think that just having a group of people who are proud of what they are doing, and who like the intellectual challenge . . . is helpful in this women's college setting.

Respondents also mentioned the critical mass of women faculty as an important feature of Bryn Mawr. In this vein, one professor commented: "A critical mass of [women] faculty is even more important than having a critical mass of [women] students. My feeling is a mass of faculty would . . . be in a position to ensure that . . . discriminatory practices and so on didn't exist, to ensure that the climate is safe for others." Several of the male faculty members indicated that the presence of strong women faculty members had a positive impact on them, by changing the way they subsequently treated women students. As one professor commented, the presence of women in his department "mellows any incipient sexism that one might have."

Interestingly, two individuals mentioned the idea that the important thing about having a critical mass of women is that it allows members of the community the freedom to be different from one another. A professor explained that there is no female stereotype that holds at a school like Bryn Mawr:

> The critical factor is having enough of a particular kind of these people so that they can develop heterogeneity. The critical mass allows them to no longer feel their primary identification with the group. . . . If I was designing a college, I would make as a serious first principle of the college an insistence on the value of heterogeneity. Any successful biological system is successful precisely because of the diversity it

contains; the more different kind of things you have interacting, the more adaptable, flexible, creative a system is.

In fact, many of the respondents indicated that the "women's collegeness" of Bryn Mawr is something that they almost "take for granted." As one student explained, "Bryn Mawr just completely eliminates the element of gender. . . . So you get four years where that is not even an issue in your mind." An important component of Bryn Mawr is that, in general, those at the institution have historically rejected the notion of "difference feminism"; the idea that women learn differently from men and that instruction must be tailored to the "special needs of women." One administrator, for example, suggested that "Women need a women's college not because they are different or they learn differently or they are not ready for prime time, but because they need women alone. A place where they are not going to have to just put up with all the distractions of the other world."

Awareness of Social Realities

Equality in sex roles is just not questioned.

Constituents at Bryn Mawr were very aware of how women are treated in the larger world. They talked about sexism and the glass ceiling, and they actively worried about how their students will cope with the discrimination they will face in graduate school and in the job market. Many claimed that the fact that Bryn Mawr is organized around the notion that women are capable helps women students combat societal sexism.

According to one faculty member, "The major merit of a women's college is that you have bureaucrats who, in effect, are concerned with women's issues, and they have the power. Exercising that power, they set up a structure of governance here which requires of people that they show certain sensitivities." In this vein, an administrator stressed the importance of Bryn Mawr creating

> a situation where equality in sex roles is just not questioned. . . . Women don't take things for granted and they are aware that you have to build in some safeguards to see that an institution does not do business as usual, and that male models don't simply take over in the classroom or in the way in which extracurricular life is structured.

According to many respondents, one of the ways that Bryn Mawr and other women's colleges differentiated themselves from coeducational institutions was by recognizing the possibility that men and women may respond differently in classroom situations. In fact, constituents seemed to be very aware of the studies that found men participated more than women in coeducational classrooms. Recognition of this phenomenon influenced many of the students interviewed to come to a women's college like Bryn Mawr. In particular, one young woman picked Bryn Mawr because she believed that it was important to "be in an environment where professors and the administration are more conscious of the situation of women in the classroom and how much attention they get, and how much attention they ask for." Several constituents indicated that because courses at Bryn Mawr are predominantly or exclusively filled with women, "the women themselves feel differently in a class where they can speak more freely." As one student commented, "I didn't feel social pressure to sacrifice attractiveness for intellect."

Involvement Opportunities

It's a given that women will do it.

Many of those interviewed talked about the benefits for students involving themselves in a variety of extracurricular activities, particularly in the student Self-Government Association (SGA). Bryn Mawr has the oldest student self-government system in the country, established in 1892. All Bryn Mawr undergraduates are members of the SGA, which takes on more responsibility than typical student government associations. As one student explained, the SGA is self-regulating; its control "extends beyond organizing parties and fund-raisers. We collect dues. We have a budget for clubs and organizations on campus. We appoint people to sit on administrative and faculty committees." An administrator had this to say about the SGA: "There is no professional staff to run student activities and to deal with student discipline; there is just no climate for that. And that sort of vacuum is very handy to motivate students to do for themselves."

The word "trust" was commonly used by respondents to describe the impact of Bryn Mawr's Self-Government Association. As an alumna stated:

> There is a long tradition here of empowering students, in the sense of making them feel that they have a strong voice in running the college. . . . There are all kinds of decisions which we share with students here, where other places would say, "I can't believe you talk to the students about that." . . . [There is] that sense of a democratic institution where all the constituencies ought to be involved in decisions and where students have wisdom and maturity to contribute to decision-making.

Aside from the SGA, several respondents talked about how the fact that Bryn Mawr is a women's college encourages students to become involved in extracurricular activities. As one faculty member commented, "If something needs to be done, students do it. There is no looking around for someone else to do it. It's a given that women will do it."

Tempered Support for Students

Sometimes I worry that we take too-good care of them.

Three-quarters of those interviewed indicated that caring and support from faculty and administrators is an important part of Bryn Mawr's success. In general, respondents talked about how faculty and administrators make themselves available to students, how they talk to students about both academic and personal concerns, and how they actively mentor students. This idea was captured particularly well by a faculty member who stated, "Both intellectually and personally, kids can get treated pretty individually around here. . . . For kids who are floundering either personally or intellectually, this can be a pretty supportive place. . . . A lot of kids really blossom here. They are really shy little girls . . . then after about six months, they are raising hell." Faculty at Bryn Mawr pride themselves on taking "this fierce personal interest in their students—who assist them not just here, but all through their graduate careers."

At the same time, however, respondents also expressed the idea that support should be tempered because, ultimately, students are responsible for themselves. For example, one faculty member suggested that the institution "takes very, very, very good care of our students." He added, however:

> Sometimes I worry that we take too-good care of them. When they get out there in the cruel world, it's not the same, and they come back rather indignant, saying, "Well, the graduate school doesn't seem to care." And we say, "Of course they don't care, but that is how it is." We sometimes worry that we are not preparing them for that very well.

Another faculty member expressed a similar notion:

> We take our students in the early years and try very hard to be helpful, supportive, and encouraging to them without being condescending to them. But, on the other hand, we are essentially giving the students the message that they have to make it on their own. We are not going to be holding their hands through every step of the way. We expect a certain maturity and initiative on their part. . . . You could make an argument that is good because if students get the idea from the beginning that they have to have some initiative in this process, then that is a good thing to have learned. That bodes well for any future success they may have.

The combination of support and personal responsibility, according to one faculty member, means that "faculty here may let the students explore more on their own . . . if they are going along well, give them some guidance . . . and provide the necessary skills, references, and direction, and then the students who take advantage of these things will go on."

Inclusion in the Curriculum

Women's issues are all over the place.

While the majority of constituents mentioned the positive impact of having students learn about women's history, of reading works by women authors, and of validating the contributions of women scholars, most also commented on the institution's ambivalence about straying too far from the traditional canon. As such, most admitted that women's studies as an academic field was slow to come to Bryn Mawr and that even though women, as a topic, are now part of the curriculum, students are still required to partake in a "highly structured traditional curriculum."

The history of Bryn Mawr as an institution dedicated to the notion of "providing women with the same educational opportunities as men" is at the root of the institution's ambivalence toward emphasizing women in the curriculum. Bryn Mawr, according to an administrator, has been "gender-blind rather than gender-focused for a lot of its history." Similarly, an alumna from the early 1970s explained Bryn Mawr's curricular ambivalence in these terms:

> When I was a student . . . there was a real resistance, in some ways, to focus in on women's studies and women's history here because of the kind of feminism that founded Bryn Mawr, which was all about not acknowledging gender differences very much. Women just have to go for what men have gone for, and that's the way you prove you can do it. The more you talk about women having different needs or needing to hear about women's history, the more you are talking about something that will ultimately be weighted second best. . . . We are certainly not way out on the cutting edge.

When the institution began to include women's issues in the curriculum in the 1980s, it did so following a "mainstreaming policy." As one faculty member stated, "What Bryn Mawr is trying to do is bring feminist and gender studies into every relevant department of the college, infuse the curriculum with it, rather than just setting up a separate department or major. The goal is to have everyone talking about difference, rather than having a department on difference." In fact, though there is a program in feminist and gender studies, it does not offer a major. According to one student, undergraduates are even discouraged from creating an independent major in feminist and gender studies. Specifically, the student mentioned a faculty member who asked students at a women's studies meeting to consider "what doors might be closed off to us were we to go into feminist and gender studies." The student added that although the faculty member's comments may have been accurate, she was disappointed because the faculty member did not encourage students to push the boundaries.

Today, according to most of the constituents interviewed, "women's issues are all over the place. . . . Your chances of discussing women in a class even if the word 'women' isn't in the title is about 95 percent." At the same time, according to a faculty member, the change to a more "feminist" curriculum was accomplished not by hiring new professors, but

> by the radicalization of the older, existing faculty who have gotten into the women's studies field. So there has been a considerable amount of internal revision. At the same time, because it is still largely a faculty trained in a previous dispensation, we still are at least half-way loyal to the traditional canon, although we express our loyalty in increasingly devious ways.

The result of this ambivalence led one student to claim that "while the space is open for discussion, this is not a place that embraces the concept of women's ways of knowing."

Conclusion

Bryn Mawr is unlike any other college in the country. Still heavily influenced by its founding dean, M. Carey Thomas, Bryn Mawr attracts women who are capable of succeeding academically and provides them with an environment that actively encourages and demands this kind of achievement. The characteristics that set Bryn Mawr apart include its historical mission to provide a rigorous undergraduate education for women; an effort by faculty members to have high academic standards and high expectations for students and to treat students like colleagues and scholars; the presence of motivated, bright, and capable women role models; a critical mass of high-achieving, competitive students; a recognition of the social realities facing women; and providing leadership and involvement opportunities for women. The pervasiveness of these six institutional characteristics was highlighted by almost every individual interviewed. Two other factors—personal support for students and inclusion of women in the curriculum—were also cited as important in facilitating student success. However, several respondents indicated that these two traits might clash with Bryn Mawr's history of de-emphasizing gender differences.

BENNETT COLLEGE

Bennett is a small, residential, four-year liberal arts college affiliated with the United Methodist Church, located in Greensboro, North Carolina (see the Supplement to Chapter 5 for details regarding the demographics at Bennett). The campus was built around a central green, which is surrounded by buildings of various ages and styles. Bennett is in the process of being renovated, one building at a time. Though the buildings are of different architectural styles, one is struck by how well they seem to fit together, creating a very comfortable, welcoming environment. At the apex of the main green sits the campus chapel, physically and spiritually the institution's center. Within the chapel is the Bennett Black Madonna, an inspiring stained glass window that depicts the essence of Bennett College, a place that takes African American women seriously.

Bennett has not always been a women's college. Founded in 1873 as a coeducational college and seminary for newly emancipated slaves, Bennett experienced serious financial difficulties in the early 1900s. As a result, the institution was taken over by the Women's Home Missionary Society and the North Carolina Board of Education. In 1926, under the mandate of these agencies, Bennett College reorganized as a college for African American women. The current institutional mission, which has not changed substantially since the 1950s, is as follows:

> The purpose of Bennett College is to maintain distinction as an institution of higher learning by offering women an education conducive to excellence in scholarly pursuits, preparation for leadership roles, and life-long learning in a contemporary society. . . . The college advances cognizance of African American heritage, international awareness, and the preparation of world citizens. . . . Overall, excellence in performance is valued as the foundation for the achievement of mission and educational goals and is the primary emphasis in all teaching and learning endeavors at Bennett College.

During the campus visit, faculty members, administrators, students, and alumnae were interviewed to determine, from their perspective, why Bennett College has produced such a high proportion of successful African American women. There was a high degree of consistency in responses. Comments were sorted into 10 categories, presented in order of importance (as indicated by how much constituents emphasized them):

- High academic expectations
- Personal support and advising
- A supportive peer culture
- A strong institutional mission
- A critical mass of African American women
- Inclusion in the curriculum
- The presence of role models
- An emphasis on giving back to the community
- Extracurricular involvement opportunities
- Awareness of societal realities facing African American women

High Academic Expectations

You are phenomenal women.

Every respondent interviewed discussed how important it is for students to gain confidence in themselves and in their abilities. They each described how they thought students gained feelings of self-worth. Underlying all of the theories on bolstering self-confidence was the fundamental belief that students at Bennett College have the potential to succeed. From all indications, this belief system has been an important and consistent part of Bennett College since its inception. Responses about high expectations fell into four categories: understanding where students are when they arrive at Bennett, reiterating the idea that students can succeed, not giving up on students when they experience difficulties, and encouraging students to apply for graduate programs.

Faculty and administrators at Bennett were realistic about who their students are and about what kind of experiences they had before they came to college. Recognizing the potential lack of academic preparation and the effects of racism and sexism on students, respondents all echoed the idea that Bennett takes "students . . . from where they start to where you want them to be, by whatever means possible." As one faculty member stated:

> We are dealing with a group of people who for all kinds of reasons, historical and otherwise, have been deprived, not only intellectually but economically, and therefore a group of people whose self-expectation is very low. . . . So, it becomes very important to bring them to develop a consciousness of their capabilities.

The approach most frequently mentioned for getting students to feel good about themselves involved the Bennett community telling students that they have potential, telling them that they are capable, and telling them what is expected of them. The idea, according to one faculty member, is that "you can be told something so much and for so long that pretty soon you start to believe it, and you will act it out."

Many of the faculty members talked about the positive impact of "Bennettizing." "To be 'Bennettized' is really to believe in more than the potential of students. . . . You believe that these students can learn, can be the best, and are expected to be the best, and you do whatever it takes to get them where they need to be." One of the most moving comments about the importance of reiterating the notion of expectations came from a senior. She talked about Bennett students being called "phenomenal women" after the Maya Angelou poem of the same name. She added:

> That is continually told to you from the time you step on the campus to the day you leave. And, I truly believe that we speak life and we speak

death to one another by saying "I am this," "I am that." If you are continually told that you are stupid or ignorant, you will begin to perform in that capacity. If you are told you are phenomenal, excellent, then you will perform on that level. And, I truly believe that is what these young women hear night and day. "You are phenomenal women," "you are exceptional," "you operate in a spirit of excellence." This is continually told to them, and I think that puts them in the mind-set to see themselves that way. It sets the tone.

In addition to telling people what is expected of them, respondents also made it clear that it is important to help students achieve the skills necessary to meet the institution's high academic standards. Respondents stressed that having high expectations requires persistence from students, and it also requires that the faculty not give up on them prematurely. According to one professor, "The emphasis is placed on helping students succeed, not on screening out the ones that shouldn't be here." Similarly, a science professor compared Bennett's philosophy with that of many other colleges. He stated, "One of the differentiators is that the expectation at a majority school is that you have the 'right stuff' from day one. . . . The bar is set pretty high for the first jump." He added that if a student were interested in sciences at a majority college, "If she were good, but not exceptional, she would be dropped. . . . Their orientation is distinction, differentiation, grooming the best." At Bennett, however, "there is more of an attempt made to be supportive, particularly in the early courses. If you have the interest and *some* ability, you are going to find some level of success, and then you can slug it out in the higher level courses to see if you really have the right stuff." He added that "Bennett cares about high quality work, but the point where you cut people off is further along here. . . . You may start out a little slower in some classes, I don't think it means you end slow." The faculty made it clear that they do not accept substandard work. In the words of one faculty member:

> Bennett takes in a lot of students who probably wouldn't get into other colleges based on their SAT scores and their grade point averages. . . . But, we aren't going to just pass the buck and put a Band-Aid over them. When they leave Bennett College, they are going to be prepared to compete with everybody else out there who has gotten a bachelor's degree.

A majority of respondents also mentioned the importance of reminding and sometimes "nagging" students about graduate school. For example, one alumna stated, "People encouraged you to go to graduate school every day. 'When are you going to do it?' 'How are you going to do it?' And, it was not always in a question form. They talked to you in a way that told you this is what is expected of you." Several faculty members also talked about how much time they spent picking up the phone and asking graduate schools to send admission forms and information. Administrators explained that they regularly invited deans of graduate schools and current graduate students to campus to help students learn about the next step. Others stated that they actively provided their students with information about summer research projects to enhance the students' chances of getting into graduate school. At the same time, a number of faculty and administrators demonstrated their expectations of students by inviting them to attend academic and professional conferences, believing that "it is important to immerse them into certain socialization activities." One student told a story about how the president of the college helped to support and encourage her:

> When I received my LSAT scores, I was very disappointed, very depressed. . . . I talked to the president and she asked me how the application process was going. I told her it was not going anywhere because I decided not to apply. The first thing she said was, "Yes, you are going to apply. You have the grades, you have the leadership, you have the ability, not everything is based on the LSAT scores." . . . It was not an option not to apply.

As a footnote to this story, the student had already received one acceptance to law school.

Strong Support for Students

We will push you, we will push you.

The amount and type of support given to students was another theme constantly expressed by members of the Bennett community as being important to the success of their students. According to a faculty member, students have access to support from the president on down to the housekeepers. Students are provided with "individual nurturing and attention to details . . . attention to students who seem to be slipping and attention to the gifted who need all of the encouragement they can get."

Here are some examples of the extent to which the Bennett community supports students. One faculty member noted, "I am going to apply as much support and encouragement over the course of the semester as I can and be as understanding of students that are coming up to speed as I can without compromising academic integrity." For some individuals, support comes in the form of listening to students' problems and offering advice. One faculty member said, "I find myself telling students that they need to get more sleep, commiserating with them about how many hours they have to work. Students feel like they can just drop in to get cheered up, which I don't mind. I was never expected to do that at my other college." Another faculty member explained, "Students get a lot of individual attention, perhaps, at times, more than they want. It gets so individualized that professors have been known to go to dorms and say, 'Get up and get to class.'" One faculty member suggested that Bennett faculty "can't just let students fail." She added, "I need to go to that student after the first instance and say, 'I think you are having a problem.' Sometimes I'll call them in for a conference; sometimes I write notes on their papers; sometimes I call their parents. . . . They may still end up failing, but . . . I feel a strong sense of responsibility for the success of my students."

For many of the faculty members and administrators, supporting students means going out of their way to help them. One administrator described faculty dedication as "missionary zeal." She added:

> Our clientele, basically, are students who have potential, who know why they are here and have some semblance of where they want to go. So that says to us, if this is where these young ladies need to be at the end of this experience . . . then okay, I'll come over here on Saturday morning and tutor them in chemistry, or I'll stay here in the afternoon. . . . When a student comes in and says, "I want you to know that I finally passed that Spanish test," you know it's because somebody on the faculty or staff or someone in her residence hall said, "You can do this, just change your priorities."

Respondents frequently used family metaphors when talking about supporting students at Bennett. Some faculty and administrators, for example, talked about their role as parental figures for the students. Specifically, one faculty member stated, "There is a lot of parenting going on here. . . . It is a very tricky line to walk between how much parenting to do and to let people sink on their own. There is a line you have to reach when you say, 'You are on your own now, and I can't save you, but I have given you every opportunity to save yourself!'"

Finally, a student described a ritual that symbolically represented Bennett's dedication to support and encouragement. According to this student, during convocation, "Our president will have the faculty stand and they will read a statement saying, 'We will push you, we will push you.' And, we reply, 'We will pull you, we will pull you.'" Through this ritual, the student added, "We tell them, 'We want the knowledge. We want to be educated. We want to know.' And with that sort of environment, it is very much conducive to your being successful and going on to graduate school."

Supportive Peer Culture

Students develop a kinship with each other.

Just as students receive support from administrators and faculty, students also support one another. In fact, a majority of respondents at Bennett described the importance of having a supportive student culture. As one student explained, "You battle, but you always try to support. In reality, you are part of a team." Just as family metaphors described the relationship between faculty and administrators and students, they were also used to describe the relationship among students. Sisterhood at Bennett has become formalized through ritual. Bennett, for example, practices what they call the "sister class arrangement," in which each first-year student is "sistered" to a junior, and each sophomore is "sistered" to a senior. This arrangement is designed to help students support one another and to encourage and formalize peer support.

Interestingly, one of the most effective and commonly used methods of having faculty help and support students, the "belle system," relies on the close connections and support among students at Bennett. The belle system gets its name from two sources—first, Bennett students are known as "the Bennett Belles," and second, it is a pun on the name of the telephone company—Bell Telephone. The belle system involves telling one student to tell another student that she needs to see a professor or that a professor is concerned about her. It was described as an "effective grapevine communication system." According to those who use it, the belle system works because "students are motivated to help and support each other."

Focused Institutional Mission

An institution dedicated to the struggle of African American women.

Institutional mission was said to play a significant role in Bennett's ability to graduate successful African American women. Noteworthy about Bennett's mission is its singular focus. "There is a well defined mission here . . . [and] there is an attempt made to live the mission." The mission of the college is to serve a specific clientele—African American women. "It's not just being a small college educating women. It's being an institution dedicated to the struggle of African American women." This dedication to educating African American women was described as "unshakable." Indeed, respondents referred to themselves as "specialists" in the field of educating and working with African American women.

Frequently, respondents commented that Bennett's mission is to use whatever means necessary to "move a student from where she is to where she needs to be, in order to be successful." This exact sentiment was expressed by several respondents. More specifically, people at Bennett equated success with attending graduate school, with obtaining good jobs, and with giving back to the community. To achieve this part of Bennett's mission means to encourage and to support students in all of their endeavors, whether they be academic or social. An administrator summed up the importance of commitment to the mission of the institution by saying, "I think you have to buy into the concept, embrace the philosophy and be committed more than anything else, and that is what we do. . . . People who work here believe that, people who study here know that, and they know they are going to leave here fully prepared to take on the world."

Many of the things that Bennett strives for in its mission, in fact, have become part of formalized tradition and ritual on campus. One faculty member commented that the amount of formalized recognition at Bennett was "incredible." He added that they observe "honor day, senior day, and good student day," among others. Another faculty member had given a lot of thought to the effect of this type of ritual. She explained:

> On this campus, we understand that ritual is not extraneous to one's education. It's an acting out of the value system and symbols which people hopefully are living out every day in the classroom and on the campus. Ceremony is taken very seriously. It is part of building self-esteem, part of validating the educational experience and validating your institution, so that you feel special as a student.

The belief is that "tradition can breed success." As one student explained, "When I listen to alumnae tell me about how the college was, and what made them be who they are, you discover a certain aura about Bennett that makes you want to succeed. You don't want to fail and do something to that heritage and tradition."

Critical Mass of High Achieving African American Women

For the first time in my life I was in the majority.

Many of those interviewed talked about the impact of having a large group of African American women in all roles within the institution. The effect, in general, is that as a black woman at Bennett, you don't feel marginal. One professor commented, "The school is designed for black females. You have a majority of faculty of your race, which makes a difference. You are at an institution where you are wanted. . . . You can be who you want to be here." An administrator stated, "Because this is a college for African Americans, you don't get discriminated against, you are given a sense of self-worth, and you are taught that you are special."

One member of the Bennett community expressed the belief that for the first time, Bennett women "get the chance to be surrounded by African American women who all have similar achievement goals." She added, this is "the first and only time that this will happen in their lives. . . . [As a student,] you have a group of students who look like you, who come from similar backgrounds, and who all have the same high achievement goals. This is it, this is your chance." An alumna offered this explanation of the benefits of critical mass:

> My experience as a student here was that I felt like I had died and gone to heaven. I grew up in Ohio and went to a large predominantly white high school. . . . Suddenly, here I was with 600 young black women, with black teachers, male and female, all of whom were saying "you can succeed," "we believe in you.". . . For the first time in my life, I was in the majority. . . . To suddenly be within a system which you know is for you, of you, and because of you—that is a heady experience for the minority in America. For the person who is in the minority, that is a dream.

Inclusion of African American Women in the Curriculum

To know where they are going, they must know who they are.

With the exception of one required women's studies course and one required black history course, the formal curriculum at Bennett College is like the curriculum at any private liberal arts college in America. "Our curriculum is designed to help people go to graduate school and get good jobs. As such, we need to prepare them to know the same material as other students, so they can do well on the standardized tests." At the same time, however, most respondents voiced the importance of learning about African American and women's history and culture as a means to empowerment. Professors, students, and administrators mentioned the inclusion of African American and women's issues in the classroom as an important component at Bennett.

One of the ways that African American and women's issues are included in the curriculum is through a professor's examples. According to one professor, "You don't need to have African American or women in the course title for the course to include African Americans or women as a topic. . . . The mere fact that this place is black . . . dictates to instructors that they should include African American women as examples." Another professor added that because the majority of students and faculty are African American, they "have the same frame of reference—see through the same lens."

For most respondents, the main avenue for students to learn about their history and culture has traditionally come through the co-curricular activities and the informal curriculum. Specifically, women at Bennett have always been required to attend Chapel—also known as Lyceum, Vespers, and the Academic Cultural Enrichment Series (ACES). Regardless of its name, these mandatory programs were said to be the most consistent vehicle through which Bennett women identify with, and learn about, others who are similar to them. According to one long-time administrator and alumna, "It's the extracurricular activities like the cultural programs that students are exposed to that makes us different."

Whether a part of the formal curriculum or a part of the co-curriculum, there was no disagreement among constituents about the importance of exposing students to the significant contributions of women, African Americans, and African American women:

> In order for students to know where they are going, they must know who they are. They must believe in that, embrace that, and feel good about that. And, being African American is who they are, and so we focus on that as an aspect of their development. . . . It is important for people to know not only who they are, but where they fit into the whole context of the American culture.

Role Models

Once you see successful people . . . success becomes familiar.

Just as it is important to learn where you come from, many respondents indicated it was important to actually meet and get to know successful people whom you can emulate. As such, the presence of role models was a frequently cited reason for Bennett's success. Individuals considered the following groups of people as potential role models: faculty and administrators working at Bennett, alumnae of Bennett College, and "the high level of visible people brought to campus through various programs." Regardless of who the role model is, constituents agree that role modeling is important to facilitate the success of students, particularly African American women. According to one professor, role modeling "is very important in African American life because there are too many negative images that have to be confronted." Similarly, a faculty member commented, "Most blacks need to . . . see people of their own kind that have reached a pillar of achievement." An administrator added that "once you see successful people who look like you, success becomes familiar territory." The importance of role models is best summed up by the response of a faculty member who stated:

> I know coming here as a professor I was real impressed with the number of African American women brought to campus and how it validated me as a black woman to see these people who achieved. [For students] to be exposed to lots of black women who they would never have the opportunity to come into contact with is powerful. To have these people come in who are so successful who are just like them, many of whom will tell stories that are just like their stories . . . is influential. It just proves that you don't have to be born into a well-educated family or into a lot of money to achieve, and I am convinced that this plays a very important role.

Commitment to Community Service

It's not just about self-achievement.

When asked what Bennett does to facilitate the success of its students, a surprising number of respondents talked about Bennett's commitment to community service. Currently, students must log 40 hours of community service as a requirement for graduation. While this is a new requirement, constituents made it clear that community service and activism have always been an important part of Bennett. Several explanations were offered by constituents for why community service helped students succeed. One faculty member explained that working in the community helps with students' "total development." Another commented that "community involvement sets up role models for them." Still others discussed the leadership skills that the students acquired by being involved in the community.

The most frequently heard explanation for why community service is important had to do with making students feel connected to the community beyond the campus. As one faculty member explained, "The college offers more than just an education, it is a vital force in the community. I think because the students see that . . . they develop a commitment to improving what is around them, as opposed to just getting by." In other words, Bennett teaches you "it's not just about self-achievement, it's about achievement in the black community." Similarly, a faculty member explained, "Most of us at Bennett feel very strongly about the fact that a person should give back to humanity." A student added, "The purpose of the college is real in today's society. Someone needs to be there to progress the race as a whole, and women in particular, and that is an important goal. . . . The college focuses a lot on taking the initiative to do things on your own that benefit both yourself and your community."

Involvement Opportunities

Black women get to be the leaders.

Administrators and students were more likely to talk about opportunities for extracurricular involvement and leadership than were the faculty. All who mentioned it as a factor, however, agreed that Bennett's size in combination with the college's emphasis on developing leadership skills were significant contributors to the success of Bennett graduates. One administrator commented, "There are a relatively small number of bodies available to hold leadership positions, to participate in class discussions, to attend conferences and special events with faculty members, and to get internships. These opportunities get spread around to a wide range of students."

The fact that Bennett is both a women's college and a predominantly black institution was mentioned by several respondents as a positive factor in terms of student involvement. All of the student opportunities available are filled by African American women. As one faculty member commented, "They are all black females, and so you are going to get female [leaders] out of the process here. This can be very empowering." An administrator added that because Bennett is a black women's college, "within student organizations, black women get to be the leaders, the committee chair. . . . This gives you courage and confidence so that you can tackle things in the real world." In a similar vein, an alumna said, "Women have an opportunity to be creative, to develop their leadership skills, without having to compete with men until they get to the larger society. And by that time, they are pretty well equipped to do that."

The opportunities for student involvement at Bennett seem endless. Respondents mentioned participating in student government, sororities, clubs, and athletics; holding internships and on- and off-campus jobs; volunteering; attending conferences and other special events; and being resident advisers, peer mentors, and tutors. According to one administrator, students were even invited to the faculty-staff retreat. The effect of all of these opportunities, according to one professor, is that "students are very mature in [leadership] when they leave here." As one student stated, "Bennett gives you the opportunity to participate. You can't sit back and do nothing and expect something from it. . . . I tell the young ladies, 'If you don't participate in all the activities that are here, then you can't expect to succeed.'"

Awareness of Social Realities

Things that we do here would be out of line elsewhere.

Because Bennett's clientele is primarily African American women, several members of the Bennett community talked about how important it is for these women to understand issues of sexism and racism. While understanding this issue from an academic standpoint has already been discussed in terms of the formal curriculum and in terms of the Academic Cultural Enrichment Series, several individuals mentioned how these issues affect such things as campus policies.

For example, Bennett practices *in loco parentis*, which is demonstrated through the existence of curfew and very strict drinking and smoking policies. According to one faculty member:

> *In loco parentis* is about being proactive rather than passive. . . . This tradition springs from the need in the black community to prepare young people for the racist society in which they live. And, one of the best ways to do this is through very careful nurturing and through parental programming. Actually, it's not so much programming as it is

brainwashing—being clear to them what is needed if they are going to succeed.

This need to prepare young women by explaining the realities of racism and sexism is not new at Bennett. In fact, according to one professor, Willa Player, one of the institution's founders, wrote her dissertation on how African American women need to

> face squarely the problem of discrimination in America and the fact that these young women are going to face problems that they would not have if they had been European American. . . . Given all of that, there are certain things that we do here that would be out of line elsewhere, because we know that the need is there. You need to give them a support system, a kind of grid that underlies their self-esteem and maturity.

Conclusion

Bennett is an institution with a singular focus—a place that takes African American women seriously. The 10 reasons offered to explain Bennett's success are all deeply tied to the institution's mission. Everything Bennett does, every person it employs, every course it offers, and every program it organizes seems consciously designed to facilitate the success of its students. Intricately connected to Bennett's mission is the institution's strong belief in "moving students from where they are when they enter the institution to where they should be by the time they graduate." Members of the Bennett community take this idea seriously and provide their students with copious encouragement and support. Campus members truly believe Bennett students are "phenomenal women," and they do everything in their power to make sure the women students know this, too. Through high academic expectations and strong levels of support from all campus constituents—from inclusion of African American women in the curriculum and the exposure of students to strong role models, to a commitment to community service and involvement opportunities, to providing an awareness of the racism and sexism found in the larger society—Bennett College enacts and lives its institutional mission in a way that enhances the success of its students.

SEVEN LESSONS FOR LEARNING

Many lessons can be learned from such different colleges as Bryn Mawr and Bennett. Founded for different reasons, serving different populations, each takes the students who enter seriously and fosters their success. These two campuses provide important insights for other colleges—coeducational institutions and change colleges—to follow if they wish to take women seriously. A brief summary of the main traits responsible for creating an environment that facilitates the success of women students illuminates important differences and similarities between Bennett and Bryn Mawr and provides an opportunity to make connections between the two cases and with the wider literature regarding campus climate.

Lesson 1
Clarify and Communicate the Mission

The power of a strong, focused mission to educational quality has been discussed often in the literature (A. W. Astin 1985; Kuh, Schuh, and Whitt 1991). One of the key elements common to both Bryn Mawr and Bennett is the existence of a strong, focused mission. Constituents at both colleges know the mission, believe in the mission, and live the mission. Members of the Bennett community reiterated the importance of being a college dedicated to serving African American women, while Bryn Mawr constituents stressed the importance of the college's emphasis on educating high-achieving women. The effect of serving a narrowly focused student body was likened to the notion of Virginia Woolf's "room of one's own." The singular focus on meeting the needs of a particular group of students puts both campuses in a unique position in comparison with postsecondary institutions that have to respond to the needs of a wider range of students. Tradition is an important means of conveying the content of the mission to students. For example, Bryn Mawr's emphasis on earning a doctoral degree is expressed through events such as Lantern Night and the May Day hoop races. Bennett's mission of encouraging student success is demonstrated through the frequent recognition students receive and through such activities as the sister class arrangement and the "belle system." These traditions symbolically reinforce the expectation that students at these colleges will be successful.

Lesson 2
Believe Students Can Achieve—and Hold Them to It

High academic expectations are known to be one of the key institutional traits associated with facilitating student success. In *Involving Colleges,* for example, Kuh, Schuh, and Whitt qualitatively examined how campuses foster student learning and development outside the classroom. They found that one trait common to successful institutions was the presence of faculty members who "assume that all students can learn anything, given the proper circumstances" (Kuh, Schuh, and Whitt 1991, 284). Faculty and administrators at Bryn Mawr and Bennett have high expectations of their students, though they express these expectations differently.

Bennett, with its non-selective admissions policies, follows a "value-added model" of education that is geared to bring students from where they are when they enter to where they should be when they exit. One means to the achievement of this goal is to tell students repeatedly that they can succeed, that they are capable, and that they can do—or be—anything they want. At Bryn Mawr, particularly in traditionally male fields, many of the faculty members described conveying high expectations in ways quite similar to the approach used at Bennett. Specifically, Bryn Mawr faculty talked about not giving up on students who were having academic difficulties and reiterating the notion that, as women, they are capable of achieving even in male-dominated fields. However, in other academic areas at Bryn Mawr, high admission standards become inextricably linked to high expectations. Many at Bryn Mawr emphasized the idea that student success is related to how good students are when they enter the institution. Respondents believed that the better the student is when she enters, the more one can expect of her while enrolled, and the more successful she will eventually become. Those at Bryn Mawr said they treated their students like scholars and colleagues, engaging them in research and other active learning experiences. Institutions that take women seriously while taking into account students' precollegiate experiences are models of ways to take women seriously.

Lesson 3
Make Students Feel Like They Matter

Some degree of personal support on campus is pivotal for student success. Schlossberg's (1989) theory of mattering puts the importance of support into perspective. Mattering, which is measured by student perceptions, occurs when students feel that they are noticed, that what they say or do is important, and that they are appreciated. Even though the levels of support differ between Bryn Mawr and Bennett, it is clear that students at both campuses feel that they matter. At both schools, the norm was for faculty to take a personal interest in student success—"to get involved in their lives." One-on-one interaction between faculty and students characterized both institutions; faculty promotions and pay raises were connected to faculty working with students. The *Involving Colleges* study (Kuh, Schuh, and Whitt 1991) also talks about the importance of mattering, although the authors use the term "ethic of care" to describe support given to students. Students at "involving colleges" perceive "that faculty care and are interested, responsible and available" (286).

Lesson 4
Provide Strong, Positive Role Models

Given M. E. Tidball's research (1973b) demonstrating a connection between women achievers and the ratio of women faculty to women students, it is not surprising that members of both campuses emphasized the importance of role models in explaining the success of Bryn Mawr and Bennett. Both campuses provide environments in which members of underrepresented groups are central and present in diverse roles throughout the institution. Students, alumnae, campus visitors, administrators, support staff, and faculty members all were identified as important role models for students. Members of both campuses explained that role models were important because they conveyed to women students the idea that "I can do that too" and created a "visual correlation between image and possibility."

Lesson 5
Have Enough Women to Form a Critical Mass

Respondents at both campuses also mentioned the importance of having a critical mass of students who are similar to one another. Tidball wrote about the concept of critical mass, explaining it as being "enough to produce a response that is self-generating" (M. E. Tidball 1983, 6). She further explained that in higher education, the term connotes the "necessity for enough women on a campus to make their presence felt." The benefits of having a critical mass of similar students, according to respondents across the sites, include the following: students do not feel marginalized and in the minority, they feel comfortable and safe, they feel like they have voice, they feel like part of the campus community, and they feel freer to express differences within the group. While having students of similar backgrounds around was said to be important, more specifically, respondents mentioned the critical importance of being surrounded by driven, motivated, talented students who come from similar backgrounds. A faculty member at Bryn Mawr, for example, talked about the importance of having a place where intellectual women "find camaraderie and colleagueship of other women who are trying to do the same thing." Similarly, a professor at Bennett stated, "Here, you have a group of students who look like you, who come from similar backgrounds, and who all have the same high achievement goals."

Lesson 6
Provide Ample Opportunities for Student Leadership

Of all of the factors listed, the area of increased involvement opportunities at women's colleges has been given the most attention in the wider literature. Research by Whitt (1994) and the *Involving Colleges* study (Kuh, Schuh, and Whitt 1991) both emphasize how women's colleges provide involvement opportunities for their students. Involvement, as defined by A. W. Astin (1977), entails the investment of psychological and physical energy in tasks, people, and activities. Astin's theory of involvement suggests that students learn by being involved. Whitt's case studies of students at three women's colleges identified the ways that women's colleges provide extensive opportunities for women to assume leadership positions. Whitt's research findings echo the situation found at both Bryn Mawr and Bennett. Students at both campuses had a large range of opportunities to be involved in extracurricular activities. These opportunities, according to respondents, helped students develop strong leadership skills, kept them active in their institutions, and generally facilitated their overall success. At both institutions, respondents suggested that because they were women's colleges, women were not only expected—but obligated—to hold all of the available leadership positions.

Lesson 7
Include Women in the Curriculum

Though not widely studied, a review of the literature on the impact of diversity initiatives indicates some positive outcomes associated with addressing issues of race, gender, and social class in the curriculum (Appel, Cartwright, D. G. Smith, and Wolf-Wendel 1996). As such, it was not surprising to find that members of both the Bryn Mawr and Bennett campuses mentioned the importance of learning about gender and racial issues in both the formal and informal curriculum. However, respondents at both campuses also emphasized the importance of providing students with a "traditional" curriculum. A faculty member at Bennett College explained that their curriculum is essentially mainstream because "we need to prepare them to know the same material as other students so they can do well on the standardized tests." Nonetheless, members of both campuses emphasized the importance of exposing students to their own history, literature, and backgrounds. Women are infused into the curriculum at both institutions, providing students with role models and knowledge about where they come from. This inclusion in the curriculum was also credited with helping students become aware of racism, sexism, and classism faced by those in the "real world." Faculty at both institutions explicitly tried to "equip students with knowledge" to combat social problems such as the glass ceiling, while providing a temporary haven for women to gird themselves to face external realities.

CONCLUSION

The characteristics identified as key to the success of both Bryn Mawr and Bennett in producing graduates who eventually earn doctorates parallel findings from other sources on the traits connected to productive institutions. High expectations, support, presence of role models, critical mass of high-achieving students, opportunities for extracurricular involvement, inclusion of women in the curriculum, and a recognition of the social realities facing women in the "real world" are all traits associated with institutions that facilitate the success of their women students. Bryn Mawr and Bennett provide for these needs in different ways, exemplifying the fact that women's colleges—though they take women seriously—are not all alike. Differences in race, ethnicity, socioeconomic status, and life experience influence what students need and how colleges should respond. In addition, while separate examinations of the characteristics of each institution are illuminating, it is important to understand that the whole of these institutions is greater than the sum of their parts—one cannot just take a single element and look at it in isolation. Instead, it is the combination of characteristics, the aura of these institutions, that makes them unique and makes them able to facilitate the success of their students. Further, these institutions are only two examples of the many women's colleges that take women seriously. Other colleges, in other contexts, have other means by which to facilitate the success of their women students. Nonetheless, the examples offered by institutions like Bryn Mawr and Bennett on ways to take women seriously offer concrete lessons for other colleges to follow.

PART THREE

· · · · · · · · · · ·

Legacies from Women's Colleges Serve As Institutional Models

From the lessons presented in Part Two devolve the legacies to be handed on to *all* colleges and universities that would aspire to educate women. Some legacies relate especially to life on campus and include actions of, and interactions among, students, faculty, administrators, friends, and guests. The focus is the campus culture and the embodiment of the college's mission, along with an appreciation that it is the *totality* of the environment, as embedded in the very organizational structure, that has a bearing on graduates' subsequent success—by whatever measure. Other legacies come from off the campus or continue well beyond the college sojourn. These are legacies generated by governing boards that set the mission of the college and oversee its ongoing application and by alumnae associations that support graduates in their careers, families, friendships, and fellowship with one another and with their college for as long as they live. All of these actions and behaviors are powerful components that combine to create the ethos—even the mystique—of women's colleges, and all are valuable models for higher education institutions in general to appropriate and adapt for the benefit of the women and men who participate in their institutional life.

CHAPTER 6

New Legacies from the Campus

It is assumed that coeducation means the equal education, side-by-side, of women and men. Nothing could be further from the truth.
—Adrienne Rich, 1979

This section of the book begins with the premise, supported in the prior chapters, that women's colleges have been successful at taking women seriously. The evidence is found in a wide variety of studies using numerous methodologies, in the historical legacies of these institutions, and in colleges of differing size, selectivity, and type. Because of this record of success, and because of the long history of experience with women, women's lives, and women's learning, these institutions can inform understanding of women's education more generally, and beyond that, they can serve as models for women's education in higher education.

While only a small percentage of women can be accommodated in women's colleges, understanding the advantages these institutions provide women can benefit coeducational colleges interested in taking both women and men seriously. However, just as being a women's college does not ensure success for the institution or for all its students, there are possibilities for coeducational institutions to develop their potential for students' success. The imperative of taking women seriously requires that those possibilities be intentionally developed for all.

THE ROLE OF ORGANIZATIONAL STRUCTURE

In this context, it is important to turn to the crucial question, "What about these environments promotes success?" If we are to think through the newest legacies of women's colleges for women's education more generally, answering this question is a central task. Despite the diversity in women's colleges, two fundamental characteristics distinguish them—the composition of their student body and their institutional purpose. Within each of these two definite characteristics, a number of elements that contribute to success can be identified.

Composition of the Student Body

At its most obvious, the undergraduate student body of women's colleges is composed primarily of women. What, then, does the presence of mostly women do for the life of a campus? What does the absence of men as matriculated students mean in the day-to-day life of the college? The research reviewed in prior chapters highlights four legacies that emerge as profoundly important to educational success from the presence of women as *the* students on campus: spaces and locations, centrality of women's issues, diversity of roles, and positive peer-group influence. Importantly, these legacies often have parallel importance for others related to the institution—faculty, staff, administration, trustees, alumnae, friends, and visitors.

Spaces and Locations   The first legacy is the element of spaces and locations for the educational enterprise. Whether in the classroom, on the playing field, in residence halls, or on the campus, there are an abundance and variety of locations where women's voices are heard, where women's expectations are high, where competition and cooperation are seen, and where women— because it is their space—can expect to be treated with respect. In light of the considerable research that identifies these features as the best kind of environment for learning and growth, and clear evidence that these qualities cannot be taken for granted in institutions, the significance of such spaces and locations cannot be underestimated.

One of the most critical elements of student-body composition emerges in the classroom, where women at women's colleges experience an environment composed primarily of women. Research is mounting that shows the positive impact of woman-only classrooms for women. Thus, even in coeducational institutions, math and science classes in which there are only women have resulted in greater persistence, success, and enthusiasm for those subjects. In women's colleges, this pattern is present throughout the curriculum. Some researchers have shown that in such environments, women tend to participate more frequently. Others have pointed to the collaborative learning experience that extends beyond the classroom. Many suggest that the presence of women in such large numbers creates an expectation that women can and will succeed. Significantly, whatever societal messages still remain—about what women can or should do—evaporate as students experience personally, and by observation, the many women who perform in all areas. Whatever vulnerability to stereotyping remains regarding women's interest and persistence in math and science, for example, is not an issue in physics, chemistry, engineering, and mathematics programs and courses in which women are present and successful in the same way that they are present and successful in psychology, history, literature, and art.

The research and general literature also highlight the important impact of leadership opportunities for women, the significance of the residential environment, and the impact of a long history in women's colleges associated with athletics. The history of American higher education suggests that athletics was an activity of men on coeducational campuses. In contrast, at women's colleges, active team and individual sports activities constitute an important part of campus life. In general, women's college campuses have created an environment of ownership, of leadership, and of activities that counter many stereotypes of female behavior (Horowitz 1987).

As noted in prior chapters, research in higher education contains a great deal about the "chilly" climate women face on coeducational campuses. This area of study concerns the atmosphere for women on a campus as a whole, as well as in specific academic areas or programs. In areas of a campus where women are in a significant minority, the atmosphere is most apt to be chilly toward women. This can also be true in areas in which there are currently many women students, but where the faculty and institutional history do not reflect contemporary changes. Thus, concern about the chilly climate is often raised in such areas as engineering, the "hard" sciences, and professional fields such as medicine and law (Guinier, Fine, and Balin 1997). A chilly climate can have a powerful, negative impact on a student's level of engagement, on her ability to focus on the tasks to be accomplished, on her ability to survive challenges, and on her belief in her capacity to succeed. Environments that explicitly or tacitly support stereotypical notions that women have lesser capacities, facilitate those results, whether or not the institution intends that to be the outcome. As in the classroom, the potential of women to be successful in athletics—despite its long history at women's colleges—is only now being recognized in other institutions and in the national view. It took Title IX and litigation to shift athletic opportunities significantly for women in higher education. Prior to that, most campuses were willing to assume that lack of interest, affinity, and ability influenced the lower levels of participation by women in college sports.

Women's colleges have demonstrated a powerful capacity to engage women, to place women in environments and contexts in which other women are succeeding and are functioning, and to communicate in multiple ways that the environment is dedicated to ensuring success—rather than to explaining failure. While this may not realistically reflect the "outside world," there is considerable evidence to suggest that learning in this environment builds capacity and strength in skills, the sense of self, and the support systems to succeed. Rather than being "protected" environments, "these are environments in which the judgment of competence and talent are based on competence and talent rather than gender" (M. E. Tidball 1980b, 13).

Discussions about spaces and locations for women to excel, succeed, and thrive are relevant, as well, to women staff, faculty, and administrators of women's colleges. At such institutions, women in all positions are unlikely to be marginalized or made to be tokens. Discussions of new scholarship for women will be less risky. Thinking through how policy and curriculum impact women is likely to be welcomed and seen as central to the institution. The legacy of women's colleges is a legacy of taking women seriously, not only in *special* places but in *all* places.

The challenge, then, for coeducational institutions committed to women's education is to think about and act upon these issues explicitly and intentionally.

Centrality of Women's Issues   A second consequence of the composition of women's colleges is that in an institution whose students all are women, the central issues are defined and framed by women's experiences. Women are at the center—no apologies needed. Indeed, for it to be otherwise would be irresponsible. Discussions about career paths begin with the question of women's career paths. Programs need not apologize for questions about gender or for a focus on women. Athletic programs are built to encourage women, and resources need not be disputed in terms of what they might take away from men's sports. Even when gender is never mentioned, it is clear that women are the central focus. What does this mean? It means that the questions can be different—though they need not be. (It means that resource allocation need not be centered in debates about gender and who is more important.) Women's colleges do not need to apologize for introducing gender-specific issues.

A coeducational institution might respond that it is committed to *all* students, both women and men. The challenge for such an institution is that, in most cases, "all" most readily applies to men, and women may be excluded. Because of concern about women's issues and the neglect of them on many coeducational campuses, there are frequent efforts to raise woman-specific questions or to focus attention on women. However, discussion often seems to pit women's issues against what has traditionally been done. This is occurring now, for instance, in discussions about gender equity in women's sports. Years of unequal allocation are ignored as arguments are put forth that suggest that men's athletics will suffer if women's athletics advance. The negative response on campus is predictable, and advocates for women find themselves viewed as anti-men.

Women's issues on coeducational campuses are also often addressed through the establishment of women's centers, women's studies, and other programs for women. For years, these efforts have been very important because they provide locations and spaces on campuses for women's issues. The problem is that on many campuses they are seen as marginal and are often vulnerable to budget cuts. Moreover, they are often defined as necessary in terms that suggest women's weakness, as opposed to being defined in ways that acknowledge the institution's inadequacy in addressing women's issues and concerns otherwise. Indeed, these programs provide essential and important perspectives on women, women students, and women's scholarship.

Diversity of Roles   The third result of the composition of the student body centers on the diversity of roles that are assumed by women students. Increasingly in our society, women in all contexts are diversifying what they do and where they do it. It is equally clear, however, that large sectors of the economy, significant parts of college enrollments, and major levels and fields of employment are gender-segregated. At women's colleges, whatever roles students perform—from managing the physics laboratory, to maintaining audiovisual equipment, to running student investment portfolios, to performing in athletic competitions—must be handled by women. Not only does that provide role models for students, but it also allows for a diversity of styles. More important, women in these roles are seen not as exceptions, but as taking part in the variety of roles an individual can assume.

A diversity of roles, then, mitigates against making simplistic assertions about women. So much of the recent literature on women takes on a debate mode between an essentialist argument (that women are different and thus require different approaches) and a gender-equity argument (that women are treated differently but are not essentially different). This dichotomy is false and leads to simplistic and stereotyping statements and conclusions. On many campuses where women's diversity is fostered and featured, similarities and differences can be seen that mandate much more complex treatment both of individuals and of groups.

Indeed, the literature on tokenism (Kanter 1976) suggests that simply being the only woman in a situation can be very difficult. It creates great stress, makes it difficult to succeed, and often requires responses that are not entirely consonant with an individual's own style and approach. Women politicians must pay particular attention to how they dress, for instance, as must women CEOs. To be too "feminine" is to come across as weak or not serious; to be too "masculine" is to not be a women. For such women, discussing "women's issues" might compromise one's position, and mentoring women might be seen as playing favorites. To be a token is to be seen as a symbol of all—and invisible as an individual. In women's colleges, women students succeed and fail as individuals and their success or failure need not impact other women who follow. How often has it been said, "We tried a woman in that position, and it didn't work out." That phrase would never be articulated on the campus of a college for women.

While quite relevant to women students, the issues of tokenism and of diversity in roles, styles, and interests can have dramatic impact for women faculty, staff, and administrators, as well. The diversity of women's voices, the issues related to women, and the ability to function as an individual can be facilitated in women's environments that have more women both in number and proportion and, thus, achieve a better gender *balance* at the faculty, staff, and administrative level than at coeducational institutions.

The legacy of women's colleges, then, suggests that coeducational campuses must be careful to create opportunities—and more—for women in diverse roles. Gender segregation by functions and roles supports larger societal images. If women are not majoring in fields traditionally dominated by men, then more inquiry about how to reverse that pattern needs to be considered. If women are not engaging seriously in leadership or in athletics, that, too, needs to be reversed. Similarly, hiring practices must ensure a diversity of women in roles throughout the campus. The legacy requires attention to having diverse women in a spectrum of roles—and the avoidance of a single woman intended to satisfy the need for "gender representation." More women are required, especially, in positions of high visibility.

Positive Peer-Group Influence   The literature on the impact of college on students rightly emphasizes the significant role of the peer group. To a significant degree, the climate, values, and activities of students are influenced by the presence of peers. This is most strongly apparent on residential campuses with a more traditional age cohort. In these environments, with many students in the age range from 18 to 22, there is the combined influence of being in an age cohort in which peer influences are particularly important and the tendency to establish intense relationships in residential environments. Students on residential campuses also spend significant numbers of hours each week in activities that are outside the sphere of influence of faculty and administrators—or families, for that matter. The *positive* power of peer relationships is also apparent at women's colleges, as revealed in the prior chapters. To the degree that women on the campuses of women's colleges are involved with other women in studying, participating in research, talking about their futures, developing community life, serving in leadership positions, participating on athletic teams, and clarifying issues of concern to women, the entire ethos and influence develops women's interests and talents, whatever they may be. This talent development outcome can be observed, historically, even on campuses where the peer influence is decidedly traditional in terms of women's roles and expectations. Thus, though the extant culture may have promoted traditional values, the research suggests that the results, in terms of educational aspirations and career attainment, have often not been traditional. This observation is also noted in significant histories of women's colleges (Palmieri 1995; Horowitz 1984).

Many women's colleges have been proactive in incorporating women of all ages and socioeconomic status on campus. Many even enable single mothers and their children to live on campus and participate fully in college life. These programs broaden the notion of "peer group," create opportunities for intergenerational relationships, and provide many diverse kinds of experiences for women who otherwise might not have the opportunity to participate in a collegiate experience.

Perhaps the most striking outcome of the influence and relationships among peers are the strong friendships and mutual-support systems among women that develop during college and then continue as powerful networks of alumnae. These networks, while featured for their professional advantages by institutions and researchers alike, are important simply as enduring statements about the strength and role of friendships among women. The legacy is established as generations of classmates turn into sisters.

These profound and potent elements of the education environment occur naturally as a result of the student body's composition. When combined with an intentional and focused purpose, a number of other important themes emerge.

Institutional Purpose

Often neglected in the discussion of the important elements for the success of women's colleges, and yet perhaps the most important, is the presence of an institutional purpose that is dedicated to the education of women. Once again, however, this is an element that can be merely rhetorical—or it can permeate the institution. Look, for a moment, at the difference. In colleges with focused and defined missions that permeate the culture, the institution's values, decisions, physical environment, symbolic behaviors, rituals, and history all combine to create a presence deep into the day-to-day life of its students, faculty, and staff. The purpose is also intentionally reflected in curriculum decisions, architectural design, publications, and at numerous decision-making points day-to-day and over the long term. In addition, embedded in the purpose of serving women's education is the mission of educating students.

For many campuses today, even the education of students is marginal to other institutional purposes such as research and the pursuit of prestige. An institution committed to women students and their education is an institution with a generic and general commitment to students in general. As more is known about the success of women's colleges, seven important themes emerge that relate directly to the purpose and the resulting culture of these institutions.

Faculty and Staff Composition and Attitudes   Among colleges across the nation, women's colleges are the most balanced in the ratio of women to men in virtually all ranks and divisions of faculty and administrators. Thus, not only do women students have a large variety of women demonstrating the potential and success of women throughout the institution, they also see a large number of men participating with women in governing the institution and believing in women's capacities in all fields. Indeed, several studies, described in the earlier chapters, have demonstrated that men at women's colleges have distinctly more favorable attitudes toward the education of women than men at coeducational institutions (M. E. Tidball 1976b; Women's College Coalition 1981). Moreover, in terms of the benefit to women faculty and administrators, a broad balance in representation means that no single woman is under pressure to succeed on behalf of all women. Some women succeed and some do not, but the result is not seen as representative of all.

As of 1997, 87 percent of U.S. women's colleges had women presidents (compared with 16 percent of all other coeducational institutions). Indeed, as noted in Chapter 1, great strides were made in this area from 1969 to the present. In addition, some colleges—Wellesley and a number of Roman Catholic women's colleges being the most notable—have been committed to having women serve in that most visible of roles, and have had women presidents throughout their histories.

Just as the gender balance in faculty and administration at women's colleges evolved, exemplary women's colleges today are working to achieve a similar degree of balance in the diversity of women's experiences, including racial, ethnic, and class diversity. The research discussed in Chapter 3 demonstrates the important role that women's colleges, including Historically Black women's colleges, have played in the achievement of women of color, as have other special-purpose institutions. It is crucially important to create environments where there is sufficient diversity of women in all areas of the institution.

What is clear is that women's colleges have always been capable of seeing women's potential to make a contribution. Diverse search committees and a willingness to seek and identify talent play a major role. One of the most important legacies from women's colleges has been to demonstrate, time after time, that talent can be evaluated without resorting to criteria that eliminate women. In today's higher education, with its overreliance on standardized test scores, it is essential to use multiple criteria to identify talent. Institutions that do so are more equitable as a consequence, and they also provide more models for women students.

Role Models   Throughout the literature on women's colleges and women's education, the importance of role models for students is emphasized. However, the significance of role models is more complex than is accounted for in many of the discussions in the literature, in which the concept is dichotomized in a way that suggests that only women can be role models for women, African Americans for African Americans, and so on. A role model is far more dynamic, and many factors influence being a role model and mentor.

Role models are usually seen as most significant for individuals in contexts where there are few—if any—others "like" them. Without the presence of women and women of color as employees and students on college campuses— indeed, without a critical mass of such persons—a significant statement is made about whether women and women of color should be in those positions, whether they can succeed in such positions, and whether women students and students of color should aspire to them. That is, an absence of balance (a disproportionately small number of women in science departments, for example) and an absence of women in leadership positions communicates a great deal about options and choices. Moreover, as M. E. Tidball has noted, "we learn different lessons from different role models, and we sometimes learn only a very tiny amount from any given model. . . . One token woman is not a critical mass. Two dozen women faculty among 200 men is not a critical mass" (M. E. Tidball 1979, 9–10). The research strongly demonstrates the direct and positive relationship between the proportion of women faculty and the success of women students. Thus women's colleges, by their composition, communicate clearly that the options for women are varied and the doors open wide— at least in these environments.

In past times, when women were generally seen as fragile, limited in intellectual capacities, and meant only to serve, the philosophies of women's colleges stood in stark contrast to the prevailing view. Ideas about the limits of women's capability have not been entirely supplanted. In many areas, the work force remains segregated by sex, as well as by race and ethnicity. There is still profound pressure on women, particularly young women, to lower their aspirations and to aim chiefly to please others. Entering nontraditional career areas and fields of study is now more possible than ever; surviving and succeeding in such environments, however, may challenge all the strength and skill a person has developed.

Women's colleges can encourage women students to pursue any and all fields to which they aspire, and more centrally, can provide ample role models of women who have done just that, and others who support these efforts. The legacy is clear—the challenge is to transfer these accomplishments to other institutions.

High Expectations   One of the hallmarks of women's colleges has been the deeply understood high expectations of excellence by women—in the broadest sense of the community, as well as for individuals. Around these campuses are numerous reminders of outstanding achievement by women in all realms of work and life. Pictures of such women abound in libraries, in board rooms, in hallways, in publications, and in student yearbooks. Notions of excellence in these colleges are most often framed not in terms of competition, but rather with a combined sense of both individual and group aspirations. Thus, while some detractors of women's colleges use words like "safe" to characterize them, these colleges are safe only insofar as they challenge women to excel in environments in which others have also been challenged successfully. As stated earlier, they are environments in which a person's talent can be judged based on competence, not gender.

Excellence can be defined in quite different ways. As described in Chapter 5, while the ethos of Bryn Mawr focuses on the scholar-student and Bennett College emphasizes success, there is a concrete call for excellence in all that students do. Moreover, the high expectations do not assume that students enter with their talent or skills fully developed. Thus, high expectations are combined with belief in students' capacity to learn and to excel.

Belief in Students' Capacity   Another vitally important and very distinctive element of the purpose and culture of women's colleges is the belief in students' capacity to succeed. Women's colleges throughout the history of American higher education were established to refute the notion that women could not succeed in serious pursuits, whether academic or professional. In environments dedicated to women, that assumption did not and could not prevail if the colleges were to accomplish their purpose. At Salem, at Mount Holyoke, at Spelman, and at all other colleges for women, the core assumption has been that women could and should succeed.

Women's athletic success, too, has been an important part of the legacy of many women's colleges. In coeducational environments, it becomes too easy to simply regret the absence of women rather than to create environments in which it is clear that women can succeed. Having numerous women students in every field, having women faculty, and having a general ethos of excellence and seriousness have an impact on students.

Tangible and Environmental Support   From the point of view of student learning, high expectations and belief in student capacity are critical. When combined with intentional support structures, women's colleges provide a powerful framework for success and achievement. Student support is necessary for any of a number of reasons—students may have limited experience in acquiring specific skills, low expectations for high achievement, a tendency to blame themselves for failure—they may simply experience the ambivalence that can follow setting high and difficult goals. Whatever the reason, women's colleges mandate a support structure of students, faculty, and staff, as well as of alumnae, that facilitates student success.

Education for a Larger Purpose   An important theme emerging from institutions successful in the education of women is their belief that education serves a larger purpose—whether simply in the legacy of having served women throughout their history or in obligations to the wider community. This sense of purpose manifests itself in a greater emphasis on the social role of education and the role of the graduates of the institution, in programmatic and curricular involvement, in community service, and in a general ethos that links students' education to a sense of wider obligation. In this way, students see their education as serving others beyond themselves and with significance that goes beyond their own degrees. From an individual point of view, this can positively influence the quality of effort, persistence in the face of difficult challenges, and a willingness to follow through because of an obligation to others. The legacy of women's colleges includes bringing to the fore a sense of purpose, tied to the institution's mission—a value that is transferred successfully to each new generation of students.

Links to the Past   Still another characteristic of institutions successful in the education of women is their placing of their purpose in a historical context in which students are introduced to their heritage beyond their contemporary perspective. Today, where so much of what students experience is ahistorical, such an institution imbues daily life with awareness of the influence of the past. Often this is conveyed in terms of the legacies of success against which each new student will evaluate her education. At Mount Holyoke, students are introduced early to the pioneering work of Mary Lyon, who struggled to provide higher education for women in a time when women were viewed as both mentally and physically inferior to men. On Founder's Day and at graduation, students at Mount Holyoke visit Mary Lyon's grave site (located on campus) to commemorate her contributions and celebrate their heritage.

The tradition of sisterhood and friendship resonates today at Spelman, where students at the college are invited to be part of a long legacy of friendship "handed down through the generations," and where the college president is referred to as "sister president," an honorific also common on Roman Catholic campuses headed by women religious.

Student success is not, then, simply an accomplishment of the student. It is an intentional part of the past, present, and future of the institution. This intentionality has profound implications for retention, for fostering empowerment and purpose, and for creating a sense of obligation among students that their accomplishments are part of a larger enterprise, to which they should make a contribution. By engaging their mission deeply, the entire campus ethos is strengthened, as is the commitment and support from external constituencies.

Institutions that look to successful women's colleges to understand how best to serve their women students must take an in-depth look at an environment with deeply embedded interrelationships, all committed to women's success. Most approaches to improving women's education, like the research on these approaches, focus on specific aspects of a campus—such things as numbers of women in leadership, special programs, the climate of the campus, and leadership training. It is more likely, however, that the success of institutions is a function of the confluence of many factors, rather than being attributable to a single factor or approach. While many coeducational campuses approach the education of women through singular programmatic approaches, such as a women's support group in science or a lecture series on women, women's colleges employ a holistic approach—the deep connections among multiple approaches that range from the mundane to the grand—all of which contribute to success.

THE REAL WORLD?

Perhaps the most pervasive criticism of women's colleges is that they present an unrealistic view of the "real world." Embedded in that view is the notion that successful education should always take place in an environment that replicates reality. However, there is much in educational and psychological practice that suggests education occurs best in an environment that prepares students for reality, engages them in dealing with reality, but provides an environment in which that reality—unless it promotes education—does not interfere.

Women's colleges, throughout their history, have always been aware of "women's place" in the "real world." Different colleges have responded in different ways—some have explicitly countered those assumptions while others have educated women in ways to participate but not to fight. Regardless of the philosophy, institutions have grappled with those "real world" issues and strategized ways to engage women in an education environment that minimizes the stereotypes and other negative impacts of that "reality." Thus, although women's colleges are "a world apart," their goals and mission are very much centered in the reality and history of women's lives. Indeed, as M. E. Tidball has noted, "women's colleges that fully serve women and that provide examples of adult men and women working cooperatively together at all levels and in all endeavors are . . . institutions that offer students a vision of how society can operate both effectively and equitably. They are thus one of society's precious resources" (1978, 19).

THE CHALLENGE OF CHANGE

The legacies of women's colleges are emerging and they are powerful. The challenge for those committed to women's education in other contexts is to develop strategies that capitalize on the strengths and minimize the weaknesses of coeducational environments for women students. Women's colleges grew out of a struggle to provide women the full education of which they were capable. They survive today, in part, because gender inequity issues persist. But women's colleges thrive because they have been successful at creating institutions that are empowering for women. They model what colleges and universities might look like with women at the center. This legacy, properly acknowledged, is critically instructive for coeducational institutions. With women at the center, what might be? With women and men at the center—a kind of coeducation yet to be achieved—what could be?

As described in Chapter 1, the history of higher education for women in the United States began with doubts about the capacity of women to achieve, concerns about the negative impact women would have on men if they attended school together, and the need to limit the enrollments of women in many areas. Many limits on women's access to opportunities persisted until the late 1960s, when federal regulations declared them illegal. With women constituting over half the undergraduate population of most institutions, it would be relatively easy for a campus to conclude that it need not pay too much attention to the legacies from women's colleges. Indeed, many point to the percentage of women students as an indication that significant progress has been made in taking women seriously. What the research suggests, however, is that the transformation from men-only schools to institutions that serve both women and men well is not easily achieved. It requires deep understanding and a deeper commitment to self-study and change than is usually understood. Moreover, even today, there are striking and powerful examples that change will not come easily. A small example from a recent *Chronicle of Higher Education* (Gose 1997) may suffice. An article entitled "Liberal-Arts Colleges Ask: Where Have the Men Gone?" describes a strong negative reaction on many campuses to the fact that women have become a majority of the undergraduate enrollments throughout the country. Institutional leaders were quoted as "expressing concern" about the negative impact this might have on the campus, in athletics, and on such important functions as fundraising. The article describes steps being taken to attract men—even less-qualified men. The reality is that there is fear and anxiety when women assume a majority position—even, as in this case, when it is merely at the undergraduate level. Yet, in 1997, 30 years after sex discrimination was declared illegal, some campuses are suggesting that having too many women is a disadvantage, without worrying about how this might seem to the public at large. How is it that having many more men than women (a condition at most engineering schools, for example) is not cause for concern, yet, having 52 percent women is reason for open fear?

A resistance to—and ambivalence about—women remains, though it may stay deeply buried until some issue emerges. Taking women seriously then requires serious commitments and understanding on the part of the institution and its constituencies, as well as in its mission. Being serious about women will require a level of intentionality in hiring and in aspirations for students—and in the capacity to think about women and men, and the diversity among women and men, that is not easily achieved. There are some campuses, for instance, that have been focusing on the question of peer influence, both in terms of the influence of men and the influence of women. Thus, campuses that take women seriously will also take men seriously, especially in terms of attitudes and behaviors toward women. What behaviors are tolerated on campus? What kinds of jokes are treated as acceptable? What is the ethos of the fraternity and sorority system?

Moreover, in transferring this legacy to coeducational institutions, a generic commitment to high expectations and belief in students' capacity to succeed will not be sufficient unless the attention to women and men, and to women and men of all backgrounds, is intentionally developed. But intentionality is manifest not just in occasional rhetoric. It is manifest in a living history, a living legacy of larger purposes, and in the translation of purpose in both the small and the large decisions of institutional life. It is also manifest in the larger communities beyond the campus that have developed. For women's colleges, these communities of trustees and alumnae play a major role in the creation of the total environment while extending the reach of the college's influence and nurture both in time and place beyond the campus. These legacies are further developed in Chapter 7.

CHAPTER 7

Builders, Benefactors, and Volunteers

We are all a part of the continuing story of this place—students, faculty, alumnae, staff, administration, trustees, friends—all of us are founders. All of us share in the joy and responsibility of seeing to it that this place continues serving women with excellence, expertise and enthusiasm.
—M. E. Tidball, 1990

Although the day-to-day campus environment is most obviously influenced by administrators, faculty, and students, and by the guests who come as lecturers, performers, and consultants, other defining forces also are influential. These are the board of trustees, who are responsible for the existence of the college in the first instance, as well as guarantors of its robust continuation; and the alumnae association, whose purpose is to ensure that any and all who have ever been enrolled will remain part of an extensive network of mutual service and interdependent relationships. Both of these entities at women's colleges have developed ways of being and doing that have been conceived and enacted expressly for the women who are their principal constituencies. As such, they offer their insights and understandings as models for all institutions of higher education.

THE CONSCIOUSNESS OF GOVERNANCE

Members of the Board

Once upon a time, on a transatlantic flight from Paris, the board chair of a newly constituted men's change college, albeit a men's college of long standing, was speaking with an alumna of a women's college. She asked him, "How many women will you have on your board, now that you are admitting women students?" He replied that the college's bylaws permitted only two non-alumni board members, and since there would be no women graduates for several years, and none of those ready for trustee service for many more years after that, the college had no need to address this issue for some time. "But," reasoned the alumna, "with women students, you will need to hire women faculty and women administrators, and to accomplish that you will surely need more than two women on the board of trustees." Somewhat irritably, he explained again the college's bylaws. "Well, then," she asked, "why don't you amend the bylaws?"

An unlikely scenario? Unfortunately, a very common one—neither unique nor of ancient times. Recall, for example, the concern of trustees and admissions officers of many liberal arts colleges that increasing the proportion of women students would create disruptions, if not "gender imbalances," on their campuses (Gose 1997). At women's colleges, by contrast, the consciousness of trustees is well-imbued with concerns for women in all the college's constituencies, in large part because the majority of trustees are alumnae, parents or husbands of alumnae, or members of the sponsoring order of religious sisters. That is to say, women and woman-supportive men are in charge of seeing to it that women in the college environment will be well served. As a result, changing the bylaws or updating the mission statement or calling for curricular review are matters to be expected, met, and implemented when or if the education of women warrants such amendment. By virtue of those called to become members of the board, women's voices are heard and do make a difference. Just how important these voices are, and the knowledge and expertise and care that informs them, can be found in many realms, some of which are discussed in this chapter.

On boards of women's colleges, the presence of women's voices, and especially the voices of alumnae, have regularly prevailed in asserting what they know to be true about the education of women. Thus, for all of higher education, the legacy from women's colleges is this: ensure the presence of women in substantial numbers—not mere tokens—on boards of trustees. Include, particularly, women who have been personally involved in the education of women—as graduates or faculty of a women's college, as professors of substantive women's studies courses and programs, or as pioneers in any way in the higher education of women. Such trustees can make a difference for women as they demonstrate ways in which the institution can grow in its effort to take women seriously.

Clarifying Identity as the First Priority

Most frequently mentioned as the primary responsibility of a college's board of trustees is the appointment, support, and assessment of the institution's president. However, trustees at women's colleges, and women trustees of other institutions, have long known the importance of shifting the board's emphasis to refining institutional mission to ensure that women as well as men participate fully in the life of the institution. More recently, the Association of Governing Boards of Universities and Colleges (AGB) has revised its focus, as well, and has now begun to list institutional mission as "Criterion 1" among its board self-study measures (Association of Governing Boards of Universities and Colleges 1996). The reason women trustees so often advocate the establishment of this priority is self-evident: if a college is to serve the education of women, then women must figure prominently and positively in the college's statement of mission before any further decisions are made. This is, of course, already the case at women's colleges—but it must also become so for all institutions that seek to educate women.

In reviewing the mission statement, the trustees' role is first to work cooperatively with administration and faculty, and sometimes students, to determine and articulate the unique mission of the particular institution in such a way that it will have relevance and meaning in its own setting. Regular review and clarification of the mission are also responsibilities of the trustees, in keeping with the evolution of the college. Thus, though appointing the president is certainly a role of high priority, articulating the college's mission must precede it if women are to participate fully in the life of the institution. For the mission will be the basis on which the president will be selected and assessed. Articulating the mission in terms of educating women is necessary for women's and coeducational institutions alike and cannot be left to inference, since educating "men and women" (rarely "women and men") is so common a phrase that it carries very little meaning for those who are underserved.

Examples of woman-specific mission statements abound, for every women's college announces its identity in indisputably woman-supportive language. One women's college states that it is a "woman-centered college" and adds, in what is called its vision statement, "We will be a College for Women of all ages" (Wilson College 1997). Another asserts that its purpose is "to maintain distinction as an institution of higher learning by offering women an education conducive to excellence in scholarly pursuits and also preparing them for leadership roles in a contemporary society" (Bennett College 1995, 11). Still another proclaims "at the heart of the . . . College mission is a century-long commitment to the education and advancement of women and to their preparation for purposeful lives and careers" (Hood College 1997, 8). How distinctly different are these statements from the articles of endowment of Stanford University: "We have provided that the education of the sexes shall be equal, deeming it of special importance that those who are to be mothers of the future generations shall be fitted to mold and direct the infantile mind at its most critical period" (Howe 1984, 262). One must wonder how it is that this prestigious university has not revisited its reason for being or clarified what it means by "equal."

To be sure, each women's college surrounds its central fact of educating women with a constellation of particulars that establishes its special identity and purpose—to offer career preparation, to proclaim its dedication to the liberal arts, to pay specific attention to the importance of giving women leadership opportunities, among others. But all attest that their raison d'être is the education of women. Clearly this commitment is the principal guiding force for all the governance decisions that follow. The proclamation of a woman-centered mission ensures that all other roles and responsibilities of the trustees flow from this basic premise.

The legacy from women's colleges to coeducational institutions is, therefore, to recognize that unless a college or university returns to its first principles—to its original mission or charter—and makes thoughtful and penetrating revisions such that women are fully included in all aspects of the life and work of the institution, trustees and those who follow their lead will not come to terms with their responsibilities, both to the women on campus and to all women who seek higher education. Institutions that have a long history of educating men are generally seen as prestigious leaders in the society, and only to the extent that they follow the model of women's colleges in taking women seriously is there hope for the equitable inclusion of women more widely in the academic community.

Selecting the President

In the matter of presidential appointment, when the stated mission is woman-centered, the selection committee will make certain that the candidates—and above all, the finalists—are dedicated to educating women as a first priority, and that they have demonstrated their own commitment to this mission, along with their ideas and goals of what such a mission embodies. Further, since the governing boards of women's colleges are well supplied with women trustees (and faculty, students, alumnae, and staff), there will be a plenitude of women serving on search committees, making it far more likely that, for every position, women candidates will be sought and encouraged to participate (Church 1996, 76). Not only is there a greater possibility of selecting a woman officer, but women candidates who are not chosen will have had opportunities to learn about searches and about presidencies, and thus will gain useful experience for future advancement opportunities.

These valuable lessons, commonly available to men, have not been as accessible to women, except in women's colleges. An early example from Wellesley College is emblematic. The occasion was the search for a new president in 1911. The trustee subcommittee produced the following report:

> Everything that could be said [in favor of having a man become president] was brought before us. Your sub-committee, however, at a

meeting held several weeks ago decided that it would adhere to the traditional policy of the College to nominate a woman for the presidency. We found that to change that policy would be considered a severe blow to those who are in favor of the higher education of women. . . . [F]or us after all these years to change our policy *would be saying to the world that no woman could be found* to carry on the succession of women Presidents. (Howe 1984, 261–62)

Indeed, as mentioned in Chapter 1, 16 of the 18 institutions present at the Cedar Crest Conference in 1969 are still women's colleges, and *all* are now headed by women presidents. It is not that men are unsuitable for these positions. Rather it is that women's colleges are in the forefront of institutions that select women to fill important posts. Even the most cursory glance at lists of faculty and administrators of earlier eras reveals that it has always been women's colleges that have regularly and vigorously provided women academic professionals first class opportunities to use all their talents in the service of their generation.

The legacy—the message—from women's colleges to trustees in all of higher education continues the theme. Engage women in all that you do. Especially engage women when you search for a president. Recognize that the long shadow from your actions stretches across the campus to the search committees that will select deans and vice presidents, department heads and new faculty. In all searches, make clear the updated and refurbished mission that places women along with men at the center of the enterprise. Be certain, as well, that many women serve on all search committees. Where appropriate, enlist women from other institutions to fill out a committee if your institution doesn't have enough women of its own. As an interim strategy, it will call attention to the need for increasing the number of women on your own faculty and in your administration. Do not imagine that your own institution will soon have "enough" women, thereby releasing you from the responsibility of finding some in the meantime for searches. Remember Princeton's assertion that it would have a faculty of 33 percent women in 15 years, but managed to have only 14 percent some 27 years later (see Chapter 1). Including women in your institution does not just happen; it takes work and planning and, above all, a mission that explicitly acknowledges the importance of women to the collegiate enterprise.

Educating the Majority

When women are the majority of an institution, and when the institution's mission is to serve women, certain educational priorities follow. First, not only are courses taught in all areas of undergraduate endeavors, but all are open to women. Further, women are regularly encouraged to participate, especially in areas commonly inhospitable to women, such as the natural sciences. As discussed in Chapter 3, women's colleges have been the most productive among all types of institutions of higher education in graduating women who have excelled in the natural sciences and medicine. This success can be attributed ultimately to the college's mission and to the oversight of the trustees in the hiring and promoting of women faculty. For all types of colleges, the production of women scientists—or career achievers in other fields—follows directly from the number of women faculty to whom the women students have had access (M. E. Tidball 1973b; 1986b; 1989). Further, women faculty in all kinds of institutions are more concerned than men faculty with issues of importance to women, although men who teach in women's colleges are more concerned about women's education than men in all other types of institutions (M. E. Tidball 1976b). Thus the hiring, paying, and promoting of faculty, both women and men, have a great deal to do with the education of women students.

Beyond the provision of a wide selection of substantive courses, all of which are clearly open to women and in which women are encouraged to participate, there is also the fact at women's colleges of peer acceptance for whatever academic course is pursued—and faculty assistance to ensure its accomplishment. Elsewhere, the insistence by the trustees, through their role in the setting of educational policy, that all courses be open to women, that faculty advising be mindful of women's capabilities, and that faculty-student relationships be available and supportive, will mean that students will be stimulated to sample widely and discover the joy and the work of learning in the context of an environment free of sexual stereotypes. From trustees comes also the policy to provide educational opportunities for returning women, that is, women past the traditional college student age. This policy decision has become one of the most important and imitated legacies pioneered by women's colleges.

This section would not be complete without special mention of women's studies courses, departments, and majors. For many years, academics at women's colleges believed that it was not necessary for them to develop and promote such curricular materials—but that conclusion overlooked their larger role as institutional models. More recently, having realized the critical importance of their leadership in the higher education community, and having become aware of their own need to study women, women's colleges have established a wide variety of forms to engage the study of women, their productions, and their contributions. In women's studies, women's colleges have now become leaders to be emulated—from courses, to conferences, to institutes, to centers (see Chapter 1).

To Benefit Women Is to Benefit All

These, then, are legacies from women's colleges to the higher education community as they pursue educating the majority. They are but some of the ways in which women's colleges have expertise to bring to the boards of trustees of coeducational institutions. In every category of activity, trustees of coeducational institutions must affirm an institutional identity, and hence mission, that includes women, for herein lies the foundation for taking women seriously and for discerning what works for women. As builders, benefactors, and volunteers, trustees are the ultimate source of wisdom, strength, beneficence, and dedication to the colleges they have committed themselves to serving. This consciousness, so evident and prevalent among trustees of women's colleges, is yet another legacy they bring to all of higher education.

THE CONSCIOUSNESS OF SERVICE

A Place for Everyone

Trustees are not alone, however, in their dedication to the colleges they serve. The graduates of women's colleges—the alumnae—work also toward ensuring their colleges' continuation into the future. In their own ways they, too, are builders, benefactors, and volunteers. As was true for their leadership roles on campus, women's college graduates hold all the leadership positions in their alumnae associations, from local clubs to regional groups to the national board of management. Additionally, with their collegiate experiences as background, 90 percent become active in professional, civic, and philanthropic organizations after graduation (Women's College Coalition 1995). More specifically, three-quarters of alumnae continue some involvement with their colleges in a variety of roles—as intern employers; class agents for development; mentors; admissions recruiters; alumnae association volunteers at the local, class, and national levels; and members of the board of trustees. Additionally, alumnae are regularly urged to become involved in a variety of events and activities, many of which are social in nature, as a part of enjoying others who have shared an important time of their lives in a common place for a common set of reasons. One local club, for example, holds "decade brunches" each fall so that alumnae from the same and neighboring classes can keep in touch, as well as sponsoring a book club, holiday party, special tours, and a forum with the college president. These events are in addition to projects that include a book award program for outstanding high school students in the community, admissions activities for prospective students, and work for the club itself to develop membership and volunteers (Mount Holyoke College Alumnae Association 1997). The possibilities for engagement of women's college alumnae is exceptionally rich, both with respect to their colleges and also to the larger society.

Belonging

The central office of an alumnae association, geared to oversight of local activities as well as to initiating events of its own, sees to it that alumnae are kept in touch with their college and made to feel a part of a system that has room for individuals, their ideas, and their concerns. An association customarily publishes a magazine, administers alumnae records, manages a speakers' bureau, participates in an educational travel program, holds conferences both on campus and around the country for special groups, along with a myriad of other relevant projects. The majority of alumnae associations are an arm of the college's office of external relations; however, some are notable for their independence. The Wellesley College Alumnae Association has long been regarded as a model of autonomy and expertise. A sense of its character is revealed in a letter in the alumnae magazine from the association's newly-elected president:

> As Wellesley alumnae, we are united by our love for this College. In spite of differences in age, ethnicity, geography, and professions, we share a common experience and value what we learned here. That bond brings strength to our Association, the reason we have been able to help in so many ways to ensure that Wellesley maintains its place among the very finest colleges in the country. Please commit to continue our tradition of giving and serving—the students, future generations of students, and all alumnae will be the beneficiaries of your dedication. (Black 1997)

It is instructive to compare this style of interaction with that of a men's change college communicating in its magazine with both men and women graduates:

> [The President] and the Trustees have formulated a plan to make this college one of the top five undergraduate institutions nationwide; the success of each component of the plan is dependent on the success of every other component. In other words: in order to attract highly qualified students, we must raise its prestige. In order to raise its prestige, we must fix internal problems. In order to fix internal problems, we must raise money from alumni. In order to raise money from alumni, we must clearly outline our objectives, reassert amongst our students, faculty, and administrators why this community has been established, and then take the collective plunge into proving it.

Both of these excerpts call for graduates to make a financial contribution to their college; the Wellesley letter encourages alumnae to commit to service, as well. Further, the Wellesley letter conveys a greater sense of partnership between alumnae and their college, a sense of belonging to a larger purpose where each one has a valued role, where the contributions of each one are taken seriously. It should not be surprising to learn that, in a national ranking of alumni giving per student, Wellesley ranked first among the top 20 institutions (Chronicle of Higher Education 1993). These findings confirm an earlier assessment that showed Wellesley at the top of 15 institutions on a list that included five women's colleges (Butterfield 1992).

Perhaps differences between women's and coeducational colleges, in which the comparisons are made between monetary contributions from women only at women's colleges and from both women and men at coeducational institutions, may be appreciated in light of research on giving patterns among women. It has been commonly assumed that men graduates give more to their colleges than do women. For example, Duke University trustees have voiced concern that, as a result of an increasing proportion of women students, the university will receive less in alumni gifts and will experience diminished prestige and political influence (Greene 1987). The research, however, has revealed that giving patterns and reasons for giving not only differ between men and women, but that "the most loyal are alumnae of established Catholic women's colleges, like the College of St. Catherine in St. Paul, Minn. Next come graduates of nonreligious single-sex colleges, and last are women who attended coed schools" (Matthews 1991). Surely there must be an important relationship between monetary generosity and a sense of belonging to an institution, a sense that one's college is taking women seriously, that one's college is taking each woman seriously. And with a sense of belonging and of being taken seriously comes loyalty and its derivative, generosity. "Nowhere," proclaims a Spelman College brochure, "is the meaning of friendship better demonstrated than in Spelman's recent fund raising campaign. . . . Every donor constituent group at Spelman, from alumnae and students to friends of the College, contributed to its success" (Spelman College 1996b, 13).

Women Friends

The idea of belonging leads to an appreciation of the importance of friendships among women, regularly cited as emblematic of the women's college experience. This is a truly unique opportunity that comes to women in women's colleges. The sharing of self that transpires during the college years is of unprecedented durability. The time together in a common place with common goals—the camaraderie during an important developmental period of one's life—all conspire to form bonds that can last forever. Over and over again, women's college graduates celebrate the friendships related to their sojourn at their college; relationships that refresh them, renew them, and make them glad. Time and distance may preclude face-to-face interaction, but important and significant alumnae friendships have proved powerfully enduring (M. E. Tidball 1980b, 14).

The alumnae association provides expert assistance for the maintenance of these relationships. Primarily through periodic class reunions, but also through class newsletters and class notes in the alumnae magazine, friends and classmates have a built-in way to keep in touch with one another.

There is yet another dimension of a woman's life that endures after graduation that has import for women more broadly. This is the fact that women in women's colleges have had many opportunities to learn first-hand the competence of other women with whom they share the campus—competencies that are not related to the fact of one's biology, or femaleness, or sexuality. As a result, these alumnae will later find themselves comfortable in respecting the talents and capabilities of their women professional colleagues, and their judgments about other women's suitability for various appointments will be both credible and trustworthy. Thus women's college alumnae will have key roles in the advancement of other women in their careers (M. E. Tidball 1980b, 14). Add to this the extensive career networks established among women's college alumnae, and another ingredient of their career progress and success becomes apparent.

What legacy for other colleges can alumnae associations of women's colleges offer? Most importantly, they can suggest and encourage coeducational institutions to honor the presence of women as persons who are not men. Currently, every aspect of being a graduate of a coeducational institution—from homecoming weekends, to the content of alumni magazines, to nominations for alumni trustees, to the structure of class reunions, to the very fact that all graduates are collectively tagged with a masculine noun—reminds women that they are but guests in an institution to which they do not truly belong. For these reasons, the legacy would speak first to those aspects of the campus culture that celebrate male athletic teams, conformist student behaviors, and social activities, all of which have been shown to inhibit women's aspirations (Pascarella 1984).

FIRST THINGS

Alumnae are extensions of the women who were once students, even as the institution's behavior toward them as alumnae is but an extension of its behavior towards them while they were students. Thus, for an institution to honor, support, and facilitate its women graduates, it must first honor, support, and facilitate its women students—meaning honoring all women on campus. To do these things requires the consciousness of the trustees to accept and respond to the legacies they have been offered by the two constituencies of women's colleges discussed in this chapter—the board of trustees and the alumnae association—for these are clearly closely interwoven in their basic missions.

For coeducational institutions, there is no shortcut. There is no simple or simplistic way. Women in coeducational colleges, like women in women's colleges, need a wealth of women role models and encouragement and support to study in all fields, and they must be given opportunities to belong and to develop friendships with other women, eventually being welcomed as graduates who matter. To do these things, colleges that would serve women as well as men must be prepared to make fundamental changes in the ways they perceive women and men on campus and the relationships between them. In sum, coeducational institutions must provide a coherent *total environment* that actively and deeply takes all women seriously—students, faculty, administrators, staff, trustees, alumnae, guests, and friends.

PART FOUR

· · · · · · · · · · ·

Women's Colleges and the Meaning of Taking Women Seriously

Truth, whatever its frame of reference, may be sought by a variety of means, ranging from the concrete and experimental to the abstract and ideational, but in any last analysis it will always contain an element of mystery. No one approach can answer all the questions or provide complete proof. However, the recurrence of a theme, regardless of the setting of the particular college or university, provides the kind of evidential material that bespeaks truth. Here, the recurrent theme is the fact that women's colleges are preeminent contributors of achieving women to the wider society. From their distinguished history to the lessons and legacies presented here, women's colleges are a unique and valuable national resource for the education and employment of women. They have repeatedly demonstrated their commitment as they have encouraged, empowered, and rewarded women. In sum, they have become foremost examples of what it means to take women seriously. Celebrating, supporting, and emulating women's colleges for their contributions to women and to higher education must therefore occur regularly and often by all who would participate in the development of an equitable and humane society.

CHAPTER 8

Priorities, Patterns, and Principles

It is never too late to be what you might have become.
—Mary Ann Evans (1819–80)

M any things have become apparent as the chapters of this book have unfolded. Among them is an increasingly clear appreciation of the challenge that arises from attempts to communicate what has been learned from many divergent sources to readers coming from widely different experiences and perspectives. In this effort, the overarching goal has been to provide at least the essence of what it means for institutions of higher education to take women seriously. The issues are far greater than the simple sum of their separate parts. The effort of finding, collecting, and presenting the available material surrounding taking women seriously speaks to the very theme of this book. That is, if women *were* being taken seriously, it would not have been so difficult to produce relevant material on institutions that do so, bringing it forth for edification and action. Indeed, it would probably already have been accomplished many times over. But it has not—which says something important about the status of women in American higher education.

It is hoped that this book will change that for its readers and for all among whom they have influence. For *everyone* has a stake in the education of women. This is because women of all backgrounds constitute the largest untapped source of talent in our nation, and educated women the surest hope for the development of a humane, equitable, and productive society. Women's colleges offer the clearest and most complete vision of what education for women can be and should be so that the gifts of women can be duly received and incorporated into the ongoing life of the larger community (M. E. Tidball 1980b, 12).

PRIORITIES

First Women

Acquiring an appreciation of the contexts in which the higher education of women has taken place, and especially in which women's colleges have been active, provides a framework within which to appreciate the considerable contributions of these institutions. The founders of women's colleges cited as exemplars stand before us to this day with their courage, their vision, and their enormously hard work. By whatever criteria—young Elisabeth Oesterlein's barefoot walk from Pennsylvania to North Carolina, Mary Lyon's tireless search for the pennies and dollars that would ensure an endowment for her school before it opened, Mother Guerin's harsh voyage from France to the wilderness of southern Indiana, Susan Mills's venturesome experiment in the far west, Sophia Packard and Harriet Giles's exploration of education for southern black women, and Indiana Fletcher Williams's legacy on behalf of her beloved daughter—all of these women dedicated their lives and their persuasive energies to their unshakable belief that women were educable and that the country and the world would be the better when they were given the full benefit of higher education opportunities. These defining stories must continue to be told, else meanings located in the originating events are lost, and with that, the impetus necessary for future generations to take women seriously.

Reaching Out

The priorities of these pioneering women clearly materialized through their perspicacity and foresight: the fruits of their labors resulted not only in quality education for millions of women in women's colleges, but also in the establishment of hundreds of women's colleges both in the United States and abroad that continue to serve as institutional models of places that take women seriously. Like a pebble dropped into a pond, the work of these early founders in behalf of women has generated ripples of benefit not only to those who attended the early women's colleges, but to *all* women wherever they may participate in higher learning.

Women's colleges such as Cedar Crest, Wellesley, and Immaculata, along with the Women's College Coalition, have been among the institutions that have taken leadership in developing conferences, workshops, and symposia to increase understanding of what works for women in *any* higher education setting, and to recommend courses of action that will make taking women seriously possible. All women's colleges have regularly appreciated that, for women students to benefit optimally from the higher education environment, it is mandatory that there be a multitude of women faculty and administrators, trustees, and guests—women of a variety of backgrounds and lifestyles, some struggling and some secure in their identity—all taken seriously. Furthermore, *all* women are viewed as important to the education enterprise, and *all* are accorded respect, justice, and colleagueship. These priorities are consistent with the findings of human resource studies that regularly demonstrate that in order to flourish, even outstanding talent requires training, direction, provision for a sphere of action, and rewards (Committee on the Education and Employment of Women in Science and Engineering 1983, 1.1).

Going Public

Attempts to encourage educators to appreciate the vital role played by women's colleges included portions of the Carnegie Commission on Higher Education's *Opportunities for Women in Higher Education*. Its editors wrote:

> These accomplishments of the graduates of women's colleges are worthy of emphasis, not only as they bear on decisions of women's colleges . . . but also—and far more significantly in terms of potential influence—as they suggest how changes in policies and faculty attitudes in coeducational institutions could affect the accomplishments of their women students. (Carnegie Commission on Higher Education 1973, 74)

Yet even with this endorsement from so respected an institution as the Carnegie Commission, little attention or action resulted. Women and the encouragement of their talents have not merited a high priority in most environments. Still, what was known in women's colleges was now before the higher education community.

Shortly after the Carnegie report, the president of Wellesley College, in an invited response to the Department of Health, Education, and Welfare, stated:

> Unfortunately, the proposed Title IX guidelines read as if both sexes had suffered past discrimination in equal measure. This is not so. It has not been *men* who have been excluded from participation in, denied the benefits of, or subjected to discrimination in society. It has been *women*. The talents and resources of women are being lost to society. (Newell 1974)

The response to this statement, presented by the president of Brigham Young University before the U.S. Congress as the delegated representative of the higher education community, was an opposing view carrying the implication that all collegiate institutions supported his stand (Jamison 1975). Apparently, women were not to receive high priority, much less be taken seriously, except by other women.

Voicing her dismay at the continued negative ambiance on campuses around the country, Florence Howe noted, "Residence on the campuses of old and distinguished coeducational or formerly male colleges has convinced me anew of the maleness of higher education; of what I can only call at best the continued *toleration* of women, as faculty, administrators or students. . . . I am talking about the general tenor of campus life" (Howe 1984, 233). So it is that the communication of fact or even firsthand experience has not regularly merited positive action on behalf of women in higher education. Indeed, the communication of fact has frequently resulted in apathy if not antagonism.

How difficult it is to write of these things without voicing a complaint! Yet to omit them is to fail to bring forth the great contrast between institutions that take women seriously and those that do not. It is a matter of reordering priorities, a matter of restructuring the foundations, a matter of reformulating board bylaws—or whatever else it takes to bring women truly and fully into the mainstream of institutional life. Forthrightly acknowledging the struggles may be painful to note—and even more painful to see—but by doing so, by taking women seriously, a new and enlightened beginning for all people can ensue.

PATTERNS

So many patterns, so many insights, emerge from the examination and analysis of the most recent decades of American higher education. Formidable increases in the sheer number of individuals participating in collegiate education, along with enormous societal perturbations, have had significant impacts on all social institutions. Among those most vulnerable to the wide shifts in the patterns of national life have been small, independent colleges, and among the small colleges, some institutions particularly affected by change have been those whose first priority is the education of women. That so many women's colleges have continued to serve as models of what works for women is thus truly a significant accomplishment.

Patterns of Reorganization

In order for women's colleges to continue their role as foremost educators of women, it was necessary for them first to break with the patterns of collegiate education common to most small colleges before the middle of the 1960s: small, residential, liberal arts, and church-related being the most frequent characteristics. Only relatively few remain that way. Identifying the most essential characteristics of each institution in its role as a college for women became a top priority. Missions were reevaluated and reformed, collaborative efforts for governance were instigated, and new ways of reaching out not only to traditional but also nontraditional publics and potential participants were devised.

These activities were undertaken by virtually all women's colleges. Impressively diverse results emerged that nonetheless all retained at the core the basic mission of taking women seriously. A new consciousness developed in which the importance of women on faculties and among administrators and trustees was reaffirmed. The significance of women faculty to women students was realized, and the roles and value of men faculty at women's colleges discovered and celebrated (M. E. Tidball 1976a).

Although there was no longer a standard institutional organization for most women's colleges (as there had been in an earlier era), there were instead the adaptations to the sea changes in American society and higher education. These led not only to significant renewal and refreshment, but to a realization that the patterns basic to taking women seriously remained. Only the outward conventionalities were abandoned or reframed with a new understanding and intentionally.

For women's colleges, there emerged not only the revitalized residential, liberal arts college, in which the definition of liberal arts had been reformed to include such studies as computer science, but also many new shapes and emphases. Especially among the Roman Catholic colleges, there was an enhancement of the mission to serve the underserved, now seen as women of color, women from the inner city, single mothers, women workers who could not attend during customary classroom hours, and women with particular career-related requirements that could be met only by collegiate level studies. Many women's colleges also opened their doors to men for nonresidential classes during evenings and weekends. Virtually all women's colleges established academic programs for "returning" women, that is, women older than 22. The many new forms and the increased diversity of options for the education of women nonetheless continued to be based on the imperative to take women seriously.

Patterns of Research

At quite another level, along with conventional research methodologies, new tools were developed and applied to questions of what works for women. Principal among these were the disaggregation of data by sex and by institution type in order to study the situation for women apart from men, in all categories of institutions, in all constituencies of institutional life, and in terms of institutional productivities of achieving graduates. In these efforts, data repeatedly demonstrate that the environment of women's colleges is reliably associated with positive outcomes for women, testifying to the assertion that "wisdom . . . begins with the will to disaggregate, seeking to give proper weight to settings that make a difference" (Clark 1987, v).

Some of these outcomes relate to individual students, such as increased aspirations, overall satisfaction with campus life, involvement in extracurricular activities, opportunities for leadership, and enhanced self-confidence and self-esteem. Other outcomes refer to postcollege accomplishments; in these, women's colleges regularly produce the largest proportion of women career achievers and participants in graduate and medical education. Not only is the productivity of women's colleges disproportionately greater than their selectivity in admissions, but it is also consistently greater for women than that of any other category of higher education institution.

It must be added that the great outpouring of research that investigates environments for the education of women has regularly felt constrained to make use of definitions and endpoints that have traditionally been assigned by men to be the kinds of results that count. For example, measuring institutional productivity, as a highly quantitative and objective approach, was devised in part in response to critics' objections to "anecdotal" evidence; however, as a methodology outside the traditional realms of social science research, it has regularly been suspect. Alternatively, interrogation of survey databases based on respondents' opinions and attitudes has grown with ever-increasing complex statistical methods of analysis, in spite of the subjectivity of the original input material; yet these have been the reigning methods of sociological/psychological research with which one has had to comply in order to be heard at all. More recently, as research that seeks to understand what works for women has begun to gain some credibility, case studies are appearing as a formal means of gathering evidence; time will tell how acceptable case studies will prove to be. Regardless, researchers interested in learning what works for women continue to explore many routes to that end, even though their findings have often met with a not insignificant degree of disapprobation.

What has emerged from these prototypical attempts to gain an understanding of what is essential for the education of women is not a singular "best way" to do research to produce a "scientific answer." Rather, it is the recurrence of a theme regardless of the setting, or the type of investigation, or the institution in which the work was accomplished, that provides the kind of evidential material that bespeaks truth. Thus from these multiple perspectives has emerged a common theme, and that theme is the extraordinary contribution of women's colleges to the participation of women in a multiplicity of national and international leadership roles (M. E. Tidball 1998).

Patterns of Productivity

Other patterns that have become apparent from the new research are those associated with the doctoral field participation of women compared with that of men, participation distributions that are consistently different from each other, regardless of the type of baccalaureate institution from which the doctorate recipients graduated. Further, the large majority of college environments are more nurturing of men than of women. This becomes clear by studying patterns for both women and men from the same institutions. The men proceed more frequently to substantive postcollegiate accomplishments than do the women, even when the graduates come from the most productive institutions in the country.

These differences in patterns of productivity raise a warning to coeducational institutions that they still have much to incorporate into their environments if they would truly take women seriously. Only by recognizing the existence of different productivity patterns for women and men is the way opened to learning the underlying reasons and devising ways and means for ameliorating any inequities they may signal (M. E. Tidball, 1993).

Discovering Wholeness

In all, these several patterns at different levels call to mind characteristics of chaos theory, in which the power of consistency among different scales leads at last to an appreciation of the importance of the whole (Gleick 1987, 115). Here are the different scales, all of which repeat the same theme of taking women seriously, albeit in differing ways, making it possible to identify a principle that applies universally (Ferris 1988, 385). Here there is a certain underlying consistency, even if it is not immediately apparent to the casual observer. What goes on in the boardroom with respect to women—the priorities of trustees and search committee members, the approach to hiring at all levels, and the criteria set for student admissions and staff qualifications— is intimately related to how and what professors teach and students learn. It is intimately related to how faculty see themselves in terms of competencies and self-respect, and how students develop self-confidence and self-esteem. It is intimately related to alumnae loyalty and the establishment of life-long friendships and support networks. Analogously, what goes on in the classroom, in the residence halls, on the playing fields, and what goes on in the alumnae association, and what goes on in the development office and the budget office, all contribute to outcomes for every member of the community. That is, in order to understand what is happening with respect to institutions that take women seriously, one must not imagine that there is any one way to meet the challenge. Rather, one must consider the *whole*, the totality of the interrelated functions and groups of individuals whose actions, beliefs, and energies are combined and interwoven in a multicolored tapestry that is incontrovertibly committed to taking women seriously.

PRINCIPLES

Priorities and patterns lead unerringly to identifying the principles upon which the education of women is to be built by all institutions that would join the effort to educate women. Clearly the task is neither simple to devise nor straightforward to implement. Women's colleges—by virtue of their long history in dealing with the education of women, and most important, their creative adaptation to larger changes in the society and higher education across many eras of national life—are the natural institutional models of what works for women. But like women as individuals, they are regularly overlooked—invisible and inaudible—because they are but a small proportion of the higher education community. Not only are women's colleges a small proportion, but most are also small in size as individual institutions. Thus, they are doubly disadvantaged in a society in which large, if not largest, is beautiful as well as best, and in which institutions are measured and promoted by whatever they offer that can be counted and recorded in college guides and popular magazines.

Yet what works for women resides within the *wholeness* of the environment, originating from a mission in which women are taken seriously (M. E. Tidball 1996). It has to do with creating a community in which women have a clear sense of ownership, knowing that they make a difference and knowing that they matter and that they truly belong and always will. What is essential is not to be found in quantifiable categories except for that which has heretofore not been quantified by those who assess the value of various institutions, namely, to what extent is there a *critical mass of women* as trustees, administrators, faculty, staff, students, graduates, guests, and friends.

In Table 13, two lists summarize what is and is not essential for taking women seriously. The nonessentials are all most certainly important aspects of institutional definition, and each can and does contribute in a positive way to the overall capabilities of an institution. For example, no one would belittle the potential importance of a large endowment. But having a large endowment is not *essential* to taking women seriously.

What has emerged from the writing of this book is that the essentials for taking women seriously are to be found in the vision of the leaders of an institution who know that what is most important are those characteristics that form the infrastructure upon which a thriving community of women is built. That is to say, the majority of those things that are most important, most essential, for the education of women are not countable. Examples of these include high expectations for excellence in all dimensions of community life; a wealth of spaces and places where women's voices are heard; personal responsibility as exemplified in the operation of an honor code, along with a large measure of trust and responsibility; the celebration of traditions and institu-

---

TABLE 13

INSTITUTIONAL CHARACTERISTICS RELATED TO TAKING WOMEN SERIOUSLY

Essential

Visionary leadership committed to the education of women
Critical mass of women in all constituencies
Belief in women's capacities and high expectations
Places and spaces for women's voices to be heard
Opportunities for women's leadership in all aspects of institutional life
Celebration of traditions and institutional history
High degree of trust and responsibility
Active and empowering alumnae association

Nonessential

High selectivity in admissions
Large endowment
High faculty compensation
High proportion of faculty Ph.D.s
Extensive library holdings
Conformist student behaviors

---

tional history that tie the present to the originating events, thereby assuring a future with depth and meaning; and an ethic of service that grows from a larger purpose beyond self.

It is for all these reasons—the priorities and patterns that have illuminated the principles—that the principles, in turn, lead to infinite possibilities. These possibilities are not only for the education of women as full participants in national and international life, but for the education of men as well. Surely men, too, can benefit from the truths unmasked through the study of what works for women (M. E. Tidball 1984).

As a result of gaining a closer understanding of the context in which women's colleges have been founded, have grown and, most importantly, have adapted to the changing scene all around them; as a result of reviewing research relevant to institutional support for women and discovering that all approaches lead to a common end that points to women's colleges; and as a result of bringing forth for others those characteristics of women's colleges that lend themselves to serving as models for educational environments that support all participants; a new opportunity to enliven, enrich, and extend the educational community has been created. Further, beyond that new community there is now a revitalized opportunity for educators in all settings and in all constituencies to be key contributors to the development and expression of an equitable and humane society.

ADDITIONAL
RESOURCES

•••••••••••••

SUPPLEMENT TO CHAPTER 1

Connecting with Global Issues

In Chapter 1, *taking women seriously* applied principally to women in higher education in the United States during the last half century. However, women's colleges and women's organizations in the United States also have a long history of involvement in the education of women worldwide. Many graduates of women's colleges have set out for foreign lands, not only as teachers and missionaries but also as founders of girls' schools and colleges for women. For example, daughter institutions of Mount Holyoke College alone include those in Iran, Spain, and South Africa, as well as in India and Turkey (Green 1979, 345). And while women's access to higher education internationally varies with the culture, economy, and politics of any given country, many women have nonetheless found ways to acquire an education (M. E. Tidball 1977a).

COMING OF AGE

Recent reports of women's education in other lands include their attendance at Ahfad University, in Sudan. First opened as a school for girls in 1907, the institution evolved through high school and college status before becoming a university—the only women's university in Africa. In addition to their formal academic studies, the 4,500 women students learn "leadership qualities" and "initiative." According to their male president, trying to make women more independent through education is facilitated by having an environment in which all the students are women (Useem 1998). In a study on the role of women's colleges in India, several important ways in which women are taken seriously, including both academic and non-academic aspects of education, network building, and leadership development, have been detailed (Singh 1996).

In both of these contemporary examples, it is important to note that an integral part of the education of women is the appreciation that the intersection of individual, institution, and environment—the totality of interrelated aspects of education in its broadest sense—is regularly found to be critical for the education of women. Thus, these international observations add further weight to the repeated finding from the United States that taking women seriously demands a systems approach that includes all constituencies and their interactions (M. E. Tidball 1993).

A WIDER HORIZON

Any discussion of women's education outside the United States must focus more broadly upon issues of work and health, in addition to education itself. The interrelationships among these elements of women's lives have regularly been mentioned, but women continue to struggle for acknowledgment and action. Toward these ends, the recently published wall chart, *1998 Women of Our World*, has included data on several aspects of women's lives (Population Reference Bureau 1998). It is noted that, worldwide, more men than women are literate, although since the 1980s, the gap between girls and boys enrolled in secondary schools has narrowed (from 80 girls enrolled per 100 boys to 90). Further, the accompanying text discusses important issues highlighted at the International Conference on Population and Development in Cairo, as well as at the more recent Fourth World Conference on Women in Beijing. The topics include wage inequities; family planning; maternal mortality; AIDS; domestic violence; and disadvantages faced by adolescent women, elderly women, and women who are heads of households.

Contributions from Women in the United States

In the middle of the 1980s, the American Council on Education, through its Office of Women in Higher Education, recruited 36 women educators to summarize the status of higher education for women in the monograph *Educating the Majority* (Pearson, Shavlik, and Touchton 1989). Justifications for a "New Agenda for Women," articulated in the last chapter of the volume, were encapsulated in 15 guidelines presented as a means to improve the status of women in American higher education. These guidelines, reprinted in Table 14, are clearly applicable to all sizes of institutions of higher education, including small colleges. Several years later, revisions of language and five additional recommendations were developed (Shavlik and Touchton 1992,

47–55). The revised and additional guidelines still focused on education issues, but a subtle shift had occurred: the new guidelines seemed directed toward the complex environments of large institutions, to the exclusion of small colleges. A subsequent, more obvious change in emphasis came about as the result of worldwide interest in the status of women as encouraged by the United Nations.

TABLE 14

GUIDELINES FROM *EDUCATING THE MAJORITY*

1. Seek a strong commitment from the leadership of the institution to understanding and addressing the concerns of women students, faculty, staff, and administrators.

2. Correct inequities in hiring, promotion, tenure, and salary of women faculty, administrators, and staff.

3. Provide a supportive campus climate for women.

4. Make a permanent institutional commitment to women's studies.

5. Review all policies for effect on majority women and minority women and men.

6. Integrate impact studies into planning processes, whether long range or short range.

7. Give specific attention to sexual harassment.

8. Prepare an annual status report [on women].

9. Initiate a campus values inventory.

10. Develop an institution-wide concern for children and families.

11. Appreciate the value of diversity.

12. Make leadership development and commitment to fostering women's leadership joint priorities.

13. Establish or reaffirm the commitment to a Commission on Women.

14. Appoint a high level person whose formal responsibilities include advocacy for women on campus.

15. Create a center for the exploration of community and personal relationships.

Source: Pearson, Shavlik, and Touchton 1989, 446–56.

THE UNITED NATIONS
FOURTH WORLD CONFERENCE ON WOMEN

In September of 1995, the United Nations Fourth World Conference on Women took place in Beijing, China, with more than 30,000 in attendance. At approximately the same time, more than 50,000 members of non-governmental organizations (NGOs) and concerned individuals from all over the world convened in Huairou, just outside Beijing, to discuss the same issues as those on the agenda of the United Nations conference. The outcomes of these conferences were summarized by the staff of the Office of Women in Higher Education in a 28-page pamphlet titled, A *Commitment to the Future: Higher Education and the United Nations Fourth World Conference on Women*. This excerpt from their preface encapsulates the essence and significance of what was accomplished.

> The results of the Conference were profound. Delegates approved and representatives of 189 countries signed the *United Nations Platform for Action*, a forward-looking document dedicated to the proposition that "the empowerment of women is the empowerment of society." The document consists of two parts, "The Beijing Declaration," which commits the signers to advancing the status of women, and the "Platform for Action," which specifies actions to be taken by governments, organizations, and institutions in 12 critical areas of concern to women. (Shavlik, Touchton, and Hoffman 1997)

The document addresses the role of higher education in the implementation of the *Platform for Action*. All of these items are cast in a global context. Many of the concerns presented in the platform have been characterized as "women's issues." To the extent that this occurs, they are likely to be relegated a low priority. This is true even in the United States, especially in those educational institutions that mirror public life and fail to take the aspirations of women seriously.

The following presentation has been adapted from Shavlik, Touchton, and Hoffman. The 12 critical concerns are identified by title, with a statement of the problem followed by general remarks about what education can do. The global-level policies and procedures embodied in the *Platform for Action*, intended to enhance "the empowerment of women" worldwide, are an extension of the concept of *taking women seriously* as advocated in this book.

The Twelve Critical Areas of Concern

1. Women and Poverty The overwhelming majority of the 1 billion people on this planet who live in poverty are women. The number of women living in poverty and the risk of women continuing to live in poverty are both increasing faster than the corresponding figures for men. Women's poverty is related directly to lack of access to education and to barriers that prevent the participation of women in the decision-making processes that affect their lives.

2. Education and Training of Women Women constitute two-thirds of the world's illiterate people. In countries where women have access to higher education, they often encounter conditions in the classroom and elsewhere on the campus that discourage their full participation.

3. Women and Health Women's health involves their emotional, social, and physical well-being and is affected by the social, political, and economic context of their lives. Poor women are particularly vulnerable to being denied adequate health care. There should be equal relationships between women and men in matters of sexual relations and reproduction; decisions about childbearing should be free from discrimination, coercion, and violence.

4. Violence against Women In all societies, women are subject to some degree of physical, sexual, and psychological abuse that cuts across lines of income, class, and culture, in both public and private life. The fear of violence, including harassment, constrains the mobility of women and limits their access to education and financial resources, as well as to both political and economic power.

5. Women and Armed Conflict Peace is a prerequisite for the attainment of equality between women and men, but armed conflict exists throughout the world. Eighty percent of the world's refugees are women and children, who are particularly vulnerable to violations of their human rights. Rape, forced prostitution, and "ethnic cleansing" are used as strategies of war.

6. Women and the Economy Although women contribute significantly to economic life everywhere, they are largely excluded from economic decision making. They often receive low wages for their domestic and community work, or no wages at all. Their employment, economic, and professional opportunities often are restricted by discrimination in education, training, and work conditions.

7. Women in Power and Decision Making   Despite the widespread movement toward democratization in most countries, women remain largely underrepresented at most levels of government, especially at higher levels. Globally, women hold only 10 percent of legislative positions and an even lower percentage of ministerial positions.

8. Advancement of Women   Although many countries have institutional mechanisms to promote the advancement of women, these structures and functions are uneven and inadequate in their effectiveness. As a result, women often are marginalized in government bureaucracies and lack the resources to do their jobs well. The same problem exists at the regional and international levels. Although the number of women who serve as college and university presidents has been increasing, women remain vastly underrepresented in higher education leadership despite their availability and the adequacy of their preparation.

9. Human Rights of Women   The United Nations Conference on Human Rights and the *United Nations Platform for Action* from the Fourth World Conference on Women have declared that women's rights are human rights. All human rights are universal, indivisible, interdependent, and interrelated. Their full and equal enjoyment by women and girls is essential for the advancement of women. However, these declarations will not become reality until all nations review and, if necessary, amend their laws to ensure equality and nondiscrimination, both under the law and in practice.

10. Women and the Media   Many women work in the media, but few hold decision-making positions. In most countries, the media project a negative and demeaning image of women—sometimes reflected in violent and degrading or pornographic presentation of products—that does not reflect women's diverse lives and contributions to society.

11. Women and the Environment   As consumers, producers, caretakers of their families, and educators, women play an important role in sustainable development. But they rarely have formal training as resource managers, and they largely are absent from decision-making processes that affect the environment.

12. The Girl-Child[1]   Because of the lack of protective laws, or a failure to enforce them, the girl-child in many countries is vulnerable to such practices as female genital mutilation, preference for and of male children, early marriage, sexual exploitation, discrimination in access to health care and food allocation, and all kinds of violence. In many countries, girls are neither encouraged nor given the opportunity to attend school for more than a few years; in other countries, girls are discouraged or prohibited from receiving training in mathematics, science, and technology, or advanced training of any kind.

What Higher Education Can Do

The imperatives that follow are derived from the recommendations of Shavlik, Touchton, and Hoffman. Colleges and universities must become knowledge-able about the *Platform for Action* and conversant with the 12 critical areas of concern. They must devote funds to support campus activities (including faculty research) on issues identified in the platform. Surveys must be con-ducted of how the campuses—through classes, co-curricular activities, cam-pus programs, and institutional policies—address issues from the platform. Campus commissions on "Women to implement addressing platform issues" must be created. Presidential speeches, coursework, research, and campus programming must all be used to explore the meaning and implications of the theme "women's rights are human rights." Higher education must be aware of the meetings of the U.N. Commission on the Status of Women and have them serve as a focal point for campus programs. The Internet must be utilized to research the implementation status of the *Platform for Action* in various countries throughout the world. Campuses must sponsor forums through which international students and U.S. students talk about the status of women and girls—including their own personal experiences—in their own cultures. Faculty whose students are seeking careers in education must be encouraged to become sensitive to the 12 critical areas so that new teachers and counse-lors will help eliminate the barriers to equal societal roles for girls and boys. Faculty development workshops must be programmed to encourage utilization of the 12 critical areas to enhance curricular offerings and to incorporate gender perspectives into the curriculum. Legislation and policy at all levels of government, in the United States and in other countries, must be followed and analyzed to ensure that barriers to women's advancement are eliminated. Every institution of higher education must take personal responsibility for enhancing the opportunity for women and men and girls and boys to gain respect for their mutual abilities to contribute to public and private life (Shavlik, Touchton, and Hoffman 1997, 7–18).

SOLIDARITY WITH ALL WOMEN

At the outset, it should be acknowledged that *taking women seriously* and *the empowerment of women* are not mutually exclusive; it is a matter of *both/and* rather than *either/or*. Although the two viewpoints meet in the realm of higher education, their different origins create some particularities that deserve elucidation.

The first 10 guidelines of Table 14 applied to colleges as well as universities, and as a result were not far removed from the subject matter of this book. However, as the language was revised and guidelines added, the concerns were generalized and became more focused on conditions that were primarily relevant to large educational entities. The process of creating guidelines evolved further to the point of substituting the 12 critical issues of the platform derived at Beijing as a starting point for recommendations in which educational concerns became secondary to global issues.

Although the suggestions for what higher education can do were entirely desirable and valid for many environments, they were not in the same frame of reference as *taking women seriously* in the way it has been developed in this book. Rather, the present authors have used women's colleges as exemplars of a variety of educational environments where women are taken seriously. They have advanced three mutually reinforcing streams of research data to confirm that this does indeed take place. They have analyzed many facets of the campus environment to show how taking women seriously is actually enacted among the several constituencies that make up the total environment of women's colleges. The strategies documented in this book are capable of being implemented at many levels, not only in higher education but in various kinds of institutional settings. Thus, while the *empowerment of women* cannot directly achieve taking women seriously, *taking women seriously* can substantially contribute to the transformation of the *Platform for Action* developed at Beijing from its status as an ideal into the realm of reality. In this way, connections with global issues are accomplished and solidarity with all women is affirmed.

NOTE

1. During the process of preparing for the United Nations Fourth World Conference on Women, women attending the African Regional Meeting expressed concern that in many countries, girls are not considered or treated as children; thus arose the term "girl-child." This term draws attention to the rights of girls to be considered important to their societies, to be treated with dignity, and to be given their human rights.

SUPPLEMENT TO CHAPTER 2

Tracking Frames of Reference

.

Databases of educational information are compiled from surveys of individual institutions. This process is called aggregation. Aggregated data (e.g., total enrollment figures) are of general interest, but it must be possible to separate data by institutional type before one can focus on small colleges. Beyond that, to find information on women's colleges, it is necessary to track changes within various subtypes of small colleges. The process that enables these new perspectives is the technique of disaggregation, a powerful tool in contemporary research.

Unfortunately, the extent to which this can be done is limited by the availability of data. Further, it must be acknowledged that no single data source is complete. To follow a given variable over time is not usually possible when using national databases, because decisions affecting inclusion and exclusion of data change from one time period to the next. Even an accurate count of the number of women's colleges at any given moment becomes a matter of opinion (Harwarth, Maline, and DeBra 1997, 28 n. a).

ALTERNATIVE SOURCES

Although all academic institutions report to various regulatory agencies, including the U.S. Department of Education, when this information is made available in annual publications, it is not usually possible to disaggregate the data to obtain details on individual colleges or groups of colleges of the same subtype. At the other extreme, there are data made available in very great detail through the Integrated Postsecondary Education Data System (IPEDS), but the effort involved in aggregating and synthesizing this information in order to present it in a meaningful way is substantial. A third option is to use data published in various editions of college guides where information is presented in a standard format, but two cautions apply: (1) the transfer of information is labor-intensive, and (2) the reliability of this self-reported data is reduced because institutions that compete with one another for students try to put forward the best possible showing in these trade publications. Information from all three of these data sources has been used in Chapter 2 to present the most comprehensive view possible of the molding forces that have changed the parameters of American higher education, with a particular emphasis on how these changes have impacted women's colleges.

DISAGGREGATION BY INSTITUTION TYPE

In the 1950s, the U.S. Office of Education, then part of the Department of Health, Education, and Welfare, maintained a set of institution types for both accredited and non-accredited collegiate institutions. These classifications were functional in nature and were based on curricular and organizational characteristics, as well as on statistical data obtained from the institutions. The classifications were published in an annual *Education Directory*, updated as institutions altered their characteristics, and used as a basis for the reporting in the *Biennial Survey of Education in the United States, 1952–54* (Badger and Rice 1956). For 1953, the types of institution, the number of each type, and relevant enrollment data[1] are shown in Table 15.

Without describing the table in detail, it should be noted that liberal arts colleges represented 38 percent of the institutions by number, were intermediate in size (mean enrollment) and taught 26 percent of the total annual enrollment; two-year institutions, then called junior colleges, represented 28 percent of the institutions, were small in size, and only instructed 12 percent of the annual total enrollment; teachers' colleges and other professional schools represented 24 percent of the institutions, were small in size, and dealt with 12 percent of the enrollment; whereas the large universities and technological schools that represented only 10 percent of the number of institutions matriculated 50 percent of the enrollment. These differences between number of institutions, average size for the type, and share of the total enrollment for the various categories of institutions have undergone substantial changes over the ensuing years.

In the mid-1960s, one measure of a changing climate was that the biennial surveys gave way to annual compilations under the title *Digest of Educational Statistics*. A second change, relating to data for the 1968–69 year, occurred when the Office of Education no longer attempted to identify institutions of

TABLE 15				
Type of Institution by Number and Enrollment in 1953				
		Enrollment		
Type	**Number**	**Mean**	**Total**	**Percent Annual Total**
Liberal Arts Colleges	713	796	567,534	25.6
Junior Colleges	521	510	265,799	12.0
Other Professional Schools*	253	336	84,923	3.8
Teachers Colleges	200	910	181,998	8.2
Universities	131	7,753	1,015,701	45.8
Technological Schools	53	1,931	102,332	4.6
Annual Totals	1,871	1,186†	2,218,287	100.0

Notes
* Other professional schools includes 115 theological schools listed separately in the source
† This number is not the sum of the numbers in the column above it, but is the
   (Annual Total Enrollment) ÷ (Annual Total Number)

Source: Badger and Rice 1956.

higher education by functional categories. From that time to the present, universities have been distinguished from "all other four-year institutions" and two-year institutions, but there has been no subsidiary categorization by institution type, except for the relatively more recent focus on Historically Black colleges and universities.

Fortunately, earlier compilations (Snyder and Hoffman 1995, Table 208) provided data on the number of institutions by size ranges of total enrollment; thus it was possible to divide the "all other four-year institutions" category into two broad types: "small colleges" and those larger entities that included most of the emerging "comprehensive institutions."[2]

However, combining all the colleges below a certain enrollment level does not recreate the former liberal arts colleges category; in 1963, 14 percent of liberal arts colleges had total enrollments in excess of 2,500 students. Similarly, at that time, a significant number of those institutions offering graduate programs below the doctoral level (a portion of the definition for a comprehensive institution) had total enrollments below 2,500 students. As enrollments have increased over the past several decades, the importance of the two exceptions noted has diminished.

The Carnegie Foundation attempted to re-establish a set of functional categories. However, these definitions have also changed over time. A problem is always created when more than one criterion is used to create a category, for example: (1) liberal arts colleges were classified by size, by selectivity, and by the proportion of baccalaureate degrees awarded in traditional liberal arts and science disciplines, (2) comprehensive institutions were classified by size, by the proportion of baccalaureate degrees awarded in occupational or professional disciplines, and by having master's degree programs, (3) doctorate-granting universities were classified by the number of Ph.D.s awarded and by the number of disciplines in which they were awarded, and (4) research universities were classified by giving a high priority to research, by the size of their federal support for research, and by awarding at least 50 Ph.D. degrees each year. The scheme has been revised periodically but has not entirely overcome the problem that some institutions qualify for more than one of the categories. The recent emphasis on ranking institutions of higher education undertaken by *U.S. News and World Report* has produced alternative ways, including geographical considerations, for classifying institutions in higher education. Clearly, a coherent taxonomy for institutions of higher education has not yet been achieved.

Defining "Small College"

There has never been a formal definition of "small college." In the 1950s, most liberal arts colleges (see Table 15) had total enrollments under 2,500 students, but this is not true today. Similarly, there are colleges today that have total enrollments under 2,500 students that are *not* liberal arts colleges. Therefore, provided the functional diversity among those colleges that meet a specific size (enrollment) criterion is acknowledged, it is legitimate to speak of all colleges with total enrollments under 2,500 students as small colleges. Such colleges are important in this book because most women's colleges are small colleges.

It should be noted that the data from the Small College Database[3] are not identical to the total enrollment numbers for small colleges shown in Figure 1 in Chapter 2.

A frequency distribution (number at specified interval over range) for the number of colleges at various sizes (as measured by full-time enrollment) was plotted as a histogram where the interval was set at 100 students and the range was from 0 to 1,999 students. Such a graphic representation supports the concept of small colleges as a separate entity. Using data from the four datapoints of the Small College Database (1963, 1973, 1983, and 1993), there was a consistent peak of more than 50 colleges per interval. The peak occurred at all intervals between 500 and 899 students over the 30-year period, and there was only a small drift toward larger size. Although many more students are represented in intervals above 2,000 students, the interval of 100 students is sufficiently narrow that the larger colleges and universities are spread out along the enrollment axis and no other peak occurs.

TABLE 16		
Comparison of Data from Two Different Sources		
Item	**Figure 1**	**Table 18**
Source	U.S. Dept. of Education	Small College Database
Time frame	1953; 1963; 1974; 1983; 1993	1963; 1973; 1983; 1993
Number of colleges	906; 1,031; 1,210; 1,335; 1,383	750; 748; 762; 721
Accreditation status	includes non-accredited	all accredited
Basis for size	total enrollment*	full-time enrollment
Upper limit of size	2,500	2,000
Basis for upper limit	published table	analysis of frequency distribution
Individual college data	none tabulated	more than 40 variables

Note
* Full-time enrollment plus the head count of part-time enrollment.

There are substantive differences between the data from the U.S. Department of Education and the data from the Small College Database (see Table 16). It can be stipulated that the standard deviations for the five means of the small college *total enrollment* depicted in Figure 1 are very large. This is also true of the standard deviations for the four means of the small college *full-time enrollment* from the Small College Database shown in Table 18. Therefore, either set of means (and, by extension, other derived numbers) are legitimate representations of the "true" population of small colleges. To put it another way, the colleges in the Small College Database are fewer in number than the institutions depicted as small colleges in Figure 1. Nevertheless, the former represent a legitimate subset that is large enough to justify its use in creating generalizations that apply to groups of similar small colleges.

SMALL COLLEGES

With a few exceptions, the women's colleges that are of primary interest in this volume are small colleges. Information on small colleges has not been summarized in the education literature in a systematic manner. It is of sufficient interest in understanding the impact of changes in higher education on women's colleges to provide a brief overview of small college information.

Relative Constancy of the Number of Small Colleges

For the 1963 datapoint, the Small College Database used as a primary source the first edition of *Comparative Guide to American Colleges* (Cass and Birnbaum 1964) along with a definition of a small college as one with an enrollment of less than 2,000 full-time students. All institutions listed in this compilation

were accredited by the appropriate regional accrediting association. On this
basis, there were 750 small colleges with an average size of 891 students. At
subsequent datapoints, the number of small colleges was increased by newly
accredited colleges and decreased by colleges that outgrew the small college
definition, as well as by colleges no longer listed in subsequent editions of the
primary source.

The first new finding to emerge from a review of the data in the Small
College Database was the relative constancy of the number of accredited small

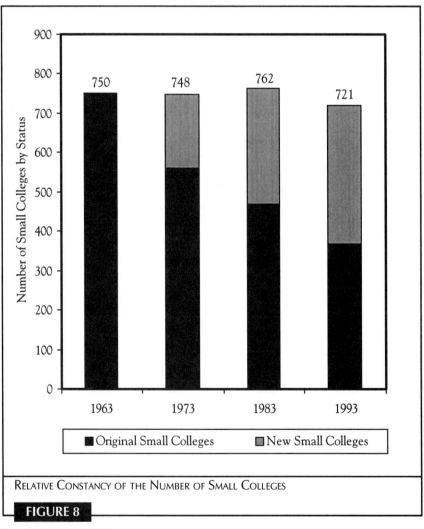

RELATIVE CONSTANCY OF THE NUMBER OF SMALL COLLEGES

FIGURE 8

Source: C. S. Tidball 1996.

colleges from one decade to another. This is shown in a stacked bar graph in Figure 8. Note that only about half of the original small colleges present in 1963 were still listed in the primary source by 1993. A more complete picture of the changes in number of institutions can be found in Table 17.

The closure of small colleges is a real phenomenon that has received some attention in the media. A parallel trend, which has had less exposure, is the increase in size of some small colleges to the point where they can no longer be considered small; this change has contributed to the growth in number and enrollment of the comprehensive institutions, many of which were public institutions that began as teachers' colleges. What has not been recognized is the emergence of newly accredited small colleges, which has tended to keep the number of small colleges relatively constant over the three decades from 1963 to 1993. The absence of substantial increases in mean enrollment from one decade to another, as shown in Table 18, is additional evidence that the small colleges do represent a separate entity.

Changes in the Number of Small Colleges by Subtype

In order to understand the impact of demographic changes on women's colleges, it is necessary to disaggregate the data by small college subtype. Such an effort has been done in Table 3 in Chapter 2, but that focus was on *student enrollment*. In this supplement, the effort will be repeated, but the focus will be on *number of colleges*. Thus, Table 18 shows the actual number of colleges and mean enrollment for each subtype from 1963 to 1993.

TABLE 17

NUMBER OF SMALL COLLEGES BY STATUS

Status / Year	1963	1973	1983	1993
Original Small Colleges	750	561	470	367
New Small Colleges	0	187	292	354
Total Small Colleges	750	748	762	721
Enrollment >1,999*	11†	123	157	213
Closed Small Colleges	0	66	104	175
Total in Database	761	937	1,023	1,109

Notes
* Small colleges that became larger than the size definition.
† These colleges had enrollments larger than 2,000 full-time students in 1963, but they dropped below 2,000 students at a later datapoint. The earlier data were added for the sake of completeness.

Source: C. S. Tidball 1996.

TABLE 18								

FULL-TIME ENROLLMENT FOR SMALL COLLEGES

College Subtype	1963		1973		1983		1993	
	No.	Mean	No.	Mean	No.	Mean	No.	Mean
Coeducational Colleges	481	961	485	1,209	532	979	503	1,025
Men's Colleges	79	926	30	1,033	17	1,081	7	1,055
Women's Colleges	173	667	106	700	85	736	60	770
Men's Change Colleges	11	1,305	56	1,243	54	1,212	65	1,284
Wom. Change Colleges	6	500	71	654	74	755	86	872
All Small Colleges*	750	891	748	963	762	949	721	1,009

Note
* The total numbers (No.) are identical to the numbers in Figure 8. The standard deviations for the four mean enrollment numbers are: 1963 = 443; 1973 = 454; 1983 = 475; and 1993 = 470.

Source: C. S. Tidball 1996.

It is possible to extract from Table 18 some estimates of how each subtype has fared during this turbulent half century. The apparent increase in the number of coeducational colleges masks the fact that many coeducational colleges closed their doors in this period. As seen in Table 17, between 1983 and 1993 there were 62 new small colleges that were all coeducational. But during this same time interval, as shown in Table 18, the sum of all coeducational colleges had decreased by 29 colleges. This means that approximately 90 coeducational colleges either ceased operations or grew beyond the size limit for a small college during that 10-year period alone.

The situation with regard to the men's colleges and the women's colleges is more complicated to analyze, but here, too, some inferences can be made to approximate the number of closures. The sum of the men's colleges and the men's change colleges[4] was 90 in 1963; that same sum was 72 in 1993. This represents a net loss of 18 colleges or 20 percent of the 1963 total. The sum of the women's colleges and the women's change colleges in 1963 was 179; that sum was 146 in 1993. This represents a net loss of 33 colleges or 18 percent of the 1963 total. Thus, both the men's colleges and the women's colleges decreased in number during the 30-year period, in approximately the same proportion.

RECAPITULATION

The database issues relating to the momentous changes that have taken place in American higher education during the past five decades have been presented. Those who attempt to create a coherent view of change over such an extended time frame must contend with differences in the way that information is tabulated even from the same source. It was acknowledged that no single source of information is adequate to present any "complete" picture. Thus, the assumptions made to resolve inconsistencies should be available to the reader who is willing to keep the constraints in mind as understanding emerges.

The frame of reference has been American higher education, but it has been necessary to disaggregate annual enrollment numbers by categories not presented in the annual compilations from the U.S. Department of Education. This has led to reliance on other sources. It was desired to understand the impact of higher education changes on women's colleges. This required defining a "new" entity, the small college, and identifying ways to track information on this group of similar colleges. Moreover, women's colleges are a subset of small colleges. Although coeducational colleges are the largest of the three traditional subtypes of small colleges, the picture has become complicated by the almost complete disappearance of men's colleges and the introduction of two new subtypes, namely, the women's change colleges and the men's change colleges. These two new subtypes were included because institutional environments measured by group demographic data for these colleges differ not only from that of the historically coeducational colleges, but even moreso from each other, in ways beyond the differences in admissions policy.

The impact of these perturbations in higher education has been momentous. All independent and church-affiliated small colleges have been squeezed. However, the women's colleges have been especially versatile, and creative adaptations have enabled them to preserve women as their first priority, that is, to continue taking women seriously.

NOTES

1. As used in presentations of statistical data maintained by the United States government, the term "total enrollment" is understood to mean full-time students *plus* a head count of part-time students.
2. See Chapter 2, Note 3.
3. The Small College Database was developed by Charles S. Tidball during the 1980s and 1990s. It contained demographic information on the universe of accredited colleges that ever had a full-time enrollment of less than 2,000 students (which currently consists of 1,109 colleges). The database is not available in hard copy but is stored in a computerized version located at the Tidball Center for the Study of Educational Environments at Hood College. Four datapoints at 10-year intervals are available: 1963, 1973, 1983, and 1993. The information consists of five fields that are present at each datapoint and six fields containing time-specific information. All data are sex-disaggregated to the extent that such information was available in the public domain. New fields for faculty information were added in 1983. Additional new fields for information on part-time enrollment were added in 1993.
4. See Chapter 2 for a complete discussion of the rationale for use of the terms "men's change college" and "women's change college."

SUPPLEMENT TO CHAPTER 3

From Baccalaureate Origins to Institutional Productivity

INTRODUCTION

The term *baccalaureate origins* has appeared in a variety of contexts. An early use of the expression occurred in an effort to refine information stored in the Doctorate Records File, a database maintained by the Office of Scientific Personnel of the National Research Council/National Academy of Sciences. There, the original data provided by the doctorate recipients was "double-checked by sending to each school of *baccalaureate origin* (emphasis added) the complete list of its graduates included in the files, with the request that they check it, correct it if necessary, and supplement it if incomplete" (Harmon and Soldz 1963, iv). The difficulties of maintaining accurate lists of undergraduate institutions over time because of mergers, closings, and changes of names are also set forth in the document cited above.

A second use of the expression baccalaureate origins is in the context of describing geography as a factor relating to doctoral productivity. Ingenious figures were developed comparing the geographic regions of the United States with such regional variables as: relative land areas, relative population, baccalaureate origins of doctorates, and doctorate producers (Harmon and Soldz 1963, 27). The underlying data were subdivided by state within each region and by broad doctoral field but not by collegiate institution.

A third use of this phrase was in the tabulation of the "Leading Forty Baccalaureate Origins Institutions in Each Decade of Doctorate Production, 1920–1961" (Harmon and Soldz 1963, 31). In Appendix 4 of the cited

162

publication, some 1,200 baccalaureate institutions were identified, even if as few as one of their graduates went on to obtain a research doctorate in the period from 1920–1961 (Harmon and Soldz 1963, 86–119). A second measure of the thoroughness of this particular source is the listing of the leading foreign baccalaureate institutions whose graduates went on to obtain research doctorates in the United States (Harmon and Soldz 1963, 36).

This third use of the term baccalaureate origins, and the methodology that links the accomplishments of graduates to particular baccalaureate environments, begins the evolutionary trail that will be followed in this supplement. Although information about specific individuals is used to develop measures of productivity, it should be emphasized that the focus of the method is on drawing conclusions about institutional environments. The researchers cited above made no attempt to adjust the information for differences in institution size or type of undergraduate college. Neither did they acknowledge sex, race, ethnicity, or other characteristics of the doctorate recipient.

Such research based on baccalaureate origins has evolved during the last four decades. At first, only staff members affiliated with those institutions that maintained databases could undertake this type of research. However, the advent of computerized lists that could be queried, and from which specialized printouts could be commissioned, has altered the landscape and made it possible for research in this field to be conducted more widely.

Components of Baccalaureate Origins Research

Several components must be considered when designing research on baccalaureate origins. The focus in such studies is not only on institutions that grant the baccalaureate degree but on those collegiate environments that nurture their students in such a way as to be especially productive in the proportion of their graduates who go on to postbaccalaureate achievement. Thus there are baccalaureate *graduates* and a number of them become *achievers*; but in order to calculate the *productivity* of a collegiate environment and compare it with others, that productivity must be adjusted for the size of the baccalaureate institution (achievers ÷ graduates).[1] A number of sources catalog achievers of various kinds; some, like the Doctorate Records File, have considerable detail about individuals, including where they went to college and when they graduated. However even this rich source does not provide either the number of graduates in the year of graduation or the size of the collegiate institution. For that information, which is needed to calculate productivity, the investigator must turn to another database containing the number of graduates for each institution and undertake the requisite calculations.

Frame of Reference

Before leaving this introduction, it would seem appropriate to contrast two approaches to data analysis when undertaking research on baccalaureate origins. The number of baccalaureate degree–granting institutions in the United States is large and growing. One way to reduce the data processing effort is to obtain random samples from compilations of achievers and determine the baccalaureate origins of those individuals before aggregating the results in order to draw conclusions. Using this approach, conventional statistical methods apply, and the use of well-established indices of significance are not only appropriate but essential. This approach has the advantage that there is no subjective element in selecting the collegiate institutions, since they emerge from the achievers selected at random. However, there is a risk of using a sampling approach, especially when dealing with smaller collegiate institutions and data from achieving women graduates of various races—some essential differences may be missed completely.

An alternative is to use a population demographic approach. By defining a population in advance—for example, those baccalaureate institutions that have had more than 2 percent of their women graduates of a specified decade go on to obtain a research doctorate by a specified date—it is possible to decrease the data processing to manageable proportions without drawing random samples from the underlying universe. Under these circumstances, the differences between productivity rates of comparable institutions are not *estimates* of differences derived from sample data but are based on data from the entire population. As such, these differences are *real* differences and it would be inappropriate to calculate a statistical index to determine whether or not such differences are "significant." This approach is much enhanced when conclusions are based not on results from a single collegiate institution but on collective data from groups of similar colleges.

Time to Degree

An issue that has surfaced in the literature on doctorate recipients—and that continues to be tabulated—is the time interval between the baccalaureate degree and the receipt of the doctorate (Thurgood and Clarke 1995, 28). This is important because the time-to-degree interval is defined in two different ways: (1) registered time, restricted to the time that the doctoral degree aspirant is actually enrolled in an academic program, and (2) total elapsed time, measured from the first registration to the date on which the degree is conferred. These measures differ from one another, but more important, they vary by field of doctorate, by sex, by race/ethnic status, and (for non-U.S. citizens) by residency in the United States. Thus, the issue of time to degree becomes a concern only for those investigators who attempt to make generalizations about baccalaureate origins from doctorate data without determining the baccalaureate year, the sex, the race/ethnicity, and the doctoral field for *each* doctorate recipient.

The methodologies of most of the studies described below have been designed specifically to avoid this potential problem. This was accomplished by defining a long time period for baccalaureate input, generally one or more decades, and making certain that the analysis linked individual graduates directly to their own achievements. Typically, this was done by starting with the achiever and making sure that all relevant information was utilized in performing both aggregation and disaggregation of the data. It is also desirable to allow sufficient time between ending the baccalaureate input and identifying achievers so that a high proportion of those who will become achievers are included in the study.

EARLY EFFORTS

It is not known exactly when baccalaureate origins began to be used as a tool to make comparisons among various types of undergraduate environments. Well before any research using such methods was published in professional journals, informal studies were conducted either by education associations, research agencies, or the colleges themselves.[2]

One early work using this approach appeared in *Science* (Knapp and Goodrich 1951). The focus of the study was on "the undergraduate origins of American scientists" and on "the factors that account for the varying achievements of American colleges and universities" in the "production of scientists." The paper is only two pages long and has no citations.[3] In spite of such brevity, many of the crucial elements of the method can be found in this work: (1) the time period over which graduates were identified, (2) the measure of achievement, (3) the time period between graduation and the achievement, (4) the basis for selection of undergraduate institutions, (5) an adjustment for the size of undergraduate institutions, (6) techniques used to decrease the data processing effort, and (7) special features of the analysis.

An assessment follows, in narrative form, of the seven crucial elements in Knapp and Goodrich's study; the data can also be found in synopsis form in Table 19. Graduates were identified over a relatively long (11-year) period, from 1924 to 1934. The authors indicate that this interval was selected to minimize any contribution to the findings of the impact of World War I. The measure of achievement was "full professional status as an American scientist." One could debate the exact meaning of the measure, but most would agree that the two criteria used—obtaining a doctorate in the natural sciences and being listed in the seventh (1944) edition of *American Men of Science*— were appropriate. The time between graduation and achievement was depen-

---

TABLE 19

SYNOPSIS OF METHODOLOGY—1951

1. Time period over which graduates were identified
   Eleven years, from 1924 to 1934
2. Measure of achievement
   "Full professional status as an American scientist"
3. Time period between graduation and achievement
   Approximately 10–20 years (dependent on year of graduation)
4. Selection of achievers
   In order to identify productivity leaders, the entire population of
   achievers graduating from 1924 to 1934 was studied
5. Adjustment for size of undergraduate institutions
   The number of achievers was tabulated per 1,000 graduates
6. Techniques to decrease data processing effort
   Data from colleges with less than 30 graduates were excluded
7. Special features
   - The analysis was restricted to data on men college graduates
   - Data were disaggregated by the following institutional types: liberal arts
     colleges (n=153), eminent universities (n=50), Catholic institutions
     (n=not specified), engineering schools (n=not specified), and agricultural
     colleges (n=not specified)
   - Although 19 institutional variables were evaluated, only 2 were found to
     be correlated to the productivity of scientists: (a) geographic location of
     collegiate institutions (far east and middle west = high productivity, New
     England and middle Atlantic = moderate productivity, south = low
     productivity), and (b) minimum cost of student attendance (low cost =
     low productivity, middle cost = high productivity, and high cost = low
     productivity).

Source: Knapp and Goodrich 1951.

dent on the year of graduation, but the 10- to 20-year period between
graduation and being listed in the seventh edition of *American Men of Science*
was long enough that most of the graduates who were to achieve "full
professional status as an American scientist" would have had sufficient time
for their names to be included in that compilation.

In any study of institutional productivity, those institutions that produce
large numbers of graduates are favored. Knapp and Goodrich developed their
productivity index as achievers per 1,000 graduates to minimize this bias and
computed individual values for each of the undergraduate institutions included. Limiting the study population to those colleges that had at least 30
graduates over the 11-year collection period was a reasonable way to decrease
the data processing effort. Details are not specified in the paper, but in order to
identify productivity leaders, it would seem that the entire population of
achievers who had graduated in the period from 1924 to 1934 was studied.

The use of a round number of "eminent universities" suggests that the selection of undergraduate institutions was done by the investigators on a subjective basis. Although the total number of colleges whose data were included is not provided, it appears that more than 300 institutions were studied; such a group of productivity leaders would be expected to have graduated in excess of 80 percent of those who would have achieved the indicated measure over the designated period.

Special Features   The decision to limit the study to men was justified by the authors "in order to eliminate any discrimination against coeducational institutions." Coeducational colleges and universities were included in the analysis, but, presumably, the number of women graduates was not part of the total number of graduates from those institutions. In actuality, during the time period of the study, the number of American women scientists was small, and limiting the study to men simplified the data processing effort. Even at that early date, a concern for what belongs in the numerators and the denominators of the productivity indices used to characterize the institutions can be seen. Data were originally disaggregated by two types: 153 liberal arts colleges that met the inclusion criterion and 50 "eminent" universities. Later, some additional institutions were added: Roman Catholic institutions (regardless of size), engineering schools, and agricultural colleges. Fourteen to 19 institutional variables were identified and calculated for the appropriate institutions.

Conclusions   Only two common factors were significantly correlated: (1) a geographic proclivity[4] among the graduates who went on to become scientists, and (2) a relationship[5] between the cost of the undergraduate education and the college's productivity of scientists. The paper discussed the difficulty of finding significant correlations between the identified differences and such institutional variables as entrance requirements, proportion of Ph.D.s on the science faculty, and attrition between freshman and senior year. Thus can be demonstrated the way the method is developed, the labor involved in identifying achievers, the focus on institutions, the adjustments that were made to make data processing efficient, the criteria used for institutional selection, the effort in finding the best correlations for the differences identified, and the difficulty of interpreting results especially in terms of what constituted the popular educational variables of the time. It should be emphasized that Goodrich was a natural scientist; he and Knapp approached this study on the social implications of where American scientists had obtained their undergraduate preparation without preconceived opinions or the desire to validate stated hypotheses. Rather, they collected data and let the numbers speak for themselves.

APPLYING BACCALAUREATE ORIGIN STUDIES TO WOMEN

> Identifying the baccalaureate origins of achieving women might seem
> to be a relatively straightforward task. It is not. Difficulties arise
> because many standard information sources are inadequate or incom-
> plete, because the definition of achievement not only is open to
> interpretation but also is limited by the resources available, and be-
> cause the number of achieving women by any measure is small and
> rendered smaller when only those achievers who have graduated from
> college are selected. (M. E. Tidball 1980a, 504)

In 1968, M. Elizabeth Tidball was a recently elected trustee of Mount Holyoke
College. She wanted to be well informed about the highly charged debate over
coeducation that was current at the time. To her dismay, no data existed to
enlighten her. Thus, in the manner of a natural scientist, she proceeded to
devise and carry out experiments in response to the question, What are the
relative rates of postbaccalaureate accomplishment for graduates of women's
colleges in comparison to women graduates of coeducational institutions? No
one had ever studied, on a national scale, the post-college career outcomes of
women as a function of institutional characteristics. Indeed, her work inaugu-
rated a new field of research that came to be known as "the social psychology
of higher education for women."

Securing publication of this interdisciplinary work was not straightforward.
Her statistical confirmation of a role model theory for women seemed "too hot
to handle." After four years of being sidestepped, never blatantly rejected, she
was finally heard by a brave editor who published most of the results, though
little of the method and none of the figures, tables, or other scholarly details
(M. E. Tidball 1973b).[6]

The study alluded to above can be summarized by using the same seven
criteria that were set out with regard to the Knapp and Goodrich article
detailed earlier. See Table 20 for the complete data in synopsis form; the text
that follows only highlights special areas of interest. The time period over
which graduates were identified was long, namely the five decades between
1910 and 1960. The measure of achievement was being listed in one of three
successive editions of Who's Who of American Women (1966–71). The time
period between graduation and the achievement for the 1,116 women who
had graduated from college was dependent on the year of graduation but
varied from a low of 11 years to a high of 61 years. There was no selection of
undergraduate institutions, rather, the random sampling of the listees determined the 59 women's colleges and the 289 coeducational institutions that
entered the database.

TABLE 20

SYNOPSIS OF METHODOLOGY—1970

1. Time period over which graduates were identified
   Five decades, from 1910 to 1960
2. Measure of achievement
   Being listed in *Who's Who of American Women* (1966–71)
3. Time period between graduation and achievement
   Varied from 11 to 61 years (dependent on year of graduation)
4. Selection of achievers
   A 2 percent random sample of achievers was selected from the primary source
5. Adjustment for size of undergraduate institutions
   Data were tabulated as achievers per graduates, multiplied by 100
6. Techniques to decrease data processing effort
   A random sample of 500 names (2 percent) was selected from each of the 4th, 5th, and 6th editions of the reference work cited above; the 384 women who had not graduated from college were excluded from further analysis
7. Special features
   - The analysis was restricted to data on women college graduates
   - Analysis of individual data in each subsample from the separate editions indicated that the entire group (n=1,116) could be treated as a single entity
   - Personal data also substantiated similarity of achievers regardless of the collegiate source
   - Data were disaggregated by the following institutional types: women's colleges (n=59), coeducational colleges and universities (n=289)
   - Productivity of achieving women was correlated positively with the number of women faculty and negatively with the number of men students
   - Analysis of productivity versus other institutional variables was performed

Sources: M. E. Tidball 1970; 1973b; 1974a; 1980a.

To eliminate a bias in favor of large institutions, for each of the women's colleges and the coeducational institutions, productivity was expressed as achievers per decade divided by the number of graduates in that decade. To reduce the data processing effort (all done by hand in that era) graduates earlier than 1910 or later than 1960 were excluded.

Special Features Only women college graduates were used in the analysis. The restriction to those women who had actually obtained baccalaureate degrees set important minimums on their motivation, financial resources, persistence, intellectual capacity, ability to complete a task, and hence their comparability.[7] Data on individual characteristics substantiated that there were no differences that could be correlated with institutional type in achievers as persons. Institutional productivity with respect to women achievers was correlated positively with the number of women faculty at the colleges attended (higher at women's colleges) and negatively with the presence of men students (higher at coeducational colleges).

The prior study, published in increments over more than a decade (M. E. Tidball 1970; 1973b; 1974a; 1975; 1980a), made it clear that, as persons, achievers graduating from women's colleges were not different from women achievers graduating from coeducational colleges; what was different was the rate at which these two institution types produced achievers, with the women's colleges producing approximately twice as many achievers as the coeducational institutions over the same period of time. For a more detailed discussion of the results, see Chapter 3.

A LANDMARK STUDY

One of the methodological concerns that surfaced as a result of the publication of the study summarized above was the long time period between obtaining the baccalaureate degree and the acknowledgement of career or volunteer success by being listed in *Who's Who of American Women*. Some who were reluctant to accept the validity of the findings countered with the erroneous suggestion that the conditions described in the research may have existed at some time in the past, but they were certainly no longer present! Thus, it became desirable to select a measure of achievement that could be documented with closer proximity to the four-year college experience.

The attainment of a research doctorate was such an achievement. Not only was this achievement less subjective than a listing in a registry, there was an available database that was in computer-searchable form, the Doctorate Records File (DRF) maintained by the Office of Scientific Personnel of the National Research Council/National Academy of Sciences, which contained information on all recipients of research doctorates from 1920 to the present. In 1975, a 5 percent random sample printout of women who received doctorates from 1920 to 1973 was obtained from the DRF. Those data were used for an analysis by field of doctoral selection for women graduates from both women's and coeducational colleges (M. E. Tidball 1980a).

Those data were also used to assist in the identification of baccalaureate institutions to be included in a subsequent study that set improved methodological standards for this kind of research (M. E. Tidball and Kistiakowsky 1976). This study was the first example of a research publication that provided data for women and men separately, also showing the productivity of a broad range of types of collegiate institutions in both absolute terms and as a percentage of the number of institutional graduates.

Once again, the seven reference quantities can provide an overview of methodology. The complete data in synopsis form can be found in Table 21; some highlights are presented in the following text. A long period was used to

---

TABLE 21

SYNOPSIS OF METHODOLOGY—1976

1. Time period over which graduates were identified
   - Six decades, from 1910 to 1969, for absolute productivity
   - Four decades (1920–39 and 1950–69) for percentage productivity
2. Measure of achievement
   Obtaining a research doctorate in the period from 1920 to 1973
3. Time period between graduation and achievement
   Varied from 11 to 63 years (dependent on year of graduation)
4. Selection of achievers
   The entire population of achievers graduating from the selected institutions was accepted into the study
5. Adjustment for size of undergraduate institutions
   - None for tabulation by absolute productivity
   - Achievers were also tabulated as a percentage of graduates
6. Techniques to decrease data processing effort
   A defined population was created that identified the 137 leaders for percentage productivity
7. Special features
   - The analysis included data for both women and men separately
   - A correction was applied for first professional degrees included in early baccalaureate listings
   - The following types of undergraduate institutions emerged from the primary productivity data: women's colleges, men's colleges, coeducational colleges, private universities, and public universities
   - Data were disaggregated by broad field of the doctorate
   - Baccalaureate institutions were ranked by the number of doctoral fields in which their graduates had received doctorates
   - Characteristics that were associated with productivity leaders for women were differentiated from those that were associated with productivity leaders for men

Source: M. E. Tidball and Kistiakowsky 1976.

identify graduates. The measure of achievement was obtaining a research doctorate in the period from 1920 to 1973;[8] the period between graduation and achievement was variable but was long enough to capture more than 50,000 women and more than 350,000 men graduates who went on to earn doctorates. The original selection of undergraduate institutions was based on two components: 100 research universities that were leaders in research and development funding and 50 highly productive four-year colleges. This number was reduced by restricting the study population to those institutions with at least 400 graduates of either sex who, during a 40-year period, went on to receive research doctorates. Productivity for the 137 leaders was presented in both absolute terms and in terms corrected for size of the undergraduate institutions. The data processing effort was reduced by using the population as defined above.

Special Features   Data for both women and men were provided.[9] The following institutional types emerged from the listings: women's colleges, men's colleges, coeducational colleges, private universities, and public universities. A number of additional variables were tabulated, including: lists of leaders by both absolute and percentage productivity, leading producers for each of five broad doctoral fields, and a comparison of those leaders by the number of doctoral fields in which they were cited. This study established that there were distinct differences in the baccalaureate origins of women and men who go on to earn doctorates. For further details on the findings, see Chapter 3.

BACCALAUREATE ORIGIN RESEARCH WITH DISAGGREGATION BY RACE/ETHNICITY

A recent study utilizing a baccalaureate origins approach provides additional applications of this methodology (Wolf-Wendel 1998). The methodology for that study is presented in synopsis form in Table 22. The starting time for the collection of graduates was 1965. Two measures of achievement were utilized: (1) obtaining a research doctorate in the period from 1975 to 1991, and (2) being listed in the 1991–92 edition of either *Who's Who in America*, *Who's Who among Black Americans*, or *Who's Who among Hispanic Americans*. A correction for institutional size was based on tabulating achievers per 1,000 students, using the mean enrollment instead of graduates. Data processing effort was reduced by using smaller defined populations of the highly productive institutions for the three groups that were the subject of the study.

Special Features   In this research, Wolf-Wendel studied only women but divided them into European American, African American, and Latina subgroups. Different measures of achievement for each subgroup were utilized, but for all three subgroups, one measure was the earning of a research doctorate, a criterion that made it possible to make comparisons with earlier work. An interesting finding from this effort is that the lists of leading institutions providing graduates that went on to outstanding achievement for the three different subgroups have very little overlap; for details, see Chapter 3. Extensive tables of descriptive statistics were provided on the three sets of highly productive undergraduate institutions. Eight sets of ranking tables for the "top 10" baccalaureate-granting institutions were created for each group. Additional analyses were conducted on these highly ranked colleges.

A final refinement of methodology in these studies is the use of quantitative data derived from productivities to assist in the selection of institutions where case studies were subsequently undertaken. The methodology of these on-site campus visits with their extensive in-depth interviews of various campus constituents is the subject of the Supplement to Chapter 5; the results from case studies at two women's colleges are presented in Chapter 5.

TABLE 22

SYNOPSIS OF METHODOLOGY—1995

1. Time period over which graduates were identified
     The starting time for the collection of graduates was 1965
2. Measure of achievement
     Obtaining a research doctorate in the period from 1975 to 1991 and being
     listed in the 1991–92 edition of either *Who's Who in America, Who's Who
     among Black Americans,* or *Who's Who among Hispanic Americans*
3. Time period between graduation and achievement
     A minimum of nine years
4. Selection of undergraduate institutions
     All U.S. institutions were ranked for each category of achievement
5. Adjustment for size of undergraduate institutions
     Achievers were tabulated per 1,000 students of mean enrollment
6. Techniques to decrease data processing effort
     Defined populations were created, which identified: (1) the 761 highly
     productive institutions for European American women, (2) the 250 highly
     productive institutions for African American women, and (3) the 131 highly
     productive institutions for Latinas
7. Special features
     • The analysis included only data for women, but three different racial/
       ethnic groups were considered separately
     • Extensive descriptive statistics were provided on the three sets of highly
       productive undergraduate institutions
     • Eight sets of ranking tables for the "top 10" baccalaureate-granting
       institutions were created for each racial/ethnic group; extensive further
       analyses were conducted on these highly ranked colleges
     • Relevant published findings that impinged on the major conclusions of
       this study were compared and contrasted

Sources: Wolf-Wendel 1995; 1998.

A NEW MEASURE OF ACHIEVEMENT

By selecting the obtaining of a research doctorate as the measure of achievement, the time period between graduation and the achievement was narrowed, but it was still some 5 to 15 years, depending on the doctoral field of study. Another investigation was devised to reduce this interval.

In 1961, a study appeared entitled "Baccalaureate Origins of 1950–1959 Medical Graduates" (Manuel and Altenderfer 1961). Because "medicine is practiced largely by men," the authors "decided to concentrate the major . . . analysis on the production of male premedical students." Two decades later, society had changed dramatically. Two new patterns in higher education had emerged: (1) many undergraduate institutions that had previously enrolled only women students or only men students began to enroll students of both sexes, and (2) there was a substantial increase in the number of women pursuing medical degrees. One result of the increase in female entrants to medical school was that, for the first time, there was a large enough population of women to allow reliable studies of the productivity for both women and men medical school entrants.

However, before any new study could be initiated, database development had to be a significant portion of the effort. Not only was there no equivalent of the Doctorate Records File for those who earn medical doctorates, there were no systematic data available to classify graduates of medical schools by baccalaureate origin and sex. After an extended effort with the staff of the Association of American Medical Colleges, a database was commissioned that made it possible to make comparisons with the 1961 study and also to encompass the new developments indicated above. All medical school entrants for each of the four years from 1975 through 1978[10] were listed by sex and by baccalaureate origin if they had received their baccalaureate degrees in the year of entry, plus or minus two years. This information had to be correlated with a second database commissioned from the National Center for Education Statistics of the Department of Education to provide the numbers of women and men graduates for all of the baccalaureate-granting institutions in the United States for the appropriate years.

The study appeared in the *Journal of Higher Education* (M. E. Tidball 1985). Its methodology is presented in synopsis form in Table 23, with some highlights discussed below. The measure of achievement was entry into an American medical school during the period from 1975 through 1978. The time period between graduation and the achievement for the majority of the graduates was a matter of months.[11]

There was no prior (subjective) selection of undergraduate institutions. Those institutions that emerged did so by meeting the minimum standards of productivity used to determine the study population. The data processing effort was reduced by restricting the analysis to a population of baccalaureate institutions that had 20 or more (at least 10 of whom were women) graduates entering American medical schools in the 1975–78 period.

Special Features   Data were presented for women and men separately. Tabulations included: (1) a comparison of demographic data for the 1950–59 medical school graduates of the earlier study with that for medical entrants from 1975–78, (2) entry rates disaggregated by institutional type, (3) rankings of leaders by number of entrants, as well as by entrants as a percentage of graduates, (4) a comparison of the baccalaureate origins of medical entrants with those of doctoral scientists, and (5) an appendix giving raw data for the 277 leading producers of medical school entrants.

Although the detailed findings as they relate to the subject of this volume have been presented in Chapter 3, it is appropriate to indicate here that the methodology supported the following items: generalizations about differences

---

TABLE 23

Synopsis of Methodology—1985

1. Time period over which graduates were identified
   Eight years, from 1973 to 1980
2. Measure of achievement
   Being accepted and actually enrolling in an American medical school during the four-year period from 1975 through 1978
3. Time period between graduation and achievement
   For most graduates, a matter of months (dependent on year of graduation)
4. Selection of undergraduate institutions
   Objective selection of institutions on the basis of a specified number of entrants
5. Adjustment for size of undergraduate institutions
   • None for tabulation by absolute number
   • Achievers were also tabulated as a percentage of graduates
6. Techniques to decrease data processing effort
   A defined population was created that identified the 277 institutional productivity leaders
7. Special features
   • The analysis included data for both women and men separately
   • The following types of undergraduate institutions were identified: women's colleges, women's change colleges, men's colleges, men's change colleges, coeducational colleges, private universities with medical schools, private universities without medical schools, public universities with medical schools, and public universities without medical schools
   • Baccalaureate institutions were ranked for both women and men by number and percent of medical school entrants
   • An appendix included raw data for the 277 leading producers of medical entrants

Source: M. E. Tidball 1985.

---

from the 1961 study; entry rates by sex for nine different types of collegiate environments including women's colleges, men's colleges, historically coeducational colleges, women's change colleges, men's change colleges,[12] private universities with and without affiliated medical schools, and public universities with and without affiliated medical schools; the identification of the most productive undergraduate colleges by absolute number and also by percentage of graduates; and a general discussion of institutional environments and student outcomes.

Further, the issue of the delay between collegiate graduation and whatever measure of achievement was selected for study was resolved. Although the influence of personal characteristics prior to college entry on postcollegiate achievement was not yet clarified, one could now be certain that the enhanced achiever productivity of the women's colleges was not the result of postcollegiate experiences.

BACCALAUREATE ORIGINS OF NATURAL SCIENTISTS

Capitalizing on the methodological improvements of previous work, the most recent findings on the graduates of the decade of the 1970s who went on to obtain doctorates in the natural sciences were published (M. E. Tidball 1986b). The methodology of that effort is presented in synopsis form in Table 24. Some highlights of the study are presented here. The time period for identification of graduates was the full decade of the 1970s; the measure of achievement was obtaining a research doctorate in the natural sciences through 1984. Although the 5- to 15-year interval between graduation and achievement is shorter than in some previous studies, there were 8,915 doctorates in the natural sciences awarded to women and 44,883 such doctorates awarded to men during this period. Once again, data were presented in both absolute terms, for 38 institutional productivity leaders for women and 35 institutional productivity leaders for men, and also in terms that corrected for institutional size. Data processing effort was reduced by using a well-crafted study population consisting of 288 collegiate institutions: the universe of baccalaureate institutions that graduated at least 10 women or 40 men during the decade of the 1970s who went on to obtain natural science doctorates prior to 1984. These numbers were selected to have the study population match the national population with regard to the proportions of women and men who went on to get doctorates in the natural sciences.

Special Features   Data for both women and men were provided and tabulations included: a comparison of national data and study data, alphabetical lists of productivity leaders disaggregated by sex, baccalaureate institutional characteristics for 10 types of collegiate environments by sex of graduate, and the relationship between the number of women graduates who obtained doctorates and the number of women faculty at the collegiate institutions they attended. The findings were compared and contrasted with pertinent previously published work. For additional details, see Chapter 3.

USING INSTITUTIONAL PRODUCTIVITY TO DEFINE THE STUDY POPULATION

A more encompassing study of the baccalaureate graduates from the decade of the 1970s who went on to obtain doctorates in all the broad fields defined in the Doctorate Records File through 1991 was initiated in the spring of 1992 (M. E. Tidball and C. S. Tidball 1994). The design of this work represents three substantive refinements in the methodology of research on baccalaureate origins: (1) calculation of institutional productivities for both women and men to determine the institutions to be included in the study population, (2) selection of the proportion of women and men for the study population

---

TABLE 24

Synopsis of Methodology—1986

1. Time period over which graduates were identified
   One decade from 1970 to 1979
2. Measure of achievement
   Obtaining a research doctorate in the natural sciences through 1983
3. Time period between graduation and achievement
   Varied from 5 to 15 years (dependent on year of graduation)
4. Selection of undergraduate institutions
   Objective selection of institutions on the basis of a specified number of doctorates
5. Adjustment for size of undergraduate institutions
   • None for tabulation by absolute number
   • Achievers were also tabulated as doctorates per graduates, multiplied by 10,000
6. Techniques to decrease data processing effort
   A carefully crafted study population was created consisting of the 288 collegiate institutions that graduated at least 10 women or 40 men during the decade of the 1970s who went on to obtain natural science doctorates prior to 1984
7. Special features
   • The analysis included data for both women and men separately
   • The productivities for women and men were tabulated for several institutional types including colleges (further subdivided into women's colleges, men's colleges, coeducational colleges, women's change colleges, and men's change colleges) and universities (further subdivided into private or public control with or without substantive graduate programs in the natural sciences)
   • The productivity of women scientists for 50 of the most productive institutions for women was highly correlated with the number of women faculty
   • Relevant published findings which impinged on the major conclusions of this study were compared and contrasted

Source: M. E. Tidball 1986b.

---

identical to that in the national population, see Table 10, and (3) disaggregation by institutional type to assure that conclusions are based on group data from similar institutions. These three refinements justify a change in nomenclature from research on baccalaureate origins to research on *institutional productivity*. This designation puts the proper emphasis on studying institutional environments rather than the students who become achievers.

The methodology for this research is presented in synopsis form in Table 25. The measure of achievement was obtaining a research doctorate through 1991. This period is seven years longer than that in the study summarized in Table 24; the additional time substantially increased the numbers in the

TABLE 25

Synopsis of Methodology—1994

1. Time period over which graduates were identified
    One decade, from 1970 to 1979
2. Measure of achievement
    Obtaining a research doctorate through 1991
3. Time period between graduation and achievement
    Varied from 12 to 22 years (dependent on year of graduation)
4. Selection of undergraduate institutions
    Objective selection of institutions on the basis of individual institutional
    productivities for women and men
5. Adjustment for size of undergraduate institutions
    Achievers were tabulated as doctorates per graduates, multiplied by 10,000
6. Techniques to decrease data processing effort
    National data are provided; a defined population with the same proportion
    of men doctorates to women doctorates as the national data was created
    which identified the 316 most productive undergraduate institutions for the
    decade of the 1970s
7. Special features
    • The analysis included data for both women and men separately
    • The productivities for women and men were tabulated for several
       institutional types including women's colleges, men's colleges,
       coeducational colleges, women's change colleges, men's change
       colleges, private universities, and public universities
    • Five broad fields in which achievers obtained their doctorates
       (education, humanities, social sciences, life sciences, and physical
       sciences) were presented graphically for men and women for national
       data and for study population data from groups of similar undergraduate
       institutions
    • Doctoral field patterns from institutions graduating both women and
       men were presented using the ratio of the productivity of men to the
       productivity of women from the same undergraduate institution

Sources: M. E.. Tidball 1994a; 1994b; M. E. Tidball and C. S. Tidball 1994; 1995.

productivity numerators without changing the denominators. The time period between graduation and the achievement ranged from 12 to 22 years; this factor is important since it differs by sex and by field of doctorate. Decreasing data processing effort was based on crafting a study population based on national data for all of the graduates of the decade of the 1970s, which indicated that twice as many men went on to obtain research doctorates as women.[13] Using this as a starting point and institutional productivity data for both men and women from over 2,000 institutions, it was possible to obtain the universe of baccalaureate institutions with more than 2 percent women graduates or 4 percent men graduates who went on to obtain research doctorates in all fields.

Special Features In addition to the innovations identified above, this study introduced a pictorial representation of the patterns of participation in the five broad doctoral fields used by the DRF. When such data are disaggregated by sex, there was a striking difference between the patterns for women and for men; see Chapter 3 for details. These sex-disaggregated field patterns were also developed for a variety of secondary variables such as undergraduate institution type; undergraduate institutional selectivity; and a new quantity, the ratio of men doctorates to women doctorates for undergraduate institutions graduating students of both sexes. The latter is a quantity that provides an objective measure of the differential climate for women and men in the same undergraduate institution and as such can illuminate issues of gender equity. Moreover, this quantity can provide an objective basis for determining collegiate institutions that take women seriously; see Chapter 3.

RECAPITULATION

At the outset, this supplement took on the ambitious task of describing the evolution of research from baccalaureate origins to institutional productivity. Using that restricted objective, the methodologies presented so far, without attempting to include all practitioners of the art, should be considered as data. It remains now to provide an overview that charts the progress in methodology of this useful analytical tool.

Clearly, the scope of the studies reviewed here goes beyond the intent of some early compilations, which were institution-driven or at least seemed to be attempting to report only on a small group of "highly successful" undergraduate institutions. Increasing the power of the method through disaggregation of data by sex, and more recently by racial or ethnic groups, has expanded the method to new horizons. Without identifying differences in the increasing number of categories of undergraduate institutions and disaggregating data by different institutional types and subtypes, progress would have remained limited. The use of alphabetical lists of productivity leaders is a refinement over the earlier practice of employing numerical rankings; it should be favored because too often the basis for the ranking is so narrow that it creates an impression of difference where none may exist.

The ability to identify collegiate variables, e.g., the proportion of women on the faculty, that could impact postcollegiate performance across different institutional types has enhanced the power of the tool. There has been evolution, too, in the definition of both the numerators and the denominators that are used to calculate productivity indices. In some early studies, there was no denominator at all; the achievers were merely counted—which, of course, favored those undergraduate environments with the largest number of graduates. This unfortunate practice has by no means been eliminated.[14]

Greater attention to available information on postbaccalaureate achievements, e.g., the fields in which doctorates were obtained, has provided new insights into the nature of undergraduate environments. Further, in the analysis of gender equity, the use of the ratio of institutional productivity for men divided by institutional productivity for women from the same institutions is an example of an additional refinement.

As statistical analysis on "random" samples drawn from collegiate populations was replaced by population demographics on carefully crafted study populations, various techniques were used to decide which institutions should be included. Since the number of women achievers was generally less than the number of men achievers, the proportion of women and men achievers in the national population became a guide for defining the study population. Although individual calculations had to be performed for many institutions, this approach to defining a study population guaranteed that achievers from all qualifying institutions were included in proportions identical with those in the national population.

The method has further evolved to drawing general conclusions based on collective data derived from groups of similar institutions. Therefore, at this point, one can legitimately abandon the term baccalaureate origins research, with its misplaced emphasis on individual achievers or individual institutions, and recognize that the real focus of this research is on institutional environments at groups of similar institutions, as measured by institutional productivity. As stated in Chapter 3, the nature of research on institutional productivity is inherently phenomenological. This enables the data to stand alone, even as interpretations of these data may change with time and fashion.

This review has documented refinements in methodology over a 45-year period. Indeed, during this interval there has been not only a substantial evolution of methods used to define institutional productivity but also an increased appreciation of this valuable approach.

NOTES

1. The number of achievers is usually small compared with the number of graduates, hence the quotient achievers ÷ graduates is a fractional quantity. The use of a factor of 100 converts the numbers to percentage productivity. To avoid decimal residuals, larger factors, e.g. 1,000 or 10,000 are also used.

2. A periodic report of 93 pages from the National Research Council tabulates doctorate-granting institutions, baccalaureate sources within the United States, foreign baccalaureate sources, and provides a variety of rankings (Office of Scientific Personnel 1948).

3. These authors proceeded to a more extensive and elaborate presentation of their findings in book form (Knapp and Goodrich 1952), but this earlier report is better suited to illustrate an overview of the method.

4. "First, a geographic gradient in the production of scientists was manifest . . . such that Middle and Far West occupied the highest position, New England and the Middle Atlantic states middle position, and the South the lowest position" (Knapp and Goodrich 1951).

5. "Second, it proved possible to demonstrate a significant relation . . . between the minimum cost of student attendance and the productivity of the institutions, such that institutions of high and low cost are inferior to those of average costs; in short, a parabolic relation obtains" (Knapp and Goodrich 1951).

6. That paper went on to become a Citation Classic in the Social and Behavioral Sciences section of *Current Contents*; it was the most frequently cited paper ever published by the American Council on Education's *Educational Record* (M. E. Tidball 1986a).

7. Data on achieving women were disaggregated by a number of personal variables including: marital status, time between receiving the baccalaureate degree and marriage, divorce status, undertaking postbaccalaureate studies, and earning a doctoral degree. This secondary analysis of individual characteristics for women in the subsamples from the three editions of the reference work indicated that there were no differences among individual subsamples such that the total group of 1,116 achievers could be treated as a single entity.

8. The data on doctorates were obtained in a commissioned database from the DRF. Unlike the 5 percent random sample of the entire DRF database previously mentioned, this commissioned database was restricted to graduates of the 137 doctorate productivity leaders identified in a preliminary phase of the study.

9. The separate identification of baccalaureate degrees from first professional degrees in reports from the Department of Health, Education, and Welfare did not occur until 1961–62; for the earlier records, these two sources of degrees were separated when necessary by using a correction factor (M. E. Tidball and Kistiakowsky 1976, n. 16).

10. This time period represented a peak of enrollment in American medical colleges that was not surpassed until the decade of the 1990s.

11. A small number of medical school entrants received their baccalaureate degrees at the end of the first medical school year and another small number did not enter medical school until a year after graduation.

12. For an introduction to the terminology of women's change and men's change colleges, see Chapter 2, Note 3.

13. The different criteria for women and men are based on the national data which indicate that, for the graduates of the 1970s, twice as many men went on to obtain research doctorates as did women. The ratio of men to women doctorates for the national data was 2.04; that for the study population was 2.08. For further comparisons, see Table 10.

14. A 1996 issue of *Money* magazine had an extensive survey of "desirable colleges" from a cost/benefit point of view but failed to make a correction for institutional size in any of its 16 research variables.

SUPPLEMENT TO CHAPTER 4

Social Science Approaches to Studying College Impact

INTRODUCTION

I n 1969, Kenneth Feldman and Theodore Newcomb published their landmark work, *The Impact of College on Students*. That book summarized 40 years of research on how students change during college. During the years following, research on the impact of college on students has grown—in part, because of the growth in the numbers going to college, the dramatic shifts in where students go to college, and the increasing diversity of students in college. As a result, Pascarella and Terenzini followed Feldman and Newcomb with *How College Affects Students* (1991), their major effort to synthesize what was known through the 1980s. Their book reflects the development of increasing sophistication in theories, in statistical methodologies, and in the use of multivariate analysis to look at the complex factors that influence the development of individuals.

While the question of how college impacts students seems simple, it actually incorporates a complex set of questions. Among them are the following: Do individuals change during college? Is this change a function of college attendance? How do these changes persist and influence later life? Do different kinds of institutions influence students in different ways? What aspects of the institution—its curriculum, its programs, its residential arrangements—have which kinds of impact? And, importantly, do the responses to these questions differ depending on which groups of students or which individuals are studied?

The methodologies available for such inquiries can never do justice to their significance. The sheer numbers of students, from hugely diverse backgrounds, attending almost 3,000 institutions (themselves incorporating significant diversity) make responding to these questions quite challenging. Moreover, there are important conceptual issues embedded in these deceptively simple questions. Nonetheless, it is the challenge of the social sciences to try to develop methods that allow the researcher, the institution, and the policy community to come to understand how and in what ways the college experience makes a difference to students. In the past 30 years, the developments in statistics and computers, along with the development of large scale databases—some of them longitudinal in nature—have permitted a variety of approaches to each of the questions listed above. More recently, scholars are also taking advantage of more qualitative techniques to permit deeper exploration of the dynamic relationship between institution, individual, and social-historical context. The combination of all these methodologies is likely to yield deeper understanding than any single study, no matter how large and no matter how sophisticated the statistics.

Most of the studies begin with the broad theoretical framework developed by A. W. Astin, in which college impact is understood to be a function of the *input* (what students bring with them); the *environment* of college, including programs, faculty, peers, and curriculum; and the *outcomes* of college. This I-E-O model has framed much of the research tradition to date (A. W. Astin 1962; 1977; 1991). The research on the impact of women's colleges is embedded in this larger research tradition. And while it tends to be primarily focused on the questions concerning a specific institution type, it is not in any way separable from the other questions about impact. Moreover, the study of women's colleges very quickly links to research focused on a variety of "single sex" questions in education, from programs for women or men, residences, and curricula, to issues of gender equity and discrimination in education. Indeed, one of the challenges of the research on women's colleges, in particular, is that it occurs in a broader social-historical context related to women and women's issues. These are often more visible than might be the case for other studies of college students—even though all research takes place in context. Significantly, the I-E-O model does not explicitly take context into account.

Moreover, the research tradition that, by necessity, uses quantitative methods, studies these large and dynamic questions in terms of single variables, trying to isolate the impact of each variable. The research reported in Chapter 4 attempts, thus, to isolate the impact of attending a women's college from all other factors that influence college achievement. While contemporary statistical methods allow the researcher to study these variables in relation to one another, the methodology itself limits the contextual frame that one can place around the data itself. That is why qualitative methodologies and critical theories that look at the context both of institutions and of individuals and groups are so important for the study of women's colleges and women's education (Guba and Lincoln 1989).

If occupational success, for example, is an important indicator of achievement for the individual—and in a collective manner, for the institution—how should one assess college impact for women's colleges whose graduates were limited by tradition, by culture, and by regulation in so many ways? If the number of graduates who are CEOs demonstrates success, how does one compare the outcomes of women's colleges? Moreover, if a college values public service, teaching, and social service, how can the success of its alumni or alumnae be compared in a society that tends to view affluence and status more highly than service? Clearly, the achievement of graduates is impacted not just by the talents of individuals and the results of educational opportunity but also by the context in which persons find themselves. Perhaps nowhere is this issue more dramatically represented than for African American women and graduates of Historically Black women's colleges. That is why M. E. Tidball's and Wolf-Wendel's research, which in some sense accepted "high status" definitions of success, have been so important. They have demonstrated the power of women's colleges even in conventional terms of achievement. The research in Chapter 4 must constantly be interrogated in terms of such issues.

METHODOLOGICAL ISSUES

A wide range of methodological issues emerge when doing any and all of these kinds of studies, whether quantitative or qualitative. Clearly the sources of data and the means for gathering data are of critical importance in studying any aspect of the college student experience. In addition to issues of controlling for individual entering characteristics described in Chapter 4, the researcher must be attentive to sample size and the relative size of samples when comparing groups, statistical questions about measuring change, and the adequacy of survey items in assessing colleges or outcomes. Moreover, as the capacity of computers to manipulate large data sets with complex statistical packages has increased, new statistical techniques are available—each with its own assumptions and limitations. Perhaps the most concise explanation of these as they relate to impact studies is included in Pascarella and Terenzini's (1991) appendix on "methodological issues in assessing the influence of college."

DATABASES

Student Databases

It is obvious, from the material presented in Chapter 4, that considerable and powerful research on students has emerged from two large national data sets. It is appropriate, therefore, to provide a brief description of each.

Cooperative Institutional Research Program (CIRP)   The CIRP studies began with the entering freshman class of 1966, initiated by the American Council on Education (ACE), under the leadership of Alexander W. Astin, and has in recent years been administered by the Higher Education Research Institute at the University of California, Los Angeles (UCLA) under the sponsorship of ACE. Until the time CIRP began, no systematic national data were available on college students except information that institutions supplied concerning numbers in attendance, sex, racial and ethnic breakdown, and degree attainment. In 1966, for the first time, a survey was developed that was intended to be distributed annually to successive classes of entering students (during their first week of college) from a selected sample of institutions. The survey since that time has consisted of responses to items serving as pretests for a number of future outcome measures on surveys to college seniors; personal characteristics such as race, gender, and religion; family characteristics; financial status; student expectations for their success in college; their plans; and a variety of attitudes and values. The survey has been administered to entering students at a stratified national sample of some 300 institutions throughout the country. The CIRP database relies heavily on "weighted samples" to ensure that the responses are given weight in proportion to their presence in the larger population. In addition to the set of core institutions, other institutions are also included, increasing the sample of institutions to approximately 600. While surveys have changed slightly since they began, the results have provided a rather consistent data source of "freshman" background characteristics, expectations, attitudes, and values for over 30 years (see also A. W. Astin, Panos, and Creager 1966; Dey, Astin, and Korn 1991).

The CIRP database also includes a longitudinal component. A sample of students from each participating institution is surveyed after four years. In addition, some entering classes have been studied after two years (and others after eight years). The follow-up survey includes questions about occupational goals, academic majors, collegiate experiences, satisfaction with a broad range of institutional qualities, and a study of attitudes and values. Because it is multi-institutional and includes such large numbers of students, this database allows researchers to study a broad range of questions concerning the impact of institutions, patterns of college-going, experiences in college, and the relation between collegiate experiences and the outcomes of college (seen from the perspective of students). Moreover, because the survey responses of the entering student can be matched with the follow-up survey, scholars and campuses have important information about shifts in individual responses. Importantly, recent databases contain institutional data such as grades and scores on standardized tests, retention and graduation information, and merged data from parallel faculty studies from similar institutions. CIRP is now the largest ongoing source of information on college students in the country. A complete description of the CIRP data is included in A. W. Astin's (1993) *What Matters in College?*

A. W. Astin's 1977 book, *Four Critical Years*, included students from the four entering classes in 1966, 1967, 1968, and 1969, followed four years later, with samples averaging 31,000 students. His 1993 book focused on the class entering in 1985, followed in 1989–90. The student sample included 24,847 students from 217 four-year colleges and universities. That study also included faculty data from the same institutions and institutional data.

For other scholars focusing on comparative studies of women's colleges, the pattern has been to use a subset of the CIRP data so that women at women's colleges are compared with women at coeducational institutions. D.G. Smith

---

TABLE 26

DESCRIPTION OF STUDENT SAMPLES FROM REPRESENTATIVE STUDIES

Author	Data Set	Cohort (Entering)	Sample Size[a]	Notes
A. W. Astin 1977	CIRP	1966–69	31,000[b]	1
D. G. Smith 1990	CIRP	1982	880	2
A. W. Astin 1993	CIRP	1985	24,847	3
D. G. Smith, et al. 1995	CIRP	1986	924	4
Kim and Alvarez 1995	CIRP	1987	3,636	5
Riordan 1992	NLS	1972	2,317	6

Notes

a   Size of sample actually used in the analysis.

b   An average sample size over the four cohorts.

1   Sample size included all students in the national sample; other institutional data for graduation and test scores were used.

2   A subset of 705 women at 4-year private baccalaureate institutions, 175 at women's colleges.

3   Includes all students in the national sample and relevant data from faculty and institutions.

4   A subset of 764 women at 4-year private baccalaureate institutions, 160 at women's colleges

5   A subset of 3,249 women at 4-year coeducational private and public institutions (not universities), 387 women at women's colleges.

6   A subset of 2,225 from "mixed gender" colleges and 92 from women who attended two years of women's colleges from the 1986 follow-up.

(1990), using the data from the 1982/86 cohort, included 705 women at private four-year coeducational baccalaureate institutions and 175 at women's colleges. D. G. Smith, Wolf-Wendel, and Morrison (1995) used the 1986/90 cohort. This study also included women at private, four-year, baccalaureate-granting coeducational institutions so that they would be more comparable to women's colleges. This yielded a national sample of 764 women from coeducational baccalaureate institutions and 160 at women's colleges. Kim and Alvarez (1995), studying the 1987/91 cohort, used 3,249 women from coeducational private and public institutions (universities were also eliminated to control for size) and 387 women from women's colleges. These samples are summarized in Table 26.

The National Longitudinal Study of the High School Class of 1972 (NLS)
The National Longitudinal Study of the High School Class of 1972 is a longitudinal survey research project of the National Center for Education Statistics. The study is designed using sampling techniques first to select a sample of high schools throughout the country and then to sample students from those high schools. The 1972 base year involved a one-hour survey of 22,652 seniors from 1,380 private, public, and church-affiliated high schools. Follow-up studies were conducted each year until 1979, and then once more in 1986. These surveys included educational status, work status, occupation, and attitudes concerning themselves, gender roles, and society.

The NLS has been used by Riordan in his study of women's colleges. Riordan (1992) selected women who had attended women's colleges for at least two years, a total of 123 women, and 92 when the 1986 follow-up was included. He compared this group to 2,225 from "mixed-gender" colleges. This study did not attempt to limit the kind of institutions for the coeducational sample but did employ weighted samples to approximate the universe of women at both kinds of institutions.

Faculty Studies
Studies of college faculty described in Chapter 4 have come from two databases, one developed as part of a national study of faculty and the other developed to investigate the views of faculty at women's colleges, in particular.

ACE Study of Teaching Faculty, 1972–73
The national study of teaching faculty conducted in 1972–73 served to replicate an earlier study of faculty sponsored jointly by ACE and the Carnegie Commission on Higher Education in 1968–69. For the 1972–73 study, a stratified sample of 301 institutions, chosen to replicate the CIRP sample, was developed and valid surveys were received from 42,345 teaching faculty. Results for the national study were weighted to reflect national norms. The survey instrument assessed values and attitudes toward teaching, institutional goals, and higher education, as well as

background characteristics and working conditions (Bayer 1973). M. E. Tidball's study of attitudes of faculty at women's colleges compared with faculty at other institutions was developed using a subset of this database. The final data set included faculty from 224 institutions: 37 private research universities, 65 public universities and colleges, 22 men's colleges, 85 private coeducational colleges, and 15 non–Roman Catholic women's colleges.

Women's College Coalition Study A database was developed by the Women's College Coalition (1981) to learn about the experiences of faculty at women's colleges. In 1980, presidents of 116 women's colleges received questionnaires to distribute to faculty in accordance with standardized instructions to ensure a random sample. Usable surveys were received from 1,271 faculty and reflected the size, selectivity, and level of the college. The survey was designed to probe perceptions about the mission of women's colleges, the institutional reward system, and faculty attitudes toward teaching, students, women's issues, and curricular change.

SAMPLING

Much of the social science research referenced in Chapter 4 relies on sampling techniques to make conclusions about students and other campus groups. That is, the researcher has relied on the responses and involvement of a smaller number to generalize to the entire population. This is in contrast to the population demographic approach used in the baccalaureate origin studies. Because it would be impossible to ask or to get an entire population of students and other members of the campus community to participate on a regular basis, social scientists most often rely on sampling techniques to study a smaller population, from which generalizations to the larger population are made. Much like public opinion polls that can predict election outcomes from as few as 1,000 voters, social science researchers rely on statistical methods to ensure an appropriate sample of participants to generalize to larger groups. In addition, periodic studies have been conducted on "nonresponses" to ensure that the sample is representative. The CIRP database, for example, has "weighted" the responses of participants in terms of institutional weights so that there is increased validity in generalizing to the total population of students. Because sampling is not easily controlled on college campuses, it is not uncommon to find some inconsistency among studies. Moreover, researchers often use subsets of larger databases to ask particular questions or to make specific comparisons. Such is the case for many of the studies reported in Chapter 4. Thus, it is critically important to understand the participants of any study, the population from which they were drawn, and the results of the study in the context of other studies on the same topic.

Sampling is also an issue in qualitative research in which the researcher is interested in exploring how and why events occur by involving participants in describing or telling about experiences through interviews, ethnographies, observation, and relevant documents. Here again, researchers make important decisions about where, as well as whom, to sample—decisions that can profoundly influence the results.

STUDYING OUTCOMES

In asking about the impact of college on students, the researcher or policy-maker, parent, or student, is interested in what happens to the student as a result of college attendance. Many have already discussed the complexity of this question, including the difficulty of distinguishing whether what happens in college is a result of the collegiate experience or whether it might result, as well, from simple maturation (Pascarella and Terenzini 1991). In general, the outcomes of interest include a broad array of items, including educational competence, educational achievement, attitudes and values, and behaviors. Some of these, such as degree achievement, can be studied without the participation of the person. Most of these, however, must be studied by methods of self-report, from the student or close observers.

Moreover, there is an important time frame involved. To study the long-term impact of college, one would need to wait years after college—as Riordan does in his study of career attainment. Long-term impact studies of this kind are, in fact, often accomplished archivally by studying individuals years after college and linking that information to earlier data. While using later life measures of achievement is powerful, the researcher must also cope with all the influences that can intervene between college and that moment. As a result, others study the impact at the point of college completion using student goals and aspirations, student satisfaction, and academic achievement as important indicators of college impact.

Timing of research becomes significant in yet another way. Clearly, attending college in the 1950s was quite different than in the 1990s. For women, in particular, much has changed. During this period, women's education options—and their options once completing college—have expanded. Research on women's colleges, as well as all research on college impact, must take this into account. Significant patterns of consistency and change across and between time periods becomes very important in coming to conclusions both for students and for institutions.

It is important to note that the outcomes of college and the college experience are related. That is, a college can be studied in terms of the satisfaction students have with their college experience, but student satisfaction can also serve as an evaluation *by the student* of the college experience.

The research reported in Chapter 4 on leadership illustrates this point as well. Leadership represents both an expected outcome of college—the development of the students' capacity to perform as leaders. At the same time, the development of leadership is treated as an experience that colleges provide—an experience that results in self-confidence and later achievement. Here, then, leadership serves in both capacities.

GENERALIZING

If one is sampling only from the total population, the legitimacy of making generalizations is critical. In a study of 70 or 100 students, how does the reader know that the findings will hold for a larger population? Statistical methods, in part, attempt to let the reader know whether the result is likely to be generalizable. However, because of the issue of sampling and because of the concern about changes over time, the power of conclusions must be drawn not from the finding of a single study, but from the analysis of many studies, their methods, their sampling techniques, the institutions from which the samples are drawn, and the time periods in which the studies are conducted. Chapter 4 reflects that approach by including a wide diversity of studies drawn from many time periods, databases, and methodologies.

GATHERING DATA

Relying on campus participants to describe and reflect on their experiences often rests on methods of "self-report." While some studies use testing to assess academic achievement or inventories to study personality change, many researchers rely on self-report instruments—notably surveys and interviews—to study the college experience. The advantage of these approaches is that they validate the perceptions of the participants in the college experience and permit the study of issues such as values and attitudes that may or may not be accessible through other means. These approaches also provide an important window on how college makes a difference to students—what it is that colleges do that results in important shifts and changes. There are, of course, limits to self-report mechanisms. They are constrained by the perceptions of the person. A researcher may be interested in outcomes, for example, that may not be obvious to the respondent at the time. Self-report studies also have to rely on the variations in how people evaluate experiences. Some persons might easily indicate "very satisfied" to a question, while others may use that response only rarely. Thus the meaning of satisfaction may be somewhat ambiguous. In addition, self-report studies do not always have the credibility that other "more objective" indicators may command. In the same way, faculty surveys become an important way to study the views of a major constituency that is involved in shaping the college experience.

CONTROLLING FOR ENTERING CHARACTERISTICS

Perhaps one of the most enduring attempts in the research on college impact has been the effort to separate the impact of the college experience as a function of student characteristics from the experiences students have during college. If what happens to students is a function of who they were at entrance, the theory says, then colleges cannot "take credit" for what happens. In the tradition of quantitative social science research, this has led to the development of statistical methods that purport to separate the student from the experience through the use of statistical techniques. While this is an important tool, it raises important conceptual and political issues for women's colleges, in particular. Conceptually, such measures suggest that one can make such separations despite the obvious close interactions between individual and institutional experiences. Indeed, traditional background characteristics such as gender, race, ethnicity, and class are treated as static variables. These variables can also be constructs to which institutions and the people in those environments respond. Traditional research, for a long time, attributed women's success or failure to characteristics of being women. Issues concerning women in science were studied by studying such characteristics as women's attitudes, values, physiology, academic preparation, brain, and hormones. More recent research has suggested strongly that the role of gender can also be seen as a social construct in which institutions and people *respond* to gender. Women's treatment, the expectations for performance, models presented for success, and differential pressures to succeed can also impact student performance. If environments treat individuals differently, as a function of who they are, then research should not eliminate that factor through statistical manipulation.

Politically, as noted in Chapter 4, controlling for entering characteristics has led to efforts to sort out all those qualities students bring to college from what happens at college, most often for those institutions that are on the defensive for their existence. In contrast, elite institutions often proudly suggest that part of their success is a function of the selectivity of the institution and the resulting entering characteristics of the students. It is important to note, then, that the single variable, *women's college*, often remains an important predictor, even after all other factors are considered. Indeed, in studies that purport to dismiss the impact of women's colleges, institutional gender continues to appear as significant. Other scholars have recognized that this methodology is extremely conservative and, thus, have been cautious in assuming that negative findings in a single study are meaningful (Stoecker and Pascarella 1991).

The critique of these purely statistical efforts has led others to incorporate more holistic, and often qualitative assessments to address the impact of the entire experience. The combined efforts of quantitative and qualitative social science research often create the most credible insights into these complex and important issues. Inevitably, this requires the combined talents of many researchers investigating different but related dimensions of the questions under study.

CONCLUSION

There are many important sources of information for the reader wishing more detailed discussion of college impact research, critiques of social science methodologies, the use of multivariate analysis, and the contribution of qualitative research to illuminate central questions (A. W. Astin 1991; Light, Singer, and Willett 1990; Pascarella and Terenzini 1991). The research on women's colleges is both embedded in these research traditions and vulnerable to them. To the degree that colleges must demonstrate impact independent of students' entering characteristics, women's colleges must rise to a higher standard. Similarly, outcomes and indicators of achievement for women are not only a function of institutional and individual accomplishments, they are also a function of societal expectations and opportunities. It is in this context that the research summarized in Chapter 4 must be understood.

SUPPLEMENT TO CHAPTER 5

A Look Inside "A Look Inside"

The case studies presented in Chapter 5 are based on qualitative research conducted by Wolf-Wendel in the spring of 1994. It should be noted that the research presented in Chapter 5 was originally part of a larger research project in which six case studies were conducted. Only data from the two women's colleges are presented in this book.

The focus of the original study was on examining colleges with a demonstrated record of facilitating the success of their women students to determine the institutional traits associated with these positive outcomes. The unit of analysis is the individual institution. According to Baldwin and Thelin (1991), considerable evidence suggests that various types of collegiate institutions influence the probability that certain postsecondary outcomes will occur. How this occurs is unclear and is subject to scholarly debate. The public needs further clarification to determine how and why diverse types of colleges and universities achieve some educational goals and fall short in others. "The prescription is . . . certain kinds of research—namely, intensive case studies of selected institutions' inner workings, rounds-of-life and socialization" (Baldwin and Thelin 1991, 339). In other words, the case study method is appropriate when one wishes "to make sense out of the world's lessons" through the power of voice and observation combined with inductive analysis (Patton 1990, 138).

Qualitative research seeks answers to questions by examining various social settings and by observing individuals who inhabit these settings. Qualitative research follows several fundamental principles: (1) one conducts the study in a natural setting because context is heavily implicated in determining meaning; (2) meaning is an essential concern of the researcher; (3) data are words rather than numbers; (4) the investigator is concerned with processes and outcomes; (5) data are analyzed inductively; (6) data are used to generate theory rather than to enumerate frequencies; and finally, (7) the researcher recognizes and appreciates the value-laden nature of inquiry (Crowson 1987, Lincoln and Guba 1985; MacKay and Schuh 1991).

STEP BY STEP

One of the most important hallmarks of conducting case studies is that, because of the emerging nature of the design, it is impossible to plan for every contingency within the study. This appendix explains the following steps taken in the qualitative research component of the case studies presented in Chapter 5:

- The focus of the exploration
- The method for selecting data sources
- A description of data collection procedures
- A documentation of analysis procedures
- The steps taken to ensure trustworthiness

Focus of the Study

The initial focus of the case studies involved examining institutions that demonstrated an ability to graduate women who subsequently earned doctorates. The one-question interview protocol was designed to determine how constituents perceive institutional structures, policies, programs, and services, as well as uncover the attitudes, values, and behaviors of the people who occupy these institutional environments. A single-question protocol was selected because it offered campus constituents the freedom to voice their beliefs about their institutions, without facing the preconceived notions of the researcher (Lincoln and Guba 1985). The basic question asked of all institutional informants was—"Why do you think your institution has produced so many successful women graduates?"

Criteria for Selection of Sites

Case studies were conducted at two of the women's colleges that graduated high proportions of women who earned doctorates or who were listed in a *Who's Who* reference book. The case-study sites were: Bennett College in North Carolina and Bryn Mawr College in Pennsylvania. Bryn Mawr was the most productive baccalaureate-granting institution for white women who earned doctorates between 1975 and 1985. It was also the most productive institution for white women with doctorates in natural sciences and in the humanities. It was the third most productive institution for graduating white women with social science doctorates. It was the fourth most productive institution for white women listed in the 1992–93 edition of *Who's Who in America* (Wolf-Wendel 1998).

Bennett was the third most productive institution for African American women who earned doctorates and who were listed in *Who's Who among Black Americans*. The two highest ranking institutions for African American women were Spelman College, the other Historically Black women's college, and Fisk University, a Historically Black coeducational institution. Bennett College was chosen over Spelman because it has received less attention from the media and has had fewer write-ups in the academic literature. Further, from a resource perspective, Bennett College seems to be doing more with far less. Compared with Spelman College, Bennett is less prestigious, has lower student admission criteria, and is less financially secure. Compared with other institutions, Bennett produced the greatest proportion of African American women who earned natural science doctorates. It was the third highest ranking institution for graduating African American women with social science doctorates, with humanities doctorates, and with education doctorates.

Data Collection

The case studies drew their evidence from two methodologies: individual interviews and document analyses. Before the campus visits, letters were sent to each of the institutional presidents to obtain permission to use the institution as a site for this study. The letters also requested assistance in facilitating the visit.

Four-day site visits were conducted at each of the institutions studied. During the visit, semi-structured interviews were held with students, faculty, alumnae, and administrators. Each interview was approximately one hour in length. Approximately 35 interviews were conducted at each site. Status sampling, interviewing those who hold certain positions at the institution, was used to establish the initial list of interview participants. The following individuals or their equivalents were interviewed from each institution: the president, the chief academic officer, the chief student affairs officer, a representative from admissions and financial aid, directors of such institutional resources as the women's resource center and the office of black student affairs, the president of the faculty executive committee, the president of the student government, and representatives from the campus women's group and the African American student group. It was recognized that some of these positions may not exist at some of the institutional sites.

The case studies also utilized snowball or chain sampling, a process by which the researcher asks institutional informants to identify others on the campus to help expand the pool of respondents. Specifically, the researcher asked for the names of others whose opinions and experiences might add depth to the study. The goal of this technique was to achieve maximum variation in roles and perspectives among the respondents (Crowson 1987). The final list of those interviewed at each institution was determined by the institutional representative combined with the snowball sampling.

Along with the interview material, the case studies take into account written information from the institutions. The type of information gathered from these documents included, but was not limited to: demographics of the students, faculty, and staff; information about institutional resources; information about the institutional mission and goals; and the existence and description of specific programs and services aimed at traditionally marginalized groups. The different sites had different amounts and types of written materials available.

Analysis Procedures

The interview transcripts were analyzed and interpreted using the constant comparative approach (Strauss and Corbin 1990; Strauss 1987; Conrad 1982; Glazer 1978; Glazer and Strauss 1967). Glazer and Strauss (1967) identify four overlapping stages of the constant comparative approach that were used as a guide during the analysis. First, the collected data were coded into as many categories as possible, each representing a different broad concept. In doing so, the researcher began to consider the dimensions of each concept, their relationships with other concepts, and the conditions under which the concepts were pronounced or minimized. Second, the overall data were compared with the properties of the categories. Third, the categories and the relationships were further analyzed and refined to gradually develop "theory" by reducing these to higher-level concepts. Fourth, these concepts were refined into propositions. Through the constant comparative method, the research moved from the empirical to the conceptual and theoretical.

All appropriate measures were taken to ensure that the derived categories were internally consistent (internal convergence), but distinct from one another (external divergence) (Marshall and Rossman 1995; Guba 1981). Throughout the analysis process, the researcher also searched for negative instances and for rival structures as an internal consistency check (Glazer and Strauss 1967). Finally, the researcher stopped searching for data to generate and substantiate "theories" when "all of the major concepts and their interrelationships have been theoretically saturated"—when the researcher could find no additional data to embellish the "theory" (Conrad 1982, 281).

Ensuring Trustworthiness

The data collection and analysis of these case studies conforms to the highest standards of qualitative research by ensuring trustworthiness. Instead of demonstrating constructs appropriate to quantitative research—reliability, internal validity, external validity—this study rigorously employs a parallel set of standards more applicable to qualitative research. Qualitative research establishes the trustworthiness of its findings by demonstrating that findings are: (1) credible, (2) transferable, (3) dependable, and (4) confirmable (Lincoln and Guba 1985). Four techniques were employed to ensure trustworthiness.

Triangulation   This method involves the use of multiple data sources and multiple methods of data collection to verify information gathered by the investigator (Merriam 1988; Lincoln and Guba 1985; Whitt 1991). The credibility of a case study "depends on the degree to which it rings true to natives and colleagues in the field" (Fetterman 1989, 21). Credibility is established if participants agree with the constructions, analyses, conclusions, and interpretations of the researcher.

Member Checking   This study employed two types of member checking to ensure credibility. First, the researcher held debriefing sessions immediately following interviews to test initial understanding of the data gathered. Second, the researcher contacted research participants after the interviews to test the evolving analytical categories, interpretations, and conclusions (Whitt 1991).

Thick Description   A case study must be useful in illuminating another context if it is to be deemed transferable. Lincoln and Guba (1985) suggest that the only way to establish transferability is to create a "thick description of the sending context so that someone in a potential receiving context may assess the similarity between them and, hence, the transferability of the study" (126). This study provides the thick description necessary to inform "best" practices at other institutions.

Audit   The principal means of establishing dependability and confirmability in a study is through an audit. Dependability involves the reporting of results considering possible changes over time. Confirmability is the concept that the data can be confirmed by someone other than the researcher. As Lincoln and Guba (1985) recommend, the researcher created an audit trail—one that will allow an external auditor to examine both the processes and products of the study in order to ensure dependability and confirmability. The audit trail includes: (1) raw data, including tapes, interview notes, and documents; (2) products of data reduction and analysis, including field notes, interview and document summary forms, and case analysis forms; (3) products of data reconstruction and synthesis, including category descriptions, and case reports; and (4) process notes, including notes on methodological decisions and trustworthiness criteria (Lincoln and Guba 1985).

CAMPUS VISITS

Bryn Mawr College

Mary Patterson McPherson, then president of Bryn Mawr College, granted permission for the researcher to spend four days on campus during the spring of 1994. While on campus, the researcher conducted hour-long interviews with 10 students, 12 faculty members, and 8 administrators. Four of the administrators were alumnae of Bryn Mawr. In addition to the formal interviews, during the four-day visit the researcher also attended a residence hall meeting, visited several classes, and informally interacted with a range of campus constituents.

During the formal interviews, respondents were asked to describe why they thought Bryn Mawr was so successful with white women. There was a high degree of consistency among the responses across constituency groups. Eight institutional traits represent a summary of constituent responses at Bryn Mawr College. As stated in Chapter 5, the factors include the following: an institutional mission and history that takes women seriously; a faculty penchant to treat students as colleagues and scholars and to hold students to the highest academic standards; the presence of strong women role models at all levels of the institution; the ability of the college to attract a critical mass of motivated, bright, and capable women students; a recognition of the social realities facing women in the "real world"; extracurricular involvement opportunities; tempered personal support and advising; and the inclusion of women in the curriculum.

Bennett College

After receiving permission from Gloria Scott, the president of Bennett College, the researcher spent five days on the campus during the spring of 1994. While on campus, the researcher conducted 30 one-hour interviews with faculty members, administrators, students, and alumnae. She also attended a philosophy class in which over 20 students discussed why they thought Bennett College produced such a high proportion of successful African American women. During the five-day visit, the researcher also participated in several institutional events including Senior Day and a faculty meeting. The visit afforded the researcher the opportunity to informally interact with a wide range of campus constituents.

As explained in Chapter 5, comments were grouped into 10 factors that are presented in order of importance, as indicated by the frequency by which they were mentioned by constituents and by how much constituents emphasized them. They include: high academic expectations, personal support and advising, a supportive peer culture, a strong institutional mission, a critical mass of African American women, inclusion in the curriculum, the presence of role models, an emphasis on giving back to the community, extracurricular involvement opportunities, and an awareness of societal realities facing African American women.

DEMOGRAPHIC INFORMATION ABOUT THE TWO SITES

Table 27 provides some institutional highlights of both Bryn Mawr and Bennett. This table demonstrates some of the major structural similarities and differences between the two campuses.

TABLE 27

DESCRIPTION OF CASE STUDY SITES*

	Bryn Mawr	Bennett
Location	Pennsylvania	North Carolina
Institutional Race	Predominantly White	Predominantly Black
Institutional Control	Independent	Independent
Carnegie Classification	Liberal Arts I	Liberal Arts II
Enrollment	1,150	950
Faculty:Student Ratio	1:9	1:12
% of women students	100%	100%
% of minority students**	9%	100%
% of students receiving aid	62%	88%
Selectivity†	6	2
% of women faculty	47%	50%
% of minority faculty**	9%	70%
% of faculty w/ terminal degree	98%	63%
Tuition, Room, and Board	$24,085	$8,920
Endowment	$214 million	$9.8 million

Notes
* Numbers represent institutional estimates for 1993–1994.
** Numbers include only Latinos and African Americans.
† Selectivity measured on a scale of 1–6, with 1=non-selective and 6=most selective (Barron's Profiles 1991).

REFERENCES

American Association of University Professors. 1984. "Bottoming Out: The Annual Report on the Economic Status of the Profession, 1983–84." *Academe* 70(2): 1–63.

American Association of University Professors. 1996. "Not So Bad: The Annual Report on the Economic Status of the Profession, 1995–96." *Academe* 82(2): 14–108.

American Association of University Women. 1991. *Shortchanging Girls, Shortchanging America.* Washington, DC.

Amherst Visiting Committee on Coeducation. 1974. *Amherst Visiting Committee on Coeducation: Final Report.* Amherst, MA: Amherst College.

Anderson, R. E. 1977. *Strategic Policy Changes at Private Colleges: Educational and Fiscal Implications.* New York: Teachers College Press.

Appel, M., D. Cartwright, D. G. Smith, and L. E. Wolf-Wendel. 1996. *The Impact of Diversity on Students: A Preliminary Review of the Research Literature.* Washington, DC: American Association of Colleges and Universities.

Association of Governing Boards of Universities and Colleges. 1996. *Self-Study Criteria for Governing Boards of Independent Colleges and Universities.* Washington, DC.

Astin, A. W. 1962. "An Empirical Characterization of Higher Education Institutions." *Journal of Educational Psychology* 53(5): 224–35.

Astin, A. W. 1977. *Four Critical Years: Effects of College on Beliefs, Attitudes and Knowledge.* San Francisco: Jossey-Bass.

Astin, A. W. 1984. "Student Involvement: A Developmental Theory for Higher Education." *Journal of College Student Personnel* 25: 297–308.

Astin, A. W. 1985. *Achieving Educational Excellence.* San Francisco: Jossey-Bass.

Astin, A. W. 1991. *Assessment for Excellence.* New York: Macmillan.

Astin, A. W. 1993. *What Matters in College?* San Francisco: Jossey-Bass.

Astin, A. W., R. J. Panos, and J. A. Creager. 1966. "A Program of Longitudinal Research on Higher Education." *ACE Research Reports* 1(1): 1–42.

Astin, H. S., and L. Kent. 1983. "Gender Roles in Transition: Research and Policy Implications for Higher Education." *Journal of Higher Education* 54: 309–24.

Astin, H. S., and C. Leland. 1991. *Women of Influence, Women of Vision: A Cross-Generational Study of Leaders and Social Change.* San Francisco: Jossey-Bass.

Badger, H. G., and M. C. Rice. 1956. *Biennial Survey of Education in the United States, 1952–54.* Washington, DC: U.S. Government Printing Office.

Bailey, E. M., and K. N. Rask. 1996. *Are We Role Models? Major Choice in an Undergraduate Institution.* Hamilton, NY: Colgate University.

Baldwin, R. G., and J. R. Thelin. 1991. "Thanks for the Memories: The Fusion of Quantitative and Qualitative Research on College Students and the College Experience." Pp. 337–60 in *Higher Education: Handbook of Theory and Research,* volume VI, edited by J. C. Smart. New York: Agathon Press.

Ballou, R. A. 1986. "Freshman in College Residence Halls: A Study of Freshman Perceptions of Residence Hall Climates at Ten Colleges and Universities." *The Journal of College and University Housing* 16(1): 7–12.

Barron's Profiles of American Colleges. 1991. New York: Barron's Inc.

Bayer, A. E. 1973. "Teaching Faculty in Academe: 1972–73." *ACE Research Reports* 8(2): 1–68.

Beck, H. H. 1921. *Linden Hall 1746–1921.* Lancaster, PA: Conestoga.

Bennett College. 1995. *1995–1996 Catalog.* Greensboro, NC.

Black, G. S. H. 1997. "The New Alumnae President." *Wellesley* (Summer): inside front cover.

Boyer, E. L. 1987. "College: The Undergraduate Experience in America." *The Carnegie Foundation for the Advancement of Teaching.* New York: Harper & Row.

Bressler, M., and P. Wendell. 1980. "The Sex Composition of Selective Colleges and Gender Differences in Career Aspirations." *Journal of Higher Education* 51: 650–53.

Brown, M. 1982. "Career Plans of College Women: Patterns and Influences." In *The Undergraduate Woman,* edited by P. Perun. Lexington: D.C. Heath.

Butterfield, F. 1992. "As for That Myth about How Much Alumnae Give." *New York Times* 25 February.

Carnegie Commission on Higher Education. 1973. *Opportunities for Women in Higher Education: Their Current Participation, Prospects for the Future, and Recommendations for Action.* New York: McGraw Hill.

Cass, J., and M. Birnbaum. 1964. *Comparative Guide to American Colleges.* 1st ed. New York: Harper & Row.

Cass, J., and M. Birnbaum. 1973. *Comparative Guide to American Colleges.* 6th ed. New York: Harper & Row.

Cass, J., and M. Birnbaum. 1979. *Comparative Guide to American Colleges.* 9th ed. New York: Harper & Row.

Cass, J., and M. Birnbaum. 1983. *Comparative Guide to American Colleges.* 11th ed. New York: Harper & Row.

Cass, M., and J. C. Liepmann. 1994. *Cass and Birnbaum's Comparative Guide to American Colleges.* 16th ed. New York: HarperCollins.

Cedar Crest College. 1969. *Report of Conference on the Undergraduate Education of Women, July 8–10, 1969.* Allentown, PA.

Chronicle of Higher Education. 1993. "Higher Levels of Satisfaction among Grads of Women's Colleges Are Reflected in Their Giving Patterns to Their Alma Mater." *The Chronicle of Higher Education* 16 June.

Church, M. E. 1996. "A View from One Presidential Office." Pp. 69–78 in *Against the Tide: Career Paths of Women Leaders in American and British Higher Education,* edited by K. D. Walton. Bloomington: Phi Delta Kappa Educational Foundation.

Clark, B. R. 1987. *The Academic Life: Small Worlds, Different Worlds.* Princeton, NJ: Carnegie Foundation for the Advancement of Teaching.

Clark-Kennedy, A. E. 1929. *Stephen Hales, D.D., F.R.S.: An Eighteenth Century Biography.* Cambridge, UK: Cambridge University Press. Republished in 1965. Ridgewood, NJ: Gregg Press.

Committee on the Education and Employment of Women in Science and Engineering. 1983. *Climbing the Ladder: An Update on the Status of Doctoral Women Scientists and Engineers.* Washington, DC: National Academy Press.

Conaty, J. C. 1989. College Quality and Future Earnings: Where Should You Send Your Sons and Daughters? Paper presented at the eighty-fourth annual meeting of the American Sociological Association, in San Francisco, CA.

Conrad, C. 1982. "Grounded Theory: An Alternative Approach to Research in Higher Education." *Review of Higher Education* 5: 239–49.

Crowson, R. L. 1987. "Qualitative Research Methods in Higher Education." Pp. 1–55 in *Higher Education: Handbook of Theory and Research,* volume III, edited by J. C. Smart. New York: Agathon Press.

Curti, M. E. 1936. *Learning for Ladies (1508–1895): A Book Exhibition to Illustrate Some Ideas about Women's Education.* San Marino, CA: Huntington Library.

Dexter, E. G. 1906. *A History of Education in the United States.* New York: Macmillan.

Dey, E. L., A. W. Astin, and W. S. Korn. 1991. *The American Freshman: Twenty-Five Year Trends, 1966–1990*. Los Angeles: Higher Education Research Institute, UCLA.

Doherty, B. 1993. "Myths and Stories of Courage Empower Us." *St. Mary-of-the-Woods Alumnae News* (Summer): 2.

Feldman, K.A., and T. M. Newcomb. 1969.*The Impact of College on Students*. San Francisco: Jossey-Bass.

Ferris, T. 1988. *Coming of Age in the Milky Way*. New York: William Morrow.

Fetterman, D. M. 1989. "Ethnography: Step-by-Step." In *Applied Social Science Research Methods Series*, volume 17. Newbury Park, CA: Sage Publications.

Ginorio, A. B., and D. Wiegand. 1994. First Steps in College Science: Single Sex vs. Coeducational Programs. Final report to The Jessie Ball DuPont Fund.

Ginzberg, L. D. 1987. "The 'Joint Education of the Sexes': Oberlin's Original Vision." Pp. 67–80, in *Educating Men and Women Together: Coeducation in a Changing World*, edited by C. Lasser. Urbana and Chicago: University of Illinois Press.

Glazer, B. 1978. *Theoretical Sensitivity: Advances in the Methodology of Grounded Theory*. Mill Valley, CA: Sociological Press.

Glazer, B., and A. Strauss. 1967. *The Discovery of Grounded Theory: Strategies for Qualitative Research*. Chicago: Aldine Publishing.

Gleick, J. 1987. *Chaos: Making a New Science*. New York: Penguin Books.

Goodsell, W., ed. 1931. *Pioneers of Women's Education in the United States*. New York: McGraw-Hill.

Gose, B. 1997. "Liberal-Arts Colleges Ask: Where Have the Men Gone?" *The Chronicle of Higher Education* 6 June: 35–36(A).

Grant, W. V., and C. G. Lind. 1975. *Digest of Education Statistics, 1975 Edition*. Washington, DC: U.S. Government Printing Office.

Grant, W. V., and T. D. Snyder. 1986. *Digest of Education Statistics, 1985–86*. Washington, DC: U.S. Government Printing Office.

Green, E. A. 1979. *Mary Lyon and Mount Holyoke: Opening the Gates*. Hanover, NH: University Press of New England.

Greene, E. 1987. "Too Many Women? That's the Problem at Chapel Hill, Say Some Trustees." *The Chronicle of Higher Education* 28 January: 27–28.

Griffin, F. 1979. *Less Time for Meddling: A History of Salem Academy and College, 1772–1866*. Winston-Salem, NC: John F. Blair.

Guba, E. G. 1981. "Criteria for Assessing the Trustworthiness of Naturalistic Inquiries." *Educational Communications and Technology Journal* 29: 75–92.

Guba, E. G., and Y. S. Lincoln. 1989. *Fourth Generation Evaluation*. Newbury Park, CA: Sage Publications.

Guinier, L., M. Fine, and J. Balin. 1997. *Becoming Gentlemen: Women, Law School and Institutional Change*. Boston: Beacon Press.

Hall, R. M., and B. R. Sandler. 1982. *The Classroom Climate: A Chilly One for Women?* Washington, DC: Association of American Colleges.

Haller, M. 1953. *Early Moravian Education in Pennsylvania*. Nazareth, PA: Moravian Historical Society.

Hamermesh, D. S. 1993. "Treading Water: The Annual Report on the Economic Status of the Profession, 1992–93." *Academe* 79(2): 8–90.

Hansen, W. L. 1983. "A Blip on the Screen: The Annual Report on the Economic Status of the Profession, 1982–83." *Academe* 69(4): 1–75.

Harmon, L. R., and H. Soldz. 1963. *Doctorate Production in United States Universities, 1920–1962*. NAS-NRC Publication No. 1142. Washington, DC: National Academy Press.

Harwarth, I., M. Maline, and E. DeBra. 1997. *Women's Colleges in the United States: History, Issues, and Challenges*. Washington, DC: U.S. Government Printing Office.

Holland, D. C., and M. A. Eisenhart. 1990. *Educated in Romance: Women, Achievement, and College Culture*. Chicago: University of Chicago Press.

Hood College. 1997. *Catalog 1997–1998*. Frederick, MD.

Horowitz, H. L. 1984. *Alma Mater: Design and Experience in the Women's Colleges from Their Nineteenth Century Beginnings to the 1930s*. New York: Alfred A. Knopf.

Horowitz, H. L. 1987. *Campus Life*. New York: Alfred A. Knopf.

Howe, F. 1984. *Myths of Coeducation: Selected Essays, 1964–1983*. Bloomington: Indiana University Press.

Immaculata College. 1990. *Women's Colleges—The 90s and Beyond*. November 1–2, 1990. Immaculata, PA.

Jamison, A. 1975. Telephone conversation with M. E. Tidball, 25 June.

Kanter, R. M. 1976. *Men and Women of the Corporation*. New York: Basic Books.

Keep, R. A. 1946. *Four Score and Ten Years: A History of Mills College*. San Francisco, CA: Taylor and Taylor.

Kim, M., and R. Alvarez. 1995. "Women-Only Colleges: Some Unanticipated Consequences." *Journal of Higher Education* 66: 641–69.

Knapp, R. H., and H. B. Goodrich. 1951. "The Origins of American Scientists." *Science* 113: 543–45.

Knapp, R. H., and H. B. Goodrich. 1952. *Origins of American Scientists*. Chicago: University of Chicago Press.

Krupnick, C. G. 1985. "Women and Men in the Classroom: Inequality and Its Remedies." *On Teaching and Learning* (May): 18–25.

Kuh, G. D. 1993. "In Their Own Words: What Students Learn Outside the Classroom." *American Educational Research Journal* 30(2): 277–304.

Kuh, G. D., J. H. Schuh, and E. J. Whitt. 1991. *Involving Colleges: Successful Strategies to Fostering Student Learning and Development outside the Classroom.* San Francisco: Jossey-Bass.

Ledman, R. E., M. Miller, and D. R. Brown. 1995. "Successful Women and Women's Colleges: Is There an Intervening Variable?" *Sex Roles: Journal of Research* 33(7): 489–97.

Light, R. J. 1990. *The Harvard Assessment Seminars: First Report: Explorations with Students and Faculty about Teaching, Learning, and Student Life.* Cambridge, MA: Harvard Graduate School of Education and Kennedy School of Government.

Light, R. J., J. Singer, and J. Willett. 1990. *By Design: Planning Research on Higher Education.* Cambridge, MA: Harvard University Press.

Lincoln, Y. S., and E. G. Guba. 1985. *Naturalistic Inquiry.* Beverly Hills, CA: Sage Publications.

Lockheed, M. E., and S. S. Klein. 1985. "Sex Equity in Classroom Organization and Climate." In *Handbook on Achieving Sex Equity through Education,* edited by S. S. Klein. Baltimore: Johns Hopkins University Press.

MacKay, K. A., and J. H. Schuh. 1991. "Practical Issues Associated with Qualitative Research Methods." *Journal of College Student Development* 32: 424–31.

Manuel, W. A., and M. E. Altenderfer. 1961. *Baccalaureate Origins of 1950–59 Medical Graduates.* Public Health Service Publication No. 845. Washington, DC: U.S. Government Printing Office.

Marshall, C., and G. Rossman. 1995. *Designing Qualitative Research,* 2nd ed. Thousand Oaks, CA: Sage Publications.

Matthews, A. 1991. "Alma Maters Court Their Daughters." *New York Times Magazine* 7 April.

Merriam, S. B. 1988. *Case Study Research in Education: A Qualitative Approach.* San Francisco: Jossey-Bass.

Miller-Bernal, L. 1989. "College Experiences and Sex Role Attitudes: Does a Women's College Make a Difference?" *Youth and Society* 20(4): 363–87.

Miller-Bernal, L. 1993. "Single-Sex versus Coeducational Environments: A Comparison of Women Students' Experiences at Four Colleges." *American Journal of Education* 102: 22–54.

Mills, M., A. London, N. Mills, and R. Shepala. 1993. How Chilly Is the Forecast? An Institutional Study of the Campus Climate for Women. Paper presented at the 1993 annual meeting of the Association for the Study of Higher Education, in Pittsburgh, PA.

Moos, R., and J. Otto. 1975. "The Impact of Coed Living on Males and Females." *Journal of College Student Personnel* 16(6): 459–67.

Mount Holyoke College Alumnae Association. 1997. *Mount Holyoke Club of Greater Washington, DC* (Fall newsletter).

National Academy of Sciences. 1974. *Summary Report 1973: Doctorate Recipients from United States Universities.* Washington, DC: National Academy Press.

Newcomer, M. 1959. *A Century of Higher Education for American Women.* New York: Harper and Brothers.

Newell, B. W. 1974. *Statement to Department of Health, Education, and Welfare regarding the Proposed Title IX Regulations* 8 October.

Noe, R. 1988. "Women and Mentoring: A Review and Research Agenda." *Academy of Management Review* 13: 65–78.

Oates, M. J., and S. Williamson. 1978. "Women's Colleges and Women Achievers." *Signs: Journal of Women in Culture and Society* 3: 795–806.

Office of Scientific Personnel. 1948. *Doctorate Production in United States Universities 1936–1945.* Washington, DC: National Academy Press.

Palmieri, P. 1995. *In Adamless Eden: The Community of Faculty Women at Wellesley.* New Haven, CT: Yale University Press.

Pascarella, E. T. 1984. "College Environmental Influences on Students' Aspirations." *Journal of Higher Education* 55: 751–71.

Pascarella, E. T. 1985. "Students' Affective Development within the College Environment." *Journal of Higher Education* 56: 640–62.

Pascarella, E. T., and P. T. Terenzini. 1991. *How College Affects Students.* San Francisco: Jossey-Bass.

Pascarella, E. T., E. J. Whitt, M. I. Edison, A. Nora, L. S. Hagedorn, P. M. Yeager, and P. T. Terenzini. 1996. Women's Perception of a "Chilly Climate" and Their Cognitive Outcomes during the First Year of College. Paper presented at the 1996 annual meeting of the Association for the Study of Higher Education, in Memphis, TN.

Patterson, G. 1968. "The Education of Women at Princeton: A Special Report." *Princeton Alumni Weekly* 49: 5–56.

Patton, M. Q. 1990. *Qualitative Evaluation and Research Methods.* Newbury Park, CA: Sage Publications.

Pearson, C. S., D. L. Shavlik, and J. G. Touchton. 1989. *Educating the Majority: Women Challenge Tradition in Higher Education.* New York: Macmillan.

Population Reference Bureau. 1998. *1998 Women of Our World.* Washington, DC.

Quinn, M. 1993. "Mills, Still All-Women, Will Never Be the Same." *New York Times* 1 September: Campus Journal section.

Read, F. M. 1961. *The Story of Spelman College.* Princeton, NJ: Princeton University Press.

Reichel, W. C., and W. H. Bigler. 1901. *A History of the Moravian Seminary for Young Ladies at Bethlehem, Pennsylvania,* 4th ed. Bethlehem, PA.

Rice, J. K., and A. Hemmings. 1988. "Women's Colleges and Women Achievers: An Update." *Signs: Journal of Women in Culture and Society* 13: 546–59.

Rice, M. C. 1965. *Resident and Extension Enrollment in Institutions of Higher Education, Fall 1963*. Washington, DC: U.S. Government Printing Office.

Riordan, C. 1992. "Single and Mixed-Gender Colleges for Women: Educational, Attitudinal, and Occupational Outcomes." *The Review of Higher Education* 15(3): 327–46.

Riordan, C. 1994. "The Value of Attending a Women's College: Education, Occupation, and Income Benefits." *Journal of Higher Education* 65: 486–510.

Rowe, M. P. 1990. "Barriers to Equality: The Power of Subtle Discrimination to Maintain Unequal Opportunity." *Employee Responsibilities and Rights Journal* 3(2): 153–63.

Rudolph, F. 1962. *The American College and University: A History*. New York: Alfred A. Knopf.

Sadker, M., and D. Sadker. 1994. *Failing at Fairness: How Our Schools Cheat Girls*. New York: Simon and Schuster.

Sagaria, M. A. D. 1988. "The Case for Empowering Women As Leaders in Higher Education." Pp. 5–12 in *Empowering Women: Leadership Development Strategies on Campus*; in the series New Directions for Student Services, no. 44, edited by M. A. D. Sagaria. San Francisco: Jossey-Bass.

Scheye, P. A., and F. D. Gilroy. 1994. "College Women's Career Self-Efficiency and Educational Environments." *Career Development Quarterly* 42: 244–51.

Schlossberg, N. K. 1989. "Marginality and Mattering: Key Issues in Building Community." In *Designing Campus Activities to Foster a Sense of Community*; in the series New Directions for Student Services, no. 48, edited by D. C. Roberts. San Francisco: Jossey-Bass.

Schumacher, E. F. 1973. *Small Is Beautiful: Economics As if People Mattered*. New York: Harper & Row.

Sebrechts, J. S. 1993. "Cultivating Scientists at Women's Colleges." *Initiatives* 55(2): 45–52.

Sharpe, N. R., and C. H. Fuller. 1995. "Baccalaureate Origins of Women Physical Science Doctorates: Relationship to Institutional Gender and Science Discipline." *Journal of Women and Minorities in Science and Engineering* 2: 1–15.

Shavlik, D. L., and J. G. Touchton. 1992. "The New Agenda for Women Revisited." *Educational Record* Fall: 47–55.

Shavlik, D. L., J. G. Touchton, and E. Hoffman. 1997. *A Commitment to the Future: Higher Education and the United Nations Fourth World Conference on Women*. Washington, DC: American Council on Education.

Singh, J. I. S. 1996. *Moving beyond Access: Gender Positive Initiatives in Pace Setting Women's Colleges*. New Delhi, India: National Institute of Educational Planning and Administration.

Smith, D. G. 1990. "Women's Colleges and Coed Colleges: Is There a Difference for Women?" *Journal of Higher Education* 61: 181–95.

Smith, D. G., G. L. Gerbick, M. A. Figueroa, G. H. Watkins, T. Levitan, L. C. Moore, P. A. Merchant, H. D. Beliak, and B. Figueroa. 1997. *Diversity Works: The Emerging Picture of How Students Benefit.* Washington, DC: Association of American Colleges and Universities.

Smith, D. G., D. E. Morrison, and L. E. Wolf-Wendel. 1994. "Is College a Gendered Experience?" *Journal of Higher Education* 65: 696–725.

Smith, D. G., L. E. Wolf-Wendel, and D. E. Morrison. 1995. "How Women's Colleges Facilitate the Success of Their Students." *Journal of Higher Education* 66: 245–66.

Smith, E. T. 1974. "Survey of Independent Colleges Which Have Merged, Closed or Gone under Public Control." Washington, DC: National Council of Independent Colleges and Universities.

Snyder, T. D., and C. M. Hoffman. 1995. *Digest of Education Statistics, 1995.* Washington, DC: U.S. Government Printing Office.

Solnick, S. J. 1995. "Changes in Women's Majors from Entrance to Graduation at Women's and Coeducational Colleges." *Industrial and Labor Relations Review* 48(3): 505–14.

Solomon, B. M. 1985. *In the Company of Educated Women: A History of Women and Higher Education in America.* New Haven, CT: Yale University Press.

Solomon, B. M. 1987. "The Oberlin Model and Its Impact on Other Colleges." Pp. 81–90 in *Educating Men and Women Together: Coeducation in a Changing World,* edited by C. Lasser. Urbana and Chicago: University of Illinois Press.

Solorzano, D. G. 1995. "The Baccalaureate Origins of Chicana and Chicano Doctorates in the Social Sciences." *Hispanic Journal of Behavioral Sciences* 17: 3–32.

Spelman College. 1996a. *Transformation.* Atlanta.

Spelman College. 1996b. *Transformation: The Radiance of Self-Discovery.* Atlanta.

Steele, C. M. 1997. "A Threat in the Air: How Stereotypes Shape Individual Identity and Performance." *American Psychologist* 52: 613–29.

Stewart, G. C., Jr. 1994. *Marvels of Charity: History of American Sisters and Nuns.* Huntington, IN: Sunday Visitor.

Stoecker, J. L., and E. T. Pascarella. 1991. "Women's Colleges and Women's Career Attainments Revisited." *Journal of Higher Education* 62: 394–411.

Stohlman, M. L. L. 1956. *The Story of Sweet Briar College.* Princeton, NJ: Princeton University Press.

Strauss, A. 1987. *Qualitative Analysis for Social Scientists.* New York: Cambridge University Press.

Strauss, A., and J. Corbin. 1990. *Basics of Qualitative Research: Grounded Theory Procedures and Techniques.* Newbury Park, CA: Sage Publications.

Tannen, D. 1998. *The Argument Culture: Moving from Debate to Dialog*. New York: Random House.

Thurgood, D. H., and J. E. Clarke. 1995. *Summary Report, 1993 Doctorate Recipients from United States Universities*. Washington, DC: National Academy Press.

Tidball, C. S. 1989. "Further Thoughts on the College Enrollment Crisis." *Academe* 75(1): 7.

Tidball, C. S. 1996. *Small College Database*. Frederick, MD: Hood College.

Tidball, C. S. 1997. *Small College Database*. Frederick, MD: Hood College.

Tidball, M. E. 1970. "Women's Colleges vs. Coeducation: A Question of Creative Involvement?" *Mount Holyoke Alumnae Quarterly* 54: 176–78.

Tidball, M. E. 1973a. "Teaching: Two Sides of the Coin." *Mary Baldwin* 21: 8–13.

Tidball, M. E. 1973b. "Perspective on Academic Women and Affirmative Action." *Educational Record* 54: 130–35.

Tidball, M. E. 1974a. "The Search for Talented Women." *Change* 6: 51–52, 64.

Tidball, M. E. 1974b. "Women Role Models in Higher Education." Pp. 56–59 in *Proceedings of the American Association of University Women*. Washington, DC: American Association of University Women.

Tidball, M. E. 1975. "Wellesley Women in Science." *Wellesley Alumnae Magazine* 59(2): 1–3.

Tidball, M. E. 1976a. "Equality and Success." Pp. 192–99 in *Individualizing the System*, edited by D. W. Vermilye. San Francisco: Jossey-Bass.

Tidball, M. E. 1976b. "Of Men and Research: The Dominant Themes in American Higher Education Include Neither Teaching nor Women." *Journal of Higher Education* 47: 373–89.

Tidball, M. E. 1977a. "Access of Women Students to Higher Education." Pp. 4385–89 in *International Encyclopedia of Higher Education*, edited by A. S. Knowles. San Francisco: Jossey-Bass.

Tidball, M. E. 1977b. "Women's Colleges." Pp. 4389–98 in *International Encyclopedia of Higher Education*, edited by A. S. Knowles. San Francisco: Jossey-Bass.

Tidball, M. E. 1978. "To Nourish What Is Strong Already." *Barnard Alumnae* 67(3): 2–3, 18, 19.

Tidball, M. E. 1979. "The Importance of Women to Women." *Sweet Briar College Alumnae Magazine* 50: 7–11.

Tidball, M. E. 1980a. "Women's Colleges and Women Achievers Revisited." *Signs: Journal of Women in Culture and Society* 5: 504–17.

Tidball, M. E. 1980b. "Educating the New Majority: Women and Achievement." *Scan* 56: 12–15.

Tidball, M. E. 1983. "The Ideal Gas, A Critical Mass and Homeostasis: Three Lessons from the Sciences." *Women's Studies Quarterly* 11: 5–7.

Tidball, M. E. 1984. "Up from the Three R's: The Three S's and the Undergraduate Curriculum." *The Chronicle of Higher Education* 21 November: 72.

Tidball, M. E. 1985. "Baccalaureate Origins of Entrants into American Medical Schools." *Journal of Higher Education* 56: 385–402.

Tidball, M. E. 1986a. "Citation Classic." *Current Contents: Social and Behavioral Sciences* 18(15): 14.

Tidball, M. E. 1986b. "Baccalaureate Origins of Recent Natural Science Doctorates." *Journal of Higher Education* 57: 606–20.

Tidball, M. E. 1989. "Women's Colleges: Exceptional Conditions, Not Exceptional Talent, Produce High Achievers." Pp. 157–72 in *Educating the Majority: Women Challenge Tradition in Higher Education*, edited by C. Pearson, D. Shavlik, and J. Touchton. New York: Macmillan.

Tidball, M. E. 1993. "Educational Environments and the Development of Talent." Pp. 55–61 in *Single-Sex Schooling: Proponents Speak: A Special Report from the Office of Educational Research and Improvement, U.S. Department of Education*, vol. II, edited by D. K. Hollinger and R. Adamson. Washington, DC: U.S. Department of Education.

Tidball, M. E. 1994a. Learning to Count: Revelations from the Creative Integration of Divers Tables and Lists. Paper presented at New Perspectives on Women's Education: A Symposium on Current Research, at Smith College, Northampton, MA.

Tidball, M. E. 1994b. Population Studies Using Disaggregation As a Means of Characterizing Educational Environments. Final report to The Jessie Ball DuPont Fund.

Tidball, M. E. 1996. Gender and the Higher Education Classroom: Maximizing the Learning Environment. Paper presented at Duke Journal of Gender Law & Policy Conference, at Duke University, Durham, NC.

Tidball, M. E. 1998. Women's Colleges: Student Backgrounds and Educational Outcomes. Paper presented at A Closer Look at Women's Colleges—AAUW/OERI Invitational Conference, in Washington, DC.

Tidball, M. E., and V. Kistiakowsky. 1976. "Baccalaureate Origins of American Scientists and Scholars." *Science* 193: 646–52.

Tidball, M. E., and C. S. Tidball. 1994. Population Demographics and the Search for Gender Equity. Paper presented at Women's College Coalition Conference, at Mount Holyoke College, South Hadley, MA.

Tidball, M. E., and C. S. Tidball. 1995. Chaos in the Classroom: Patterns of Productivity for Women and Men. Paper presented at Trustee Scholar Symposium, at Skidmore College, Saratoga Springs, NY.

Touchton, J. G., D. Shavlik, and L. Davis. 1993. *Women in Presidencies*. Washington, DC: American Council on Education.

Trice, A. 1994. A Comparison of Classroom Environments in Coeducational and Single Sex Classrooms. Paper presented at Women's College Coalition Conference, at Mount Holyoke College, South Hadley, MA.

U.S. Department of Education. 1996. *Integrated Postsecondary Education Data System 1993 (IPEDS)*. Washington, DC: Office of Educational Research and Improvement.

U.S. Department of Health, Education, and Welfare. 1951. *Education Directory, 1949–1950*. Washington, DC: U.S. Government Printing Office.

U.S. Department of Health, Education, and Welfare. 1970. *Education Directory, 1969–1970*. Washington, DC: U.S. Government Printing Office.

Useem, A. 1998. "Promoting Gender Equity in a Land Ruled by Islamic Law." *The Chronicle of Higher Education* 13 March.

Ward, J. W. 1972. "The President's Recommendation on Coeducation." *Amherst College Bulletin* 62: 1–8.

Wellesley Center for Research on Women. 1979. *Educational Environments and the Undergraduate Woman*, September 13–15, 1979. Wellesley, MA.

Whitt, E. J. 1991. "Artful Science: A Primer on Qualitative Research Methods." *Journal of College Student Development* 32: 406–15.

Whitt, E. J. 1992. Taking Women Seriously: Lessons for Coeducational Institutions from Women's Colleges. Paper presented at the 1992 annual meeting of the Association for the Study of Higher Education, in Minneapolis, MN.

Whitt, E. J. 1994. "I Can Be Anything! Student Leadership in Three Women's Colleges." *Journal of College Student Development* 35: 198–207.

Wilson College. 1997. "Wilson College Mission Statement." *Have You Heard* 20(1): 1.

Wolf-Wendel, L. E. 1995. "Models of Excellence: The Baccalaureate Origins of Successful European American Women, African American Women, and Latinas." Doctor of philosophy dissertation, the Claremont Graduate School.

Wolf-Wendel, L. E. 1998. "Models of Excellence: The Baccalaureate Origins of Successful European American Women, African American Women, and Latinas." *Journal of Higher Education* 69: 141–86.

Women's College Coalition. 1981. *A Study of the Learning Environments at Women's Colleges*. Washington, DC.

Women's College Coalition. 1985. *A Profile of Recent Women's College Graduates*. Washington, DC.

Women's College Coalition. 1994. *Studies in Success: Applying Effective Models to Educating Women and Girls*, November 4–6, 1994. South Hadley, MA.

Women's College Coalition. 1995. *The Benefits of Women's Colleges*. Washington, DC.

Yin, R. K. 1989. *Case Study Research: Design and Methods*. Newbury Park, CA: Sage Publications.

INDEX

by Virgil Diodato

DATE DUE